the NEW YORK YANKEES *of the* 1950s

MANTLE, STENGEL, BERRA, AND A DECADE OF DOMINANCE

DAVID FISCHER

LYONS
PRESS

Guilford, Connecticut

An imprint of The Rowman & Littlefield Publishing Group, Inc.
4501 Forbes Blvd., Ste. 200
Lanham, MD 20706
www.rowman.com

Distributed by NATIONAL BOOK NETWORK

British Library Cataloguing in Publication Information available

Library of Congress Cataloging-in-Publication Data available

ISBN 978-1-4930-3892-3 (hardcover)
ISBN 978-1-4930-3893-0 (e-book)

♾™ The paper used in this publication meets the minimum requirements of American National Standard for Information Sciences—Permanence of Paper for Printed Library Materials, ANSI/NISO Z39.48-1992.

Printed in the United States of America

To my parents, and Carolyn, my reason for everything

CONTENTS

PREFACE

THE HISTORY OF THE NEW YORK YANKEES IS VIRTUALLY THE HISTORY of baseball. During the decade of the 1950s, the Yankees dominated the game. In the National Baseball Hall of Fame and Museum in Cooperstown, New York, bronze plaques commemorate the accomplishments of Mickey Mantle, Yogi Berra, Phil Rizzuto, and Whitey Ford. With these four players, and Hall of Fame manager Casey Stengel, the Yankees embarked on a 10-year run that would go down in the history books as the greatest decade in Yankees history, if not the greatest decade by any baseball team of all time. During the decade of dominance of the 1950s, the Yankees finished the season in first place eight times, with an average of over 96 victories each year. They won eight American League pennants and six World Series championships, including four in a row. Even the Ruthian Yankees of the Roaring Twenties never won more than two consecutive world championships. These Yankees won six World Series by an overall margin of 24–13, and in the two series they lost fell in heartbreaking deciding seventh games. While nearly all of the on-field playing rules remain the same today, the structure of baseball in the 1950s made it a vastly different game. At the start of the decade, there were no teams located west of the Mississippi River. Teams traveled by train from city to city. The two leagues each were comprised of eight teams. There was no playoff system; the first-place team from the National League and the first-place team from the American League met in the World Series to decide a champion. And the starting pitchers routinely finished the games they started.

By decade's end, however, all major-league teams were integrated and several franchises had relocated.

From 1950 to 1959, the world was changing rapidly, too. There was the invention of the hydrogen bomb, with the world for the first time facing the possibility that humans could destroy themselves completely. The Korean War blazed from 1950 to 1953. America was in the grip of the Cold War, a war of competing ideologies, which bred a constant tension between the Soviet Union and the United States. Hearings led by Senator Joseph McCarthy unsuccessfully sought communists in every part of the government, and in the process ruined hundreds of lives. Dwight D. Eisenhower was elected and re-elected president after having led Allied troops to victory in World War II. And racial tensions grew, especially in the South.

With the ever-changing world as a backdrop, the Yankees were a constant, a dependable and reliable winner. Wearing their pinstriped uniform, the organization was the embodiment of American success. In fact, critics said rooting for the Yankees was like rooting for U.S. Steel, the corporate monopoly. But sports, and baseball in particular, are a microcosm of society. Among the most noteworthy highlights on the diamond was the gradual racial integration of the playing fields. By the mid-1950s, catcher Elston Howard became the first black player on the New York Yankees—one of Major League Baseball's last teams to become integrated.

To be sure, the decade of the 1950s was a time when the country was moving toward a transformative change, and baseball was too, with the adjustment to such profound changes as night games, coast-to-coast travel, and the advent of television that brought the national pastime right into the living rooms of fans across the country. And fans that tuned in to watch the World Series, more often than not, saw the New York Yankees be crowned baseball champions once again.

1950: THE ALMIGHTY CASEY

WHEN THE NEW YORK YANKEES FINISHED IN THIRD PLACE IN THE American League in 1948, the owners of the team, Del Webb and Dan Topping, fired manager Bucky Harris. The Yankees were used to finishing first, so no one was surprised that Harris was let go. But the appointment of Casey Stengel as the new manager was shocking. When general manager George Weiss campaigned to bring Stengel on board as skipper, Stengel had had years of experience managing; he served as manager for the Brooklyn Dodgers, Boston Bees, and Boston Braves prior to joining the Yankees—but all the teams he had managed in the majors had been losers. In fact, Stengel had only one winning season out of nine when he was hired. Upon joining the Yankees, Stengel said, "There is less wrong with this team than any team I have ever managed." Nicknamed The Old Perfessor, Stengel was known for his decades of experience in baseball, and his unique collection of aphorisms about the game. "There are three things you can do in a baseball game," he said. "You can win, or you can lose, or it can rain."

Casey was most famous as a clown, not as a winner. As a player, he was most remembered for entertaining fans during games. He once kept a sparrow hidden under his cap and at just the right moment tipped his hat to the crowd so the bird could fly away. Stengel's coming to the Yankees was like a country bumpkin marrying a glamorous movie queen—the match seemed unlikely to last, let alone succeed. It didn't help that Casey told reporters upon his arrival at the Yankees spring training facility in St. Petersburg, Florida, "This is a big job, fellows, and I barely have had time to study it. In fact, I scarcely know where I am at." But those who scoffed at Casey were overlooking something. While Stengel's quips eventually became so plentiful they earned the collective nickname Stengel-ese, the Yankees manager also proved he was a master orchestrator in the dugout. He had learned his baseball during a 14-year playing career under the guidance of such astute managers as John McGraw and Wilbert Robinson. He knew more about the game than most people ever learn. When asked about his theory of managing, Stengel said: "The secret of managing is to keep the five guys who hate you away from the five who are undecided."

Casey was an innovator in the use of his entire roster and employed a system that was designed to get the most out of every man on his team. He was an early proponent of the five-man starting pitching rotation, and one of the original pioneers of platooning players. Stengel managed to exploit mismatches against his opponents by utilizing specific players against different pitchers, something few other managers did at that point in the game's history. His visionary tactics impressed the longest-serving and winningest manager in Major League Baseball history. "I never saw a man who juggled his lineup so much and who played so many hunches so successfully," said Connie Mack.

In 1949, rookie manager Casey Stengel's Yankees clung to the heels of the hot Boston Red Sox in a tight pennant race despite a long series of injuries to key players. The star center fielder Joe DiMaggio had a sore heel and didn't play his first game until June 28. Juggling the lineup to keep his players fresh, Stengel's use of smoke and mirrors had somehow kept his team in the race. On the last day of the season, the Red Sox were to play a doubleheader against the Yankees. If the Yanks could win both games they would take the flag. Boston's Ted Williams was having another great year. The Sox' two best pitchers, Ellis Kinder and Mel Parnell, were rested and ready for the Yanks. But the New Yorkers upset the odds. They won the two games and the pennant. Afterward, a humbled Stengel said, "I couldn't have done it without my players."

The first two games of the Yankees-Dodgers World Series in 1949 were as tight as the pennant race. The Yankees won the opener, 1–0, on a homer by Tommy Henrich. The Dodgers won the second game by the same score on a double by Jackie Robinson and a single by Gil Hodges. But the Yankees won the next three games to give Casey Stengel his first World Series championship. It was just a hint of lovely days to come. The unlikely marriage between Stengel and the Yanks had gotten off to an exhilarating start.

Seven months after breaking Boston hearts by winning the final two games of the 1949 season to snatch the pennant from the Red Sox' grasp, Stengel's Yankees returned to Boston for Opening Day of the 1950 season as the defending world champions. There was a lot going on that day. In Cleveland, the AL's first black player, Larry Doby, hit the major leagues' first home run of the decade, a two-run shot off Detroit's Fred Hutchinson in the first inning of a 7–6 Indians loss to the Tigers at Cleveland Stadium. Back at Fenway, Ted Williams picked up his 1949 Most Valuable Player Award before the game and Boston's Bobby Doerr presented a plaque to Joe DiMaggio to commemorate Joe DiMaggio Day held the previous October in Yankee Stadium.

During the game, Boston was less hospitable. They built up a 9–0 lead after five innings, pounding New York's starting pitcher Allie Reynolds. The Yankees scored four times in the sixth and DiMaggio made a terrific catch with two outs and the bases loaded in the seventh to keep the Sox from padding their lead. In the eighth inning, manager Stengel inserted rookie second baseman Billy Martin into the lineup as a pinch-hitter, and he promptly doubled and singled to become the first player to knock out two hits in one inning during his first game. Martin had played one inning as a major leaguer, and during that time he helped ignite a nine-run, eighth-inning rally. The Bronx Bombers deliriously celebrated a stunning, come-from-behind 15–10 victory at Fenway Park, breaking Boston hearts once again. If an opening game can set the pattern for a whole season, this might have convinced the

Red Sox that they were not going to beat the Yankees. And of course they didn't. (Hello, Curse of the Bambino!)

Casey Stengel's mission in 1950 was to deliver back-to-back American League pennants to New York for the first time in seven years, when Joe McCarthy was in charge. The great DiMaggio was back in center field, with Hank Bauer, Gene Woodling, and Johnny Lindell rotating in the left field and right field corner spots. The 27-year-old rookie Joe Collins was at first base sharing time with the veteran Henrich, and either Billy Johnson or Bobby Brown, who was back from his medical studies, took turns at the hot corner. Phil Rizzuto and Jerry Coleman were developing into the finest double-play combination in the league, with a much-improved Yogi Berra behind the plate.

Henrich was playing in his final season. Dubbed Old Reliable (after a train that ran from Ohio to Alabama) by Yankees broadcaster Mel Allen for his knack of getting a hit just when it was needed, Henrich was particularly clutch at the close of the 1949 regular season and in the first World Series game. On the final day of the campaign, he belted a home run and drove in two runs in the Yankees' 5–3 pennant-winning victory over the Red Sox. Three days later, in Game 1 of the World Series against the Dodgers, he led off the bottom of the ninth inning with a home run off Don Newcombe to give Allie Reynolds and the Yankees a 1–0 victory. It was the first game-ending home run in World Series history.

The 1950 edition of the Yankees would win Stengel style, with platooning—mainly outfielders Bauer and Woodling—and superior pitching. For starters the Yankees had Reynolds, Vic Raschi, and Eddie Lopat, and in the bullpen the redoubtable lefty Joe Page. Casey's crew faced a credible challenge from the Detroit Tigers, who held first place for much of the year under the guidance of ex-Yankees infielder Red Rolfe, now filling out the lineup card in Motown. An ineffective Page was nursing an arm injury. If they were going to overtake the Tigers down the stretch, the Yankees would need to acquire another relief pitcher. General manager George Weiss traded for husky right-hander

Tom Ferrick, who posted a record of 1-7 with Washington in 1947 and was 1-3 with St. Louis at the time of his trade to New York.

Weiss had an uncanny knack for recognizing pitchers of ability often struggling with poor win-loss records on second-division teams. He would then acquire these hurlers by surrendering prospects and occasionally cash. Ferrick was one such rough diamond, and with the Yanks he pitched to an 8-4 record and saved nine games. Over a crucial three-day period in late August, he notched a win and a save against Cleveland to propel the Yankees into first place. "Ferrick has been our most important individual performer in the drive to the top," said Stengel following the Yanks 7–5 triumph over Cleveland that gave them a sweep of the four-game series. "I don't know where we'd be without him," he added. "I know we wouldn't be where we are today."

The most significant roster move of the season, however, was the promotion of a 21-year-old left-hander who had been brought up from the Kansas City farm at midseason. His name was Edward Ford, nicknamed Whitey by Lefty Gomez, one of his minor-league managers. The son of a saloonkeeper, Ford got a $7,000 bonus from Paul Krichell, a Yankees scout for four decades. It was Krichell who first spotted and signed Lou Gehrig off the Columbia University campus. Krichell found Ford, too, then a 17-year-old first baseman in Astoria, Queens, not far from Yankee Stadium. Ford was only 5-foot-9 and 150 pounds in high school and was too small to be a position player in the majors. So he switched to pitching full time. Good move.

Ford made the Yankees squad when he was called up midway through the 1950 season after four years in the minors, moving from Yankees farm clubs in Butler, Pennsylvania, to Norfolk, Virginia, to Binghamton, New York, to Kansas City. He finally got his Yankees chance after writing Stengel a letter explaining how he could help the skipper's pitching staff. Stengel was so impressed with the cocky lefty that he brought him to New York despite Weiss's contention that he wasn't ready. Weiss, typical of his penny-pinching ways, was more concerned that he would have to raise Ford's $3,500 minor-league salary to the big-league standard of $5,000. Ford proved to be worth the extra money. He won his first nine decisions before finally getting tagged for a loss pitching in relief in the season's final week.

In addition to Whitey Ford, another rookie arrived during the season—a scrappy second baseman named Billy Martin. He had played for Stengel as a minor leaguer in Oakland in 1948, and a strong bond developed. One of Stengel's first moves was to suggest the Yankees buy the kid. They did. When Martin came up to the Yankees in 1950, he made it clear that he wanted to start. In spring training he got angry when any of the veterans came near second base. He acted like he himself was a veteran, refusing to observe the code of silence traditionally imposed on rookies. Nevertheless, everyone liked Martin, despite his cockiness. He was sassy, brazen, and audacious. Martin didn't play much his first two years on the Yankees in 1950 and '51 because Coleman was playing so well, and for those two years Martin unceasingly harangued Stengel to let him play. When Stengel finally benched Coleman in the middle of the 1951 season and started Martin, Casey batted Martin eighth in the batting order. "What is this, a joke?" he snapped. "Why don't you play the bat boy over me?" Stengel didn't mind. He enjoyed Martin's aggressive attitude. So did DiMaggio, who adopted him like a little brother, perhaps because Martin was of Italian descent and from Berkeley, California, across the bay from where Joe lived.

When Stengel took over as Yankees manager in '49, he treated DiMaggio with the respect he had earned. As DiMaggio's skills started to erode, however, Stengel reacted, and relations between player and manager would become frosty. DiMaggio was of the mind that Stengel had insulted him on several occasions. Once the manager put Johnny Mize in the cleanup spot, with DiMaggio batting fifth. That hurt. So did the idea of Stengel giving him a rest in Washington without first discussing it. As a mild protest Joe sat in the bullpen that day instead of in the dugout. At 35, Joe DiMaggio was getting old. The end was in sight. All the signs were there.

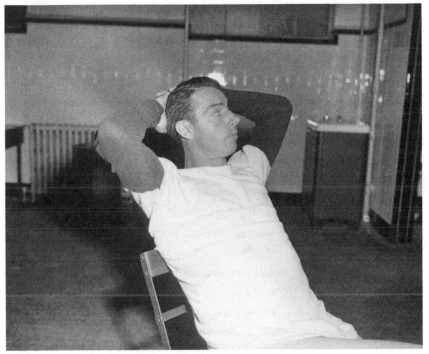

Entering his 12th major league season over three different decades with the Yankees, superstar Joe DiMaggio recognized that his playing career was winding down. COURTESY OF THE LESLIE JONES COLLECTION, BOSTON PUBLIC LIBRARY

To close out June, the Yankees lost nine of 12 games and had dropped four games behind Detroit. But the skipper had an idea to shake things up. He wanted to switch DiMaggio to first base. At the time, DiMaggio had patrolled center field masterfully since 1936. Perhaps he was using the occasion to assert his authority, to show DiMaggio that not even he was bigger than the team. Or perhaps, as he was quoted at the time, Stengel was simply trying to extend the career of a valuable player. Regardless of his motivation, Stengel went about making the change in an unusual fashion. Rather than directly approach DiMaggio on the subject, Casey asked the team's co-owner, Dan Topping, to relay the message because he knew DiMaggio couldn't refuse a close friend. DiMaggio was livid with Stengel. The two barely spoke again. Henrich, a teammate of DiMaggio since 1937 and an excellent outfielder who also could play first base, understood how DiMaggio felt. "He's worried all over," he said. "He's afraid of making a dumb play because he's not familiar with first base. It would have killed him to make a stupid play."

The Yankee Clipper played first base for one game against the Washington Senators at Griffith Stadium, on July 3. The experience was not a raving success. Although DiMaggio handled 13 putouts without an error, he looked extremely awkward on one particular play. It happened on a swinging bunt down the first base line. Joe raced in, but pitcher Tom Ferrick got to the ball first. Trying to scramble back to the bag, Joe D fell and nearly got stepped on by the runner. Cameras clicked, and the tabloid newspapers the next day carried a picture of the great DiMag crawling on his hands and knees. It was terribly embarrassing to a man known for his amazing grace in the outfield. Nowadays, of course, such a play would be shown endlessly on TV highlight reels. But veteran sportswriters of the day, who generally idolized DiMaggio, covered for him in the mainstream press. In the *New York Times*, John Drebinger wrote, "It may be reported without fear of contradiction that the Clipper acquitted himself exceptionally well." In the *Washington Post*, Shirley Povich told readers, "DiMaggio didn't botch anything around first base."

DiMaggio batted fourth his entire career after Lou Gehrig retired, at least until Stengel moved him down in the order. The prideful DiMaggio was angry, but he kept it to himself. Though clearly on the downside of his career, many still considered DiMaggio the leader of the pack. Though he battled a painful bone spur in his right heel, when he was healthy and in the Yankees lineup, pitchers couldn't sleep on him. Someone once asked DiMaggio why he played so hard day in and day out. He replied, "There might be someone in the park who's never seen me play before." In New York's 8–1 victory over the Senators at Washington's spacious Griffith Stadium on September 10, DiMaggio became the first major leaguer in the 40-year history of the ballpark to hit three home runs in one game. Joe D's achievement is all the more impressive considering that Griffith was the toughest park in which to launch a home run; for instance, in 1945, only seven home runs were hit there for the entire year. Just five days after DiMaggio's hat trick, teammate Johnny Mize blasted three homers of his own in a 9–7 loss to the Detroit Tigers. It was the sixth time Mize had hit three home runs in a game, establishing a major-league record (since equaled by Sammy Sosa). And he was the second player after Babe Ruth to accomplish a three-homer game in both leagues. Few hitters combined meticulous bat control with brute power the way Mize did. "The pitchers in the league fear no man as much," said *Newsweek* sportswriter John Lardner.

Mize split his career among the St. Louis Cardinals and the New York Giants from 1936 to 1949, with the years from 1943 to 1945 spent in Hawaii as Specialist First Class of the US Navy. A nine-time All-Star, he won four NL home run titles, a batting title, and three RBI crowns. In 1947 Mize did something unmatched in baseball history. He became the first player to hit more than 50 home runs in a season (51) while striking out fewer than 50 times (42). A first baseman through most of his career until injuries took their toll—he was nicknamed the Big Cat because of his 6-foot-2, 215-pound frame and smooth moves around the bag—Mize was no longer an everyday player. In late August 1949, the Giants sold the 36-year-old Mize to the Yankees for $40,000. He filled in at first base every now and then, giving regular Joe Collins a rest. Few players were more effective in Stengel's platoon system than Big Jawn, as Casey called him. The veteran slugger reinvented himself in his late 30s, and transformed into one of the game's premier pinch-hitting power threats, coming off the bench to produce clutch runs for a Yankees club that was destined for greatness. He went 2-for-2 with two RBIs in the 1949 World Series, helping the Yanks notch a four-games-to-one series victory over the Brooklyn Dodgers.

New York's dynasty years under Casey Stengel were defined as much by the strength of the team's bench as by their many All-Stars.

Stengel's platoon system irritated his primary starters because their playing time was affected, but it allowed part-time players to flourish. Stengel's platoon scheme would keep Mize's career going for four more years, taking the slugger into his age 40 season.

Whitey Ford finished his rookie season with nine wins, only one loss, and a sparkling 2.81 ERA. He allowed just 87 hits in 112 innings pitched and completed seven games in 12 starts, including two shut-outs. He finished second in the AL Rookie of the Year balloting to Boston's Walt Dropo, who had a monster coming-out party batting .322 with 34 home runs and 144 RBIs. Ford's contribution aided a solid corps of starters who were each at least a decade older. Raschi again was the big winner, with a 21-9 record, for an AL-best .724 winning percentage. The righty's success was even more impressive in that a collision at home plate with Indians catcher Jim Hegan in August resulted in torn cartilage in Raschi's right knee. Playing in pain, he found it difficult to put all his weight on his right leg when he pushed off the pitching rubber. Pitcher and teammates kept the injury to themselves to prevent opponents from taking advantage by bunting on him. A 6-foot-1, 200-pounder, Raschi was known to his teammates to be a fierce competitor. "Off the field he was shy and unassuming," said teammate Jerry Coleman. "Nothing like he was on the mound. There he was a beast."

Born in West Springfield, Massachusetts, Raschi's nickname, The Springfield Rifle, combined the speed of his fastball and the name of the neighboring city that was the site of the US Armory that had been producing Army rifles since 1794. Raschi was the keystone of an acclaimed, if aging, pitching staff that included Lopat (18 wins) and Reynolds (16 wins). Raschi was at his best in the big games. Perhaps his most memorable performance came on the final day of the 1949 season when he allowed just two hits over eight innings and defeated the Red Sox with the pennant at stake. "If there was only one game I had to win, the man I'd want out there on the mound for me would be Vic Raschi," said teammate Tommy Henrich.

Allie Reynolds, Vic Raschi, and Eddie Lopat: Casey Stengel's Big Three. COURTESY OF THE LESLIE JONES COLLECTION, BOSTON PUBLIC LIBRARY

The Big Three of Raschi, Reynolds, and Lopat combined for 55 victories, and the fourth starter, hard-throwing left-hander Tommy Byrne, won 15 games despite walking and hitting more batters than any pitcher in the league. He hit four batters in the five innings he pitched on July 5, equaling a league record. Calling the pitches was Yogi Berra, who started all but seven games behind the plate, while blossoming into a dangerous hitter at the dish, batting .322 with 28 home runs and 124 RBIs. DiMaggio, healthy again, joined Berra as an offensive threat with a .301 average, 32 homers, 122 RBIs, and a league-leading .585 slugging percentage. The combative outfielder Hank Bauer, a former US Marine, hit .320 with 70 RBIs in just 113 games. Mize's offensive output for the season was impressive, too; he homered 25 times in just 274 at-bats.

Hank Bauer (center) with Vic Raschi and Casey Stengel before a game at Fenway Park. Bauer was a hard-nosed outfielder who played 1,544 games in the major leagues, more than 1,400 of them with the Yankees. COURTESY OF THE LESLIE JONES COLLECTION, BOSTON PUBLIC LIBRARY

The shortstop Phil Rizzuto overcame his diminutive size—generously listed as 5-foot-6 and 160 pounds—to post his best season ever. Born in Brooklyn, the son of a trolley car conductor, Rizzuto was affectionately known as Scooter. To see him glide after a ball in the third base hole or flash up the middle to snare a grounder, the moniker was a perfect fit. At one point, he handled 238 consecutives chances at shortstop without an error, a big-league record at the time. So reliably did he make the routine play that pitcher Vic Raschi once told a reporter, "My best pitch is anything the batter grounds, lines, or pops up in the direction of Rizzuto." Stellar defense made him a difference maker, but he was also a catalyst at the top of the batting order. In 1949, he batted .275 with 110 runs scored to finish second in the AL Most Valuable Player Award voting. He peaked offensively in 1950, reaching career highs in hits, batting average, on-base percentage, runs scored, RBIs, home runs, walks, doubles, and slugging percentage. He won the AL MVP Award and the first Hickok Belt as the Professional Athlete of the Year. An article in the *New York Times* referred to him as "the dashing little shortstop, widely hailed as the 'indispensable man' of the world champion Bombers." In December, Rizzuto signed a one-year contract for $50,000, making him the third-highest-paid player in Yankees history behind Babe Ruth and DiMaggio.

It wasn't just Rizzuto and DiMaggio who had more spending power. An unprecedented postwar economic boom meant more Americans had the means and leisure time to buy cars and travel with them. In 1950 there were 25 million registered automobiles. American travel was more about the journey, and less about the destination. New categories of businesses were created to support the 1950s car culture, including roadside motels, drive-through and drive-in restaurants, and drive-in movie theaters. Americans got where they were going, and arrived looking good. The new line of Mercury Eight automobiles, featuring the all-new, state-of-the-art Merc-O-Matic transmission, was all the rage. James Dean drove a 1949 two-door coupe version in the 1955 film *Rebel Without a Cause*.

The New York Yankees, who had won the 1949 pennant on the last day of the season by bullying the Boston Red Sox, had a much easier joyride as they navigated their way through the 1950 campaign. The speeding Yanks careened into first place at the end of August and held on for dear life, winning a second straight pennant under Casey Stengel with a 98-56 (.636) record, finishing three games ahead of the Detroit Tigers. On the links, golfing great Ben Hogan won the US Open at the Merion Golf Club in Ardmore, Pennsylvania, to cap one of the most remarkable comebacks in the history of sports. Hogan had suffered severe injuries in a near-fatal automobile accident in February 1949. He not only defied doctors' expectations and returned to the golf course, he also returned to the form that helped him lead the Professional Golfers' Association Tour in money won three times during the 1940s.

Back on the diamond, the Philadelphia Phillies were surprise winners of the National League pennant. They gained the nickname the Whiz Kids from sportswriter Harry Grayson during spring training in Clearwater, Florida. The team had a roster dominated by young players, including future Baseball Hall of Famers Robin Roberts on the mound and Richie Ashburn patrolling center field. Long the National League's doormat, Philadelphia had been floundering at the bottom of the standings for decades. Fortunes improved when owner and club president Bob Carpenter took over prior to the 1944 season. His first hire was Herb Pennock as general manager. Pennock was a former New York Yankees pitching ace during the Babe Ruth era. Together, they built the young team through signing bonuses, and the investment paid off in 1950. Sadly, Pennock never got to see that team's success. He died in 1948 at the age of 53, and three weeks later, was elected to the Baseball Hall of Fame.

Manager Eddie Sawyer managed the Phillies to an 81-73 record in 1949, the first winning season since 1932, and set the stage for success the following year. In 1950, Roberts (20 wins, 11 losses) and Curt Simmons (17 wins, 8 losses) led the starters, and reliever Jim Konstanty pitched a then-record 74 games in relief. Konstanty won 16 games, saved 22, and was the NL's Most Valuable Player. Right fielder Del Ennis (from Philadelphia's Olney High School) led the team with a .311 batting average, 31 home runs, and 126 runs batted in. Ashburn batted .303 with a league-leading 14 triples. Catcher Andy Seminick had 24 home runs, while third baseman Willie "Puddin' Head" Jones hit 25. Other key players included shortstop Granny Hamner, first baseman Eddie Waitkus, and left fielder Dick Sisler.

The Phillies opened the season with a 9–1 defeat of the Brooklyn Dodgers, defending league champions, with Roberts earning the win. The early success did not last, as the team had a .500 record and was mired in sixth place at the end of April. The season soon turned around, however, as the Phillies reached third place, half a game behind Brooklyn and St. Louis, on June 1. For the remainder of the season, the Whiz Kids were in first place at the beginning of each month and opened up a seven-game lead with 11 games left. The team then lost eight of the next 10 games before facing the Brooklyn Dodgers at Ebbets Field in the season finale. The Whiz Kids won the clincher, 4–1, in extra innings, avoiding a best-of-three playoff. Sisler bashed a three-run home run in the top of the 10th inning, and Roberts pitched a complete game. The magic, however, ran out in the World Series against the Yankees.

The Phillies were pretty high and excited to be back in the Fall Classic. The last time the team had appeared in the World Series was in 1915. Grover Cleveland Alexander, a 31-game winner, defeated Ernie Shore, 3–1, in Game 1 as both pitched a complete game. The Red Sox swept the next four games, all by one run. Boston pitching was so strong in that series that a young left-hander, an 18-game winner, was not needed on the mound, though Babe Ruth did make a pinch-hitting appearance in the series opener. (He grounded out to first.)

Thirty-five years later, the Phillies were back playing in October. The first two games of the Fall Classic were played in antiquated Shibe Park in Philadelphia. Konstanty started for the first time that season in Game 1, losing 1–0 to the Yankees. The Phillies could muster only two harmless singles against Raschi. Konstanty was equally brilliant, scattering four hits over eight innings, allowing only a fourth-inning run on a double by Bobby Brown and a Coleman sacrifice fly. After Raschi's shutdown performance his teammate Brown gushed platitudes, expounding on how impressive Raschi had been, citing his perseverance to go the distance. "If he had a one-run lead going into the last third of a game, there never was a better pitcher to close one out," said Brown.

Game 2 in the City of Brotherly Love was also a classic pitching duel between Reynolds and Roberts. Stengel purposely had saved Reynolds for the game in which Roberts was to pitch. At the end of nine innings, with the score tied at one, Roberts faced Joe DiMaggio, the Yankee Clipper, leading off the 10th inning. Four straight times Roberts had forced Joe to pop up on the infield. This time DiMaggio drove Roberts's fastball on a line into the second deck of the left field grandstand, putting the Yankees up, 2–1. Reynolds, who never seemed to tire on this day, set the Phillies down in the bottom half of the inning for the victory.

A few hours after Game 2 ended, both teams boarded the train for New York City as the scene shifted to the big ball yard in the Bronx. Berra and Rizzuto carpooled from Yankee Stadium to their New Jersey homes. Yogi directed Phil, saying, "If you come to a fork in the road, take it." Meanwhile, DiMaggio hustled downtown for a late dinner at Toots Shor's, the fabled watering hole on West 51st Street in Manhattan. Joe D had his private table in the back of the establishment and a lot of newspapermen came around to interview him. He wouldn't say much about his game-winning home run because the Series was only half over. Referring to the popular eatery, Yogi Berra once said, "Nobody goes to that restaurant anymore. It's too crowded."

The majority of the Philadelphia Phillies players had never seen Yankee Stadium before, and it excited them to play in The House That Ruth Built. Down two games to none, they were desperate for an advantage on the mound and called upon the veteran left-hander Ken Heintzelman, a 17-game winner for the Phils in 1949 but a lowly 3-9 pitcher in '50. Heintzelman got the call for Game 3 because 17-game winner Curt Simmons, a member of the National Guard, was called to active duty because of the outbreak of the Korean War late in the season. With his teammates fighting to stay in first place, Simmons reported with his unit to Camp Atterbury, in Indiana. The Korean War had just started. Simmons missed the stretch drive to military training but was able to take leave to attend the World Series. Although he wasn't allowed to play, Simmons tossed batting practice to his teammates and watched the games as a spectator.

With only one run in the series to their ledger, the Phillies were anxious to get after junkballer Eddie Lopat. Casey Stengel, always thinking of the angles, decided to go with Lopat in the Stadium because he gave up a lot of flyballs that his outfield teammates could catch much easier in the Bronx than they might in the tight confines of Philadelphia's Shibe Park. Despite his regular-season stats, Heintzelman pitched beautifully and carried a 2–1 lead going into the eighth. After retiring the first two Yankees, Heintzelman flinched and walked three consecutive batters in the inning. Sawyer saw that it was time to make a change and called for Konstanty, who induced Brown to hit a groundball to Granny Hamner, the shortstop who had committed 48 errors on the season. The Phillies winced as their shortstop fumbled the ball, and the tying run scored. The Yankees continued their momentum in the ninth as Coleman singled in a run and sealed the 3–2 victory. Coleman had now personally won two games, this one and the first game in which he drove in the only run of the game with a sacrifice fly.

Despite being on the verge of another Yankees sweep, the Whiz Kids kept pace with the perennial champs, though they had lost three consecutive one-run decisions. Stengel gave the ball to Whitey Ford to pitch Game 4. After teammate Yogi Berra jump-started the Yankees attack with a run-scoring single and a bases-empty home run, Ford breezed into the ninth inning with a 5–0 lead. A shutout seemed inevitable for Ford as he forced Andy Seminick to hit an easy flyball toward Gene Woodling in left. It was a can of corn. Except the late afternoon sun blinded the New York outfielder. Woodling dropped the ball and two runs scored. Reynolds came in to get the last out, making the New York Yankees 5–2 winners and repeat champions.

Woodling, who tied Hamner for the World Series batting lead with a .429 average, was distraught over his failure to protect the shutout. He was an outstanding fielder despite the notorious sun in Yankee Stadium's left field. "I tell you, I prayed a lot out there," he once said. Ford, who had been drafted into the Army and would spend the next two years in khakis, was less concerned about losing the shutout and over-the-moon happy with the win, the first of his World Series record of 10—an accomplishment duly noted on his Hall of Fame plaque in Cooperstown. The next day in the *New York Times* Arthur Daley wrote that Ford was in complete control and had "the brass of a burglar."

Jerry Coleman, the World War II Marines flying ace, was named the outstanding player of the Series and given the Babe Ruth Award for his performance. "We won the first game, 1–0, and I drove in that run," Coleman recalled in 2012. "We won the second game, 2–1. I scored one of the two runs and DiMaggio hit a home run in the 10th to win it. In the third game I drove in the winning run in the last inning, and in the fourth game I rested." By "rested," he means he went 0-for-3. "I was exhausted," he joked.

For Robin Roberts, the 1950 World Series was his lone appearance on baseball's biggest stage. During his career, the great pitcher would pace the NL in wins four times, and innings pitched and complete games five times each. In all, Roberts won 286 games, had 45 career shutouts, 2,357 strikeouts, and a lifetime 3.41 ERA. He made 609 starts and completed a remarkable 305 of them. After the season, the baseball writers voted Jim Konstanty the winner of the NL's Most Valuable Player Award, the first relief pitcher so honored in either league. (Stan Musial finished a distant second.) Konstanty also was named by the Associated Press as Athlete of the Year, winning the award by a sizable margin over Vic Janowicz, the Heisman Trophy winner from Ohio State, heavyweight champion Ezzard Charles, and golfers Ben Hogan and Sam Snead.

The return of Philadelphia first baseman Eddie Waitkus to active duty was a relief to baseball fans everywhere. The previous season he had been shot with a rifle at close range in a hotel room and seriously wounded by an obsessive female fan. The bullet had pierced one of his lungs and lodged in the muscles of his back, injuries that required several operations. But Waitkus survived and returned to baseball in 1950. He played six seasons after the shooting, finishing his career with a .285 batting average. The encounter in the Edgewater Beach Hotel in Chicago where the Phillies were staying during a series with the Cubs was seemingly seized upon by Bernard Malamud, who placed a similar event in his 1952 debut novel, *The Natural*, which was adapted into a 1984 film starring Robert Redford as the fictional ballplayer Roy Hobbs. Despite playing a key role in the Whiz Kids rush to the pennant, the Waitkus story does not have a happy Hollywood ending. He was never really able to recover emotionally from the shooting, and his post-baseball career was difficult. He battled depression and alcoholism and endured a nervous breakdown before succumbing to cancer soon after his 53rd birthday.

New York's four-game World Series sweep over Philadelphia was the team's second consecutive world championship. It also meant that $600,000 had to be refunded to customers who had purchased tickets for the fifth, sixth, and seventh games. But Yankees owners Dan Topping and Del Webb discounted the several hundred thousand bucks their club lost by winning so fast, commenting, "We can't think of any money we're happier to lose; we'd rather win games than make money." Those were always the sentiments of the late Colonel Ruppert, who once told associates that his first obligation as Yankees owner was to give his fans a winner—only after that would he worry about his pocketbook.

Burgeoning dynasties were on the rise in other major sports during the year, as well. In basketball, the Minneapolis Lakers became the first champions of the newly formed National Basketball Association when they won the league finals in six games over the Syracuse Nationals. Big center George Mikan was the dominant force for the Lakers, who went 51-17. He averaged a league-best 27.4 points per game during the regular season, and then topped that in the playoffs by averaging a whopping 31.3 points per game. He scored 40 points in a 110–95 victory over Syracuse in the clinching game of the finals. Mikan's Lakers won four of the first five NBA championships to start the decade. In 1950, the Associated Press named Mikan the greatest basketball player of the first half-century. On the gridiron, the Cleveland Browns joined the National Football League from the defunct All-American Football Conference and made it to the title game the next six years (and seven of eight), winning three. Cleveland's Paul Brown was an innovative head coach who revolutionized the game with full-time coaching staffs, radio communication with his quarterback, extensive college scouting, and much more.

In contrast, the AL's Philadelphia franchise, the Athletics, finished last in 1950. After the season, Connie Mack, the heart and soul of the team since their 1901 inception, retired as manager at age 87 after an incredible 50 years of service—the longest by a manager or coach in any major-league sport. He remained as the A's president and named Jimmy Dykes as the new skipper. Considered a dugout's gentleman with his calm demeanor, a suit and tie, and a scorecard rolled up in his hand, Mack ended his managerial career with 3,731 wins, 3,948 losses, nine AL pennants, five World Series championships, and 17 last-place finishes.

The 1950 World Series was the last Fall Classic in which every player from both teams was white. Professional sports were integrating. Professional football integrated in 1946. Jackie Robinson made his big-league debut in baseball in 1947. Finally, professional basketball eliminated its color barrier in 1950, when a trio of players joined the NBA. The Boston Celtics selected forward Chuck Cooper in the second round of the draft, making him the first African-American player to be drafted by an NBA team. Then the former Harlem Globetrotters star Nat "Sweetwater" Clifton signed a contract with the New York Knicks. But it was Earl "Big Cat" Lloyd who became the first African-American player to take the court when he made his debut at the forward position for the Washington Capitols in an October game against the Rochester Royals.

The gradual racial integration of the playing fields was among the most noteworthy highlights of the 1950s. When Jackie Robinson broke through Major League Baseball's color barrier, the significance extended beyond the national pastime. Precisely because baseball was the national pastime, this important event reverberated throughout American society. More than 60 years later, President Barack Obama asserted: "There is a direct line between Jackie Robinson and me." To be sure, sports have always been a laboratory for social issues. Robinson integrated big-league box scores eight years before the US Supreme Court ordered the integration of public schools. So even if sports were late in opening their doors, in another way they were ahead of their time.

1951: CHANGING
OF THE GUARD

A NEW PAIR OF OWNERS MOVED INTO THE PICTURE FOR THE NEW York Yankees in 1945. The heirs of Colonel Jacob Ruppert's estate had to sell the club in a hurry, to cover their estate tax liability, forcing a sale at a time when no one was breaking down any doors to buy a ballclub. Del Webb and his partner, Dan Topping, got the biggest sports bargain of the century—the Yankees, their real estate, their farm system, and its real estate, everything, all for the war-depressed, bargain-basement price of $2.8 million.

The co-owners, however, could not have been more different.

Del Webb had been a left-handed semipro pitcher on the West Coast and had hoped in vain that a big-league team would give him a chance. Then, in 1928, he ran into a situation that changed his life. Pitching against a prison team, he drank from a bucket of contaminated water. He was stricken with a case of typhoid that hospitalized him for a year. During that time he swore off drinking alcohol and decided that he had to make his way in something other than baseball. He moved to Phoenix, then practically pioneer country, to start a construction business, and relied on influential friends to help him secure the many government contracts he received to develop real estate during the Depression. By the time World War II was in full swing, Webb had landed contracts to build internment camps where Americans of Japanese ancestry were imprisoned. If this shamed the slope-shouldered, bespectacled real estate developer, he never said a word. Soon Webb built a real estate empire of retirement communities centered in the Southwest, allowing his construction company to grow into one of the largest and the most profitable in the country. For his success Del Webb earned a spot on the cover of *Time* magazine.

Dan Topping was born into wealth and enjoyed a playboy lifestyle. As a young man he was a leading amateur golfer. Topping reached the quarterfinals of the British Amateur in 1935 and qualified three times for the US Amateur. He enjoyed telling how a journalist once had described his game. "He wrote that I had a long drive, a genial smile, and little else," said Topping. Handsome and with a perpetual tan, he was the epitome of the millionaire sportsman. As the grandson of an iron and steel magnate, he inherited the fortune that enabled him to become an owner of the Yankees for 22 years. "I'm going to buy the Yankees," Topping said shortly before buying the club. "I don't know what I'm going to pay for them, but I'm going to buy them." He had gotten into sports ownership via the late, not-so-great, National Football League team known as the Brooklyn Dodgers. With his ownership interest in the Yankees, Topping hoped to move his football Dodgers from Ebbets Field to Yankee Stadium. New York football Giants owner Tim Mara, holder of the NFL's territorial rights to New York, vetoed the move, even though the Giants then played their home games at the Polo Grounds. Topping moved the team anyway, joined the newly formed All-America Football Conference, and renamed his football team the New York Yankees. In 1950, the team folded when it was not one of the four AAFC teams admitted into the National Football League.

As people, Webb and Topping made for an odd couple. Webb, the Californian who grew up playing amateur baseball and swinging a hammer in the construction business, had little in common with the well-bred Topping, who was educated at an elite East Coast boarding school and then matriculated to an expensive private college. "Webb is the far westerner who looks as though he just shucked off his cowboy stuff," wrote Harold Rosenthal for the *New York Herald Tribune*. "Topping is an Easterner in the yachts-polo-anyone-for-tennis mold."

Nevertheless, as baseball team owners, the two arranged a surprisingly smooth working relationship. Webb labored in the background. He assumed an active role in league affairs and oversaw the daily business operations of the ballclub. He was not a presence in the clubhouse, apart from an annual appearance after yet another World Series triumph, where he might be photographed standing toward the back of the victory platform. Topping was the main man, out front and center stage, the sun-kissed face of ownership. He was often seen smiling and glad-handing at the ballpark and his name commonly appeared in bold print in the newspapers' society pages linking him to a pretty starlet. The immaculately tailored Topping was occupied primarily with getting married and remarried. He said, "I do" six times, most famously to Sonja Henie, the Norwegian figure skating champion.

After buying out Larry MacPhail, the baseball man in the organization, in October 1947, Webb and Topping remained the owners of the New York Yankees until selling the club to a television network, the Columbia Broadcasting System (CBS), for $14 million in 1964. "Best deal I ever made," said Webb.

Television was still a relative luxury to most Americans, but the medium was beginning to assimilate itself more and more into everyday life. In 1950, consumers purchased a record seven million TV sets. And in 1951, technology took a dramatic step when color television was introduced. Another major step in 1951: When the Rams beat the Browns for the NFL championship, fans across the country could watch. The DuMont Network made it the first game ever televised from coast to coast. The marriage between television and sports was still in the newlywed stage. It would prove to be a long and profitable union.

When the Yankees won the World Series in 1947, 1949, and 1950, Del Webb started to puff his chest a bit. Not bad for an old semipro pitcher now holding 50 percent of the club that had won the World Series three out of four years. Webb's Phoenix neighbors had never seen the Yankees play, however, for the team held spring training in St. Petersburg, Florida, and had every year since 1924 (with the exception of Asbury Park, New Jersey, in 1943 and Atlantic City in 1944 to 1945 during the World War II travel ban). Phoenix, since becoming a spring training site, had been the exclusive domain of the New York Giants. To impress his Phoenix neighbors, Webb arranged that for one year and one year only, 1951, the Giants and Yankees would trade spring training sites. It turned out to be an omen. Seven months later the Yankees and Giants would meet in the World Series for the first time since 1937.

Phoenix also set the stage for Mickey Mantle's debut in a Yankees uniform. Signed by scout Tom Greenwade immediately following his high school graduation in 1949, Mickey had planned to be in Florida training with the club's top minor-league team, the Kansas City Blues, when he was told to report with the major leaguers to Phoenix for training camp, which Casey Stengel called his instructional school. In Mantle the manager saw a hard-hitting, poor-fielding shortstop who would never take the job away from Phil Rizzuto, the previous year's Most Valuable Player. Scooter played with flair and a youthful exuberance—and a wad of gum on the button of his cap—but he was dead serious about winning, which made him a Stengel stalwart. But the manager was captivated with the sandy-haired Oklahoma kid with the good arm, fast bat, and blazing running speed. "Kiddo," said Stengel, "I think we'll try you in the outfield."

There were several other prospects in camp, including Gil McDougald, but by the time the club left Phoenix for a 10-day trip up and down the West Coast (the Yankees' first-ever West Coast trip), mining box-office gold out of the exhibition crowds in the minor-league parks, Mantle had become a major gate attraction, thanks to the adoring newspaper articles written about the bashful kid who hit with power from both sides of the plate, a skill which was a rarity in those days. Fans came to see him belt long home runs, and he didn't disappoint them. During a spring exhibition game against the University of Southern California, Mantle whacked three homers—one traveled an estimated 650 feet. In all, he set Phoenix afire, hitting .402 with nine homers and 31 RBIs over the Cactus League schedule. Mantle won intra-squad footraces by such wide margins that coaches suspected he'd somehow cheated. "He has more speed than any slugger," enthused manager Casey Stengel, "and more slug than any speedster. And nobody has ever had more of both of them together."

The Old Perfessor couldn't wait to unleash his newfound star on the American League. So certain were the Yankees of Mantle's impending superstardom, in spring training, they assigned him uniform number 6, an obvious progression from Ruth's number 3, Gehrig's number 4, and DiMaggio's number 5. If Mantle wasn't aware of the Yankees campaign to build him up as Joe DiMaggio's successor, he was now.

The Yankees were without Whitey Ford, one of their top pitching prospects. Ford had just begun his baseball career when he was drafted in 1950, and he was afraid the Yankees would forget about him. Hardly. The entire team showed up at his wedding in 1951, while he was in the

Joe DiMaggio and Mickey Mantle, the once and future faces of the New York Yankees, in the 1950s. NATIONAL BASEBALL HALL OF FAME AND MUSEUM, INC.

Army. Three days later, on April 17, he threw out the ceremonial first pitch against the Boston Red Sox, proudly wearing his Army uniform. It was Opening Day and the rookie Mickey Mantle blushed when a photographer asked him to pose for a picture with Ted Williams and Joe DiMaggio before the game. But Mantle was not the only member of the organization making his major-league debut that day.

For the first time, in a career that would span more than 50 years, Yankee Stadium public address announcer Bob Sheppard announced the starting lineups and introduced each player's at-bat. The first name Sheppard announced was DiMaggio—Dom DiMaggio, the center fielder and leadoff batter for the Red Sox. The Yankees lineup that day included five Hall of Famers: Mantle, DiMaggio, Phil Rizzuto, Yogi Berra, and Johnny Mize; the Sox had three more, Williams, Bobby Doerr, and Lou Boudreau. Employing a clear, concise, and correct vocal style that would go on to announce the names of hundreds of players— both unfamiliar and legendary—with equal and divine reverence, Sheppard, known as The Voice of God, became as synonymous with Yankee Stadium as its copper frieze and Monument Park.

Playing his first game in pinstripes and batting third, Mantle grounded out to second base in his first major-league at-bat. He hit a run-scoring single in the sixth inning, and went 1-for-4 and scored a run in the Yankees' Opening Day 5–0 victory over Boston in the Bronx. Right-handed pitcher Vic Raschi threw the complete-game shutout. In his first six games, Mantle collected eight hits and drove in five runs. His batting average was .320, inspiring Jimmy Cannon of the *New York Post* to roar, "I'm all out of breath hollering it up for this kid." This kid, Mantle, was just 19 years old.

The youngster's breathtaking talent was on full display when Mantle hit his first career home run off Chicago hurler Randy Gumpert in an 8–3 victory over the White Sox at Comiskey Park, on May 1. It traveled 450 feet to deep center field. The ball blasted on Mother's Day, which Mantle inscribed—"My first H.R. in the Majors, May 1, 1951, 4:50 p.m. Chicago, 6th inning off Randy Gumpert"—would be sold for $165,000 at a Sotheby's auction in 2004. The game was also noteworthy for the debut of Minnie Minoso, becoming the first black player for the White Sox. Minoso hit a home run against New York's Vic Raschi in his first plate appearance. Two days later, it was another Yankees rookie's turn to shine. In a 17–3 rout over the St. Louis Browns at Sportsman's Park, Gil McDougald tied a major-league record (since broken) with six RBIs in one inning. He hit his first career home run, a grand slam, and then added a two-run triple, as the Bronx Bombers broke out for 11 runs in the ninth inning.

An eight-game winning streak propelled the Yankees into first place in early May. Leading the way was Mantle—raw, untutored, small town–shy, but obviously able to knock the ball a country mile. And he was able to do it from both sides of the plate. His father, Mutt Mantle, who thought of everything when it came to baseball, had started him on a program of switch-hitting at age five. By May 18, Mantle was hitting .316 with four homers (two right-handed and two left-handed), and led the AL with 26 RBIs. As a left-handed hitter, Mantle pulverized low pitches, golfing them prodigious distances. Right-handed, his best swing was a level one, generated a couple of inches below the shoulders This swing produced line drives that outfielders simply couldn't get to in time.

As the season progressed, however, AL pitchers figured out Mantle's primary weakness and began to feed him a steady diet of high fastballs. As it happened, his production waned. He batted .175 without a homer over his final 11 games of May. After fanning in all five at-bats during a May 30 doubleheader in Boston, and being pulled before each game ended, he broke down in tears on the bench. Mantle's rookie season must have been nerve-racking for a rural kid. He was still only two years out of high school; he and his teenage wife, Merlyn, his high school sweetheart in Commerce, Oklahoma, were overwhelmed by the towering skyscrapers and the fast pace of the big city. On top of that, reporters from a dozen newspapers came into the locker room day after day with variations on the same question about his medical deferment from the Army due to a bone infection in his left ankle called osteomy-elitis, the result of a high school football injury, that left Mantle open to criticism that he was shirking his patriotic duty.

His father's illness added to his troubles. Mutt Mantle had been diagnosed with Hodgkin's disease, a form of cancer. The prognosis was poor. Mutt could no longer sleep in a bed; he had to sit up and try to get some rest in a chair. The kid's eyes were red a good deal of the time, and it wasn't just from the frustration of watching his batting average drop under .260 by the end of June. The low point came on July 13 when Cleveland's Bob Lemon struck out Mantle three times. That prompted Stengel to farm out the youngster to Triple-A Kansas City for more seasoning. Mantle was devastated. He struggled in Kansas City, starting off hitless in his first 22 at-bats. Then he called his father in Oklahoma. "Dad, I don't think I can play ball," he said. Mutt Mantle drove all the way to the Kansas City hotel where Mickey was staying. Mickey expected a comforting pat on the back, but when Mutt walked into the room, he began packing his son's bag, saying that he was taking Mickey home. "Thought I raised a man," said Mutt. "You ain't nothing but a coward." Mantle asked his father for one more chance. Mutt relented, then he returned to the Oklahoma mines. "I'm gonna do it for him," Mantle told himself, and he followed through on his promise. The newly focused teenager rededicated himself to baseball and eventually rediscovered his powerful hitting stroke. Over his next 40 games with Kansas City, Mickey hit .361 with 11 homers and 50 RBIs. Mickey hoped it wouldn't be too long before the Yankees recalled him to New York.

Another promising first-time appearance occurred in the spring of 1951 when the first edition of Topps baseball cards were released in a limited set of 52 cards designed to let kids play a game of card baseball. Along with a photograph and a biography of a player, each card had an at-bat result, such as single, double, flyout, and so on. Although unique among subsequent Topps sets—and packed with taffy, not bubble-gum—these cards would establish the Topps company as the leader in an upstart collectibles business and usher in an everlasting love affair between cardboard and fans.

The Yankees were chugging along at a 30-17 clip and in second place when the team became a witness to history during a game on June 8. White Sox reliever Marv Rotblatt became the first pitcher to be driven from the bullpen in a golf cart when he entered the game in the eighth inning to face the Yankees in a 4–2 Bombers victory at Comiskey Park. The New York media lampooned the move, with one report noting, "Chicago is going bush." Yankees manager Casey Stengel also objected, saying, "Yankees pitchers don't ride in golf carts, they ride in Cadillacs." Despite the negative press attention, another car arrived later in that same series, but this time, it was for the Yankees pitchers. The car was a little different, too: It was a black Cadillac hearse from a nearby South Side funeral home.

Like doubleheaders, the bullpen cart has pretty much disappeared from the game, and that's a shame because it was a true slice of Americana. It was fun to see a reliever, called on to save the day, ride into action in a golf cart topped by a ridiculous, oversized baseball cap. But the bullpens in many stadiums are located along the foul lines, a short walk from the pitching mound. And in those parks where the pens are situated beyond the outfield fences, the pitchers have gotten used to jogging to their jobs. The first chauffeured reliever, Rotblatt didn't have a long or very successful major-league career—he pitched for parts of only three seasons with the White Sox from 1948 to 1951, posting a 4.82 ERA in 74 2/3 innings—but you can't deny he made his mark. Later in the year he appeared on the quiz show *You Bet Your Life*, hosted by Groucho Marx.

Listed at 5-foot-6, Rotblatt was one of the shortest pitchers in the big leagues. But he wasn't the shortest player to appear in a major-league game—by a long shot. That distinction belongs to Eddie Gaedel, a 3-foot-7-inch circus worker, who came to the plate for the St. Louis Browns during the second game of a doubleheader against the Detroit Tigers, on August 19. It was part of a publicity stunt by Browns owner

Bill Veeck (as in wreck), who was always desperately seeking attention for his last place team. Veeck decided to stage a between-games celebration of the 50th anniversary of the American League. Hoping to drum up interest in his moribund franchise, Veeck hired the 65-pound Gaedel to provide a big finish. At the end of the proceedings, Gaedel popped out of a giant papier-mâché birthday cake, dressed in a tiny Browns uniform. The crowd roared its approval, yet the greatest promotional stunt in the history of baseball was still to come.

With the Browns due up in the bottom of the first inning of the nightcap, Gaedel bounded out of the dugout, swinging three toy bats. The announcer introduced him as the pinch-hitter for the leadoff batter Frank Saucier. That's when umpire Ed Hurley summoned Browns manager Zach Taylor for a meeting. Taylor brought out an official AL contract with Gaedel's signature on it, and waved the paper in the face of the humbled official, who had no choice but to allow Gaedel his turn at bat. So wearing number 1/8, Eddie Gaedel stepped into the batter's box, bent his 43-inch frame into a deep crouch, and created the smallest strike zone in history—about an inch and a half. Detroit pitcher Bob Cain tried to suppress laughter. Gaedel, who was under strict orders from Veeck not to swing, looked at four consecutive balls and trotted to first base, tipping his cap to the crowd along the way. Gaedel was replaced by a pinch-runner, Jim Delsing, and exited to raucous cheers.

Fans and players were hysterically laughing, but AL president William Harridge was not amused. He voided Gaedel's contract the next day, saying it was not in the best interests of baseball. Within two days, the rules were changed to ban special players like Gaedel from the game. To this day, though, you can still find Gaedel's name in the *Baseball Encyclopedia*, and his career on-base percentage is a perfect 1.000.

One of the greatest peacetime spy dramas in the nation's history reached its climax as Julius and Ethel Rosenberg were sentenced to death for revealing atomic secrets to Soviet Russia. The junior senator from Wisconsin, Joseph McCarthy, was ramping up his investigation into alleged communists he believed were infiltrating our government, our military, and our schools. The biggest sports news off the playing fields involved a college basketball scandal that rocked sports fans around the country. In mid-February, three players from City College of New York were arrested for fixing games. That is, they purposely did not try their best so games would turn out favorably for certain gamblers. The news was shocking. CCNY had been one of the feel-good stories of 1950 after winning both the NIT and NCAA tournaments in the same season. But that wasn't even the worst part. At first, most people believed the scandal was limited to games played at New York's Madison Square Garden. That turned out to be just the start, though. Eventually, the scandal spread to cities from coast to coast and was a major black eye for college sports.

Although the Yankees were winning, the mood in the locker room was not always harmonious. The relationship between DiMaggio and Stengel continued to deteriorate to the point that they now ignored each other's existence. New York beat writers who traveled with the club had no difficulty picking up on the palpable tension between player and manager. When reporters approached Stengel to question him about the volatile situation, he replied: "So what if he doesn't talk to me? I'll get by and so will he." The absolute discord between the two would hit a sour note during the July 7 game at Boston's Fenway Park. It was the dog days of summer, and Casey's club was flagging. The Yankees were only one game behind the Chicago White Sox, but they had lost four of their previous five games. Their play was uninspired. The three-day All-Star break would begin at the conclusion of the next afternoon's game, and Stengel admitted his team was fatigued. "Four or five of these players are dead tired," he explained.

Stengel's diagnosis of his team proved prophetic. In the first inning, Bobby Doerr hit an easy popup that DiMaggio misplayed, coming up short on the shallow flyball that dropped for a hit, allowing two runs to score. The next batter, Billy Goodman, hit a high flyball to right-center that DiMaggio couldn't chase down, loading the bases. From Stengel's point of view, those were two plays that a younger version of DiMaggio would have easily made. When Clyde Vollmer followed with a grand slam home run, the Yankees were deep in a six-run hole, which prompted the New York manager to make a fateful decision. He dispatched rookie Jackie Jensen out to center field. When Jensen reached center he informed DiMaggio that Casey was pulling him from the game. With a large Fenway Park crowd looking on, DiMaggio trotted from the field with his head down.

Once again, Stengel had displayed a complete lack of regard for DiMaggio's public stature. At least, that was how Joe perceived events. The skipper's decision to make the move and replace the aging superstar in the middle of the game strained an already acrimonious relationship. Following the 10–4 loss to the Red Sox, DiMaggio boiled with rage in the clubhouse as teammates looked at one another in stony silence. DiMaggio's left leg was ailing, Stengel explained, that's why he removed him from the game. Nobody was buying what Casey was selling. The Yankees lost again the following afternoon, too. More than any other team, the Yankees needed the brief rest provided by the All-Star break. They had the look of a tired team and they had limped into the midsummer respite, both literally and figuratively, having lost five of their last six, including a three-game sweep in Boston at the hands of the Red Sox. The Yankees sank into third place behind the first-place White Sox and second-place Red Sox.

Indeed, the All-Star break served the Yankees well. It allowed the players to clear their collective heads, and when the team returned to action they received a much-needed lift. On July 12, at Cleveland's Municipal Stadium, Yankees right-hander Allie Reynolds, facing only 29 batters, no-hit the Indians, 1–0, thanks to Gene Woodling's solo home run off Bob Feller in the seventh inning. Reynolds retired the last 17 batters to face him, striking out Bobby Avila to end the game.

Twice, Reynolds's baseball career took a positive turn because he listened to good advice. In college at the school that is now Oklahoma State, Reynolds was a running back on the football team and a pitcher on the baseball team. After receiving professional contract offers from both sports, he was forced to make a choice. Reynolds asked his baseball coach, Hank Iba, for help in making the decision. Iba, who would later be enshrined in the Naismith Memorial Basketball Hall of Fame, recommended Reynolds stick to pitching. "It was a fine suggestion," said Reynolds.

The beefy right-hander signed with the Cleveland Indians and reached the majors in 1943. While he possessed a blazing fastball, Reynolds couldn't always control it, leading the league in strikeouts and bases on balls over the next four seasons. By the time he was 30 years old, Reynolds had managed only a 51-47 lifetime mark for the Indians. Prior to the 1947 season, the Yankees acquired Reynolds in a trade for second baseman Joe Gordon, the 1942 AL Most Valuable Player. During spring training, the veteran Yankees pitcher Spud Chandler urged Reynolds to set up batters by changing speeds. Reynolds did just that.

In his first season with the Yankees, Reynolds went 19-8 and won his first World Series game. In 1949, he proved himself a great World Series pitcher in the series opener, throwing a two-hit shutout and outlasting Don Newcombe, 1–0. In the fourth game he retired all 10 Dodgers batters he faced to earn a save. Said manager Casey Stengel of Reynolds's dual ability to start and relieve: "He's two pitchers rolled into one."

Toward the end of the summer of 1951, the Yankees and the resurgent Cleveland Indians—winners of 13 games in a row to start the month of August—played leapfrog with each other in the standings as the White Sox and Red Sox faded badly. Rookie Gil McDougald was the team's leading hitter, and with DiMaggio not up to snuff, catcher Yogi Berra supplied most of the punch with Gene Woodling and Hank Bauer chipping in admirably. To fortify the offense, Mantle returned to fuel New York down the stretch. The kid returned to the Yankees on August 20, never to spend another moment in the minors. Now wearing the more familiar jersey number 7, Mantle batted .284 with six homers and 20 RBIs in the team's remaining 27-game charge. He hit a home run on August 29 off the ancient Satchel Paige, the famed Negro Leagues right-hander who was finishing up his legendary career with Bill Veeck's hapless St. Louis Browns.

Also that day, the Yankees traded rookie pitcher Lew Burdette along with $50,000 to the Boston Braves for right-hander Johnny Sain to bolster the pitching staff. Between 1946 and 1950, Sain won 20 games four times and led the Braves to the NL championship in '48. He and fellow pitcher Warren Spahn were so crucial to the Braves pennant run that year an enduring slogan was created around them: "Spahn and Sain, and pray for rain." As a versatile swingman for the Yankees, Sain appeared in seven games, starting four and completing one, while posting a mark of two wins, one loss, and one save down the stretch. Sain also has the distinction of being the last pitcher to face Babe Ruth in a game and the first to face Jackie Robinson. As for the young pitcher sent packing, Burdette would pay long-term dividends to the Braves and haunt the Bronx Bombers a few years down the road.

With the Indians leading the Yanks by only one game, on September 16 and 17 Cleveland was scheduled for its final visit of the season to the Stadium. To face the right-handed aces of the Cleveland staff, Bob Feller and Bob Lemon, Stengel chose Allie Reynolds and Eddie Lopat. For the opener of the two-game set, 68,760 people, the largest crowd of the season, jammed into the Stadium to see if the defending champion Yankees could stay in the race. Feller, one of the great pitching stars in the history of the game, was 22-7 going into the game, and was one of three pitchers, along with Early Wynn and Mike Garcia, to win 20 or more games for the Indians.

Reynolds was pitching the best baseball of his career, and on this afternoon he pitched brilliantly, allowing only five hits and one run. The Yanks were leading, 3–1, and in the bottom of the fifth Mantle, batting third in the lineup, doubled, and Berra, batting fourth, received an intentional walk as Feller preferred to pitch to DiMaggio. DiMaggio, burning inside because Stengel had dropped him to fifth in the order, lined a ball into the left-center field alleyway for a two-run triple and a

5–1 Yankees lead, finishing Feller and the Indians for the day. After the game a pile of Western Union telegrams were delivered to DiMaggio's locker, congratulating him on his clutch hit. "Now when I get a hit," said DiMaggio with contempt, "they send me telegrams." New York was back in first place by percentage points over Cleveland in their tug-o-war for the AL pennant flag.

The second game of the series pitted Lopat, vying for his 20th win of the season, against Indians sinkerball pitcher Bob Lemon, who already had posted 17 wins on the year and always gave the Yanks difficulty. This was another pitchers' battle. The score was tied at one run apiece. It was the bottom of the ninth inning. Phil Rizzuto was at bat. DiMaggio was on third base. Rizzuto took Lemon's first pitch, a called strike, and argued the call with the umpire. That gave him time to grab his bat from both ends, the sign to DiMaggio that a squeeze play was on for the next pitch. But DiMaggio broke early, surprising Rizzuto. Lemon, seeing what was happening, threw high, to avoid a bunt, aiming behind Rizzuto. But with Joltin' Joe bearing down on him, Rizzuto got his bat up in time to lay down a bunt. "If I didn't bunt, the pitch would've hit me right in the head," Rizzuto told the *New York Times*. "I bunted it with both feet off the ground, but I got it off toward first base." DiMaggio scored the winning run. Stengel called it "the greatest play I ever saw." As the winning run scored, Lemon angrily threw both the ball and his glove into the stands. With 12 games to go, New York now led by one full game.

In 1950, the Indians had knocked off the Tigers to enable the Yankees to win the pennant, and in '51 it was the Tigers who reciprocated and beat the Indians three straight in late September to help the Yankees. The Cleveland staff of Feller, Garcia, Wynn, and Lemon, overworked and arm-weary, folded down the stretch. With five games left in the season, the Yankees needed only one more victory to clinch their third straight AL pennant. Stengel selected Reynolds—nicknamed The Chief because he was part Creek Indian—and Raschi to pitch against the Red Sox in a doubleheader at the Stadium on September 28, which coincidentally was American Indian Day across the country.

Reynolds made sure the Yankees' pennant-clinching party would be held in grand style, as he entered the record books by becoming the first AL pitcher to record two no-hitters in the same season. The first no-hitter was on July 12, in Cleveland, against Feller and the Indians. Then, on September 28, at Yankee Stadium, Reynolds was one out away from joining Johnny Vander Meer of the Cincinnati Reds as the only pitchers to that point to accomplish the feat twice in a season. That final out was Ted Williams of the Boston Red Sox—one of the best hitters of all time—and Reynolds had to get him out twice. Williams hit a foul popup that catcher Yogi Berra dropped. Unfazed, on the next pitch, Reynolds got Williams to hit another spinning foul popup to the very same spot, and this time Berra squeezed the ball in his mitt for the final out of an 8–0 win, clinching another AL pennant for the Yankees. "When I die," team co-owner Del Webb later told Berra, "I hope they give me a second chance the way they did you."

The Yankees claimed their third consecutive pennant, a 98-65 record lifting them five games ahead of the second-place Indians, but Joe DiMaggio, 36, his body aching, was no longer the Jolter—he slumped to .263 with only 12 home runs and 71 runs batted in. Yogi Berra was the Yankees' most dangerous hitter now, with 27 homers and 88 RBIs. Mantle, in his rookie season, batted .267 with 13 homers and 65 RBIs in 96 games. Another newcomer, third baseman Gil McDougald, the only New York regular to hit over .300, was the AL's Rookie of the Year, with a .306 batting average, 14 homers, and 63 RBIs. Even with Whitey Ford in the Army, the pitching held up. The Yankees had two 21-game winners in Raschi and Lopat. Reynolds contributed 17 more wins, including seven by shutout—and two of those were no-hitters—and six saves in relief. Manager Casey Stengel, once considered a clown from his comical Brooklyn days but now revered as The Old Perfessor, smartly guided the Yankees back to their former greatness.

The Brooklyn Dodgers shot out of the gate in 1951, eager to make amends for having coughed up the National League pennant to the Philadelphia Phillies on the final day of the 1950 season. Their rival, the New York Giants, struggled to reach .500 after 40 games. Finally, manager Leo Durocher got his wish when the front office promoted Willie Mays from their Double-A squad, the Minneapolis Millers, a few weeks after he turned 20 years old. In his debut with the Giants on May 25, Mays batted third and played center field before a crowd of 21,082 against the Phillies at Shibe Park. The Giants hoped to regroup with Mays and put themselves within striking distance of the Dodgers. But Mays started off slowly, and as late as August 11 the Giants still trailed the Dodgers by 13 games. "The Giants is dead," Dodgers manager Charlie Dressen declared.

Then, on August 12, the Giants began an incredible rush. They won 16 games in a row and rolled on from there. With a little help from a sign-stealing system in the Polo Grounds consisting of a telescope and an electric buzzer, the Giants played to a 37-7 mark over the final weeks, eventually tying the Dodgers at the end of the regular season and forcing a three-game playoff to determine the NL champion.

The Giants won the first game at Ebbets Field in Brooklyn; the Dodgers took the second game at the Polo Grounds in Manhattan. Brooklyn was poised to win the third game and the pennant as it took a 4–1 lead into the bottom of the ninth at the Polo Grounds, on October 3. But then, Don Newcombe, the Dodgers ace pitcher, began to tire. The first two Giants hitters singled. With one out, Giants first baseman Whitey Lockman doubled, scoring one run and putting men on second and third. The Dodgers had two pitchers warming up in the bullpen, starter Ralph Branca and rookie reliever Clem Labine. The bullpen coach signaled that Labine was bouncing his curve, so manager Dressen chose to bring Branca into the game to face third baseman Bobby Thomson, who had hit 31 home runs already that year. Giants manager and third base coach Durocher pulled Thomson aside and reportedly told him, "Bobby, if you've ever hit one, hit one now." The Giants rookie Willie Mays was on deck, but Dressen chose to pitch to Thomson, who had already homered off Branca to help the Giants win Game 1. Thomson stepped to the plate. "I was so nervous my eyeballs

37

were vibrating," Thomson said later. The first pitch was a called strike. On Branca's second pitch, Thomson tagged the ball into the left field seats, just clearing the high wall at the 315-foot mark. New York Giants radio broadcaster Russ Hodges's call is one of the most famous in Major League Baseball history. "There's a long drive . . . it's gonna be, I believe . . . the Giants win the pennant! The Giants win the pennant! . . . and they're going crazy! The Giants win the pennant! The Giants win the pennant!"

With that one mighty swing of the bat, the never-say-die Giants, seemingly hopelessly beaten, instead won the playoff and the pennant. The Brooklyn Dodgers were devastated. It was the third time in six years they had lost a chance to win the NL pennant on the season's final day. When Thomson finished dancing around the bases in unbridled glee, he was mobbed by teammates at home plate and thousands of fans who had stormed the field. Thomson's three-run homer, known as The Shot Heard 'Round the World, won the game and the pennant, 5–4, capping one of baseball's greatest season comebacks with one of the most dramatic home runs in baseball history.

The New York Giants were riding an all-time emotional high from Bobby Thomson's miracle theatrics, and would open the 1951 World Series against the Yankees the next afternoon at Yankee Stadium. Despite a slow start, Willie Mays got untracked and won the NL Rookie of the Year Award. He completed his first big-league year hitting a respectable .274 with 20 homers. His presence helped fortify an already potent Giants lineup, which included shortstop Alvin Dark, who batted .303 with a league-leading 41 doubles; left fielder Monte Irvin, the team's first African-American player from 1949, who hit .312 with 24 home runs and a team-leading 121 RBIs; and infielder/outfielder Bobby Thomson, who batted .293 with a career-high 32 home runs. A pair of 23-game winners in Sal Maglie and Larry Jansen led the Giants pitching staff. Maglie was known as Sal The Barber because he shaved batters' chins with his inside fastball. "When I'm pitching, I own the plate," he warned.

This was the sixth time the two New York teams would be meeting in the World Series. Stengel had been a playing member of the Giants the first three times the teams battled for a championship in 1921, 1922, and 1923. The Yankees reached the World Series in 1921 and 1922, each time facing the rival Giants in a Polo Grounds World Series. The Yankees were then playing their home games in the Giants ballpark, and the teams exchanged dugouts between games. The Giants won the series both years. In 1923, each team again won their respective pennants, setting up a Yankees-Giants World Series for a third straight season. But this matchup had a plot twist. The 1923 World Series was the first Subway Series. The subway had become the main form of public transportation in the city and was a convenient way to travel between ballparks. The Yankees, in their first year in the new Yankee Stadium, gained a measure of revenge by clinching their first-ever championship in a Game 6 win on the very Polo Grounds field from which they'd been evicted.

As a player, Stengel's most memorable moments on the field occurred while playing for the Giants in the 1923 World Series against the Yankees. He hit two home runs to win two games for the Giants, but it was not enough. Babe Ruth swatted three solo home runs and Herb Pennock won two games to help the Yankees open Yankee Stadium in grand style with the first of their 27 world championships.

In the opening game of the 1951 World Series, the first all-black outfield in major-league history made its appearance when Monte Irvin, Willie Mays, and Hank Thompson took the field for the Giants at Yankee Stadium. In a curious move, Giants manager Leo Durocher replaced the injured Don Mueller in right field with Thompson, a third baseman by trade, and used veteran outfielder Bobby Thomson at the hot corner. The Giants had won one of the most dramatic pennant races in the game's history, but it left the pitching staff, mainly anchor starters Maglie and Jansen, spent at World Series time. Both had pitched in the final playoff game against Brooklyn a day earlier. Facing a similar situation as his Philadelphia counterpart had the previous year, Durocher handed the ball to a surprise starter, Dave Koslo, who had compiled a pedestrian 10-9 season record, to pitch the opener.

Mantle was playing in the first World Series game he had ever seen. Not only that, but he was the leadoff batter. He did comparatively little, drawing two walks as Koslo, a left-hander of modest abilities, beat the Yankees, 5–1, with a five-hitter. The Giants, with adrenaline still pumping, had maintained their momentum. Monte Irvin climaxed a two-run rally in the first inning with an electrifying steal of home, the first steal of home plate in a World Series since 1928, when Bob Meusel of the Yankees swiped the dish in a Game 3 victory over the Cardinals. Alvin Dark iced the game in the sixth with a three-run homer. Reynolds, who had hurled two no-hitters in the regular season but was anything but unhittable in the series opener, took the loss. It was the first opening game series loss for the Yankees since 1936, a remarkable span of ten Series in which they appeared.

The Yankees won the second game as southpaw Eddie Lopat throttled the Giants attack with his slow curves, scattering five hits through nine innings for a 3–1 victory, but Mantle wasn't around to help celebrate. He started the game with a bunt single and ended in a room at nearby Lenox Hill Hospital in Manhattan, with his father in the adjoining bed. In the fifth inning, Willie Mays led off with a flyball to right center. Mantle had been covering extra ground all season, covering for the aging DiMaggio, in the twilight of his career. According to several sources, Stengel had instructed Mantle earlier to "take everything you can get over in center. The Dago's heel is hurting pretty bad."

Mantle ran hard for the ball. DiMaggio did, too. This was the World Series, and the entire country was watching. An instant before Mantle was to glove the high fly, DiMaggio called, "I got it." In reverence, the rookie right fielder pulled up at the last second, turned on the outfield grass to slow his momentum, and fell to the turf, crumpled in a heap. The 19-year-old speedster had stepped on a drainpipe and torn ligaments in his right knee. DiMaggio caught the ball, but Mantle was finished for the Series. He had to be carried off the field and rushed by cab to the hospital for surgery—the first of a series of leg injuries that robbed him of much of his speed and plagued him throughout the rest of his career. As teammate Jerry Coleman said, The Mick had "the body of a god. Only Mantle's legs were mortal."

On the way out of the stadium, Mutt Mantle tried to help his son into the taxi that would take him to the hospital, but when Mickey placed his hand for support on his father's shoulder, Mutt collapsed from the weight, his spine already ravaged by Hodgkin's disease. The two watched the rest of the World Series from their adjacent hospital beds. Mickey had surgery and was sent home to heal. Mutt was given a grim prognosis and succumbed the following May. He was 39 years old. Mutt Mantle was denied watching most of his son's major-league career, but at least he saw Mickey switch-hit in a World Series, right-handed in the first game, left-handed in the second.

His father's death had a profound effect on Mantle throughout his career. He frequently mentioned that he would never live past 40 years of age because his father hadn't. Cancer had also claimed his grandfather and two of his uncles well before their time. For the rest of his playing days, Mantle told friends, he believed he would also die young. This fatalistic attitude haunted Mantle throughout his life, and was reflected in his poor training habits.

The series shifted to the Polo Grounds for the next three games. In the fifth inning of Game 3, the Giants held a slim 1–0 edge when the outcome of the contest turned on one of the most provocative plays in World Series history. With one out, Giants shortstop Eddie Stanky coaxed a walk off Raschi. Stanky then tried to steal second. Catcher Yogi Berra, the AL Most Valuable Player, threw a bullet to shortstop Phil Rizzuto, who was waiting by second base with the ball to tag out the would-be base stealer. Stanky looked to be a dead duck. But Stanky, an accomplished soccer player in his youth, managed in sliding to purposely kick the ball out of Rizzuto's glove. As Rizzuto chased the ball into the outfield, Stanky steamed to third. Somehow the Brat had turned a caught stealing into a two-base error.

Yogi Berra, the 1951 AL MVP, trying to leg out an infield hit during that season's World Series at Yankee Stadium. NATIONAL BASEBALL HALL OF FAME AND MUSEUM, INC.

Stengel and Rizzuto predictably protested that Stanky should be ruled out for interference, but their griping got them nowhere with the umpires. Instead of two out and nobody on, Stanky was standing safely on third with only one out. Following the imbroglio the Yanks swiftly lost focus. Two hits, an error, and a Whitey Lockman three-run homer later, the Giants had enough runs to win convincingly, 6–2. Rizzuto never forgave Stanky for outfoxing him, saying, "He plays a snarling, dog-eat-dog kind of baseball." Leo Durocher, who managed Stanky with the Dodgers and Giants, could appreciate Stanky's clever play. "He can't hit, can't run, can't field. He's no nice guy . . . all the little SOB can do is win."

The Giants were up two games to one on the Yankees. The Yankees players, certain that this series would be a sweep, as it was the year before against the Phillies, now realized that their complacency was costing them the series. Stengel had seemingly tapped late-season acquisition Johnny Sain, who had made only four starts for the Bombers that season, to pitch Game 4, but then Mother Nature intervened. A deluge of heavy rains came and delayed the Series for two days. The unexpected reprieve gave Stengel a chance to regroup his pitching staff and allowed him to roll out his Big Three once more. "The next day it rained," reported Frank Graham in the *New York Journal-American*, "and it was as if the rain cooled the Giants off, for they were not the same again."

When play resumed, the Yankees were able to return to their Game 1 starter, Reynolds, on three days rest. He was sharper this time around, and atoned for his first-game defeat by going the distance in a 6–2 victory, striking out seven, as the Yankees evened the series. DiMaggio, held hitless in 11 at-bats in the first three games, found his groove and paced the Yankees' attack with a single and a two-run homer. Maglie, starting for the Giants and pooped from his late-season heroics, didn't have much. The Yankees nicked Sal The Barber for eight hits and four runs.

The fifth game was a complete blowout as the Yankees pounded the Giants, 13–1, at the Polo Grounds. The batting star was 23-year-old infielder Gil McDougald, who hit a grand slam home run in the third inning, becoming the third player in World Series history to hit a grand slam, and the first rookie to accomplish the feat. DiMaggio had three hits and three RBIs, and Rizzuto had two hits, including a homer, with three RBIs. Lopat pitched another complete game, allowing just an unearned run to notch his second win of the series, as the Yankees were now up three games to two. Lopat had pitched all nine innings to win Games 2 and 5, allowing only 10 hits and one earned run in 18 innings.

The sixth game was a thriller right down to the wire. Hank Bauer, playing right field in place of the injured Mantle, slugged a bases-loaded triple with two outs in the sixth inning, clearing the bases to give the Yankees a 4–1 lead. For Bauer, it was the perfect time to shake off his World Series misery. In 38 previous at-bats in the Fall Classic, he had collected only five hits (all singles), for a paltry .132 batting average and only one RBI. On this occasion, the former US Marine came through with flying colors to deliver the bases-clearing triple. Then, in the ninth inning, after the Giants closed the deficit to 4–3 and with the tying run in scoring position, a racing Bauer made a sensational catch on a low line drive to end the game—and the Series. Raschi, who pitched into the seventh inning, gained credit for the victory, and received valuable relief help from Johnny Sain and Bob Kuzava.

The Yankees were world champions for the 14th time in franchise history. Mother Nature was as important for the Yankees as the hitting of Bobby Brown, who batted .357. Some World Series delays have more impact than others. Brown married his wife Sara later in the month, after postponing the wedding four days because rain delayed the Series. Phil Rizzuto batted .320 and was the World Series MVP. He became fired up and played like a demon after Stanky's famous drop kick in the third game. Though an integral part of the team's success, the formerly underappreciated Rizzuto was finally getting his due. Often overshadowed by Hall of Fame teammates, it made sense that Rizzuto was the first "mystery guest" on the old game show *What's My Line?* (DiMaggio and Mantle would appear on the program in later years as well; appearances that greatly enhanced their popularity). But those who played the game understood Rizzuto's value to his team. Ted Williams once remarked, "If the Red Sox would have had Phil we would have won all those pennants."

This Fall Classic would be the last of the Subway Series between the teams just a short walk apart across the Harlem River, the Yankees of Bronx, New York, and the Giants of the Polo Grounds, Manhattan. It had been billed as a matchup between cross-river rivals and their respective rookie stars Willie Mays and Mickey Mantle, but neither Mantle nor Mays were factors in the outcome. Mickey hurt his leg in Game 2 and missed the remainder of the series. He had one hit in just five at-bats. Willie batted just .182 with four hits in 24 at-bats, scoring only one run and driving in one. A Yankees winning World Series share was $6,500. With his share, Mickey Mantle bought his mother a more spacious house in Commerce.

1952: PLAYERS GO TO WAR

THE 1951 WORLD SERIES WOULD END UP BEING THE FINALE FOR JOE DiMaggio's baseball career. He finished the 1951 regular season with an average of .263, by far the lowest mark of his career. He hit .261 in the World Series, but contributed three extra-base hits and five RBIs. The double he lashed to right field off New York Giants 20-game winner Larry Jansen in the sixth game was to be his last hit. The Yankee Clipper was nearing his 37th birthday when World Series play ended. Following 13 seasons with the Yankees, he had posted a career average of .325 and 361 home runs. However, he felt he wasn't able to play up to his own standards anymore. Still, he ended the season up to his standards in one way: with a ninth World Series title in 10 tries.

Not long after the Series ended, DiMaggio arranged a meeting with team owners Dan Topping and Del Webb. He complained his body was aching and acknowledged his skills had deteriorated. He told them that he didn't think he could play anymore, so he had decided to retire. "I'm finished," he admitted. Topping asked Joe to think it over during his barnstorming trip through Korea and Japan, hopeful that DiMag would reconsider. Joe agreed, but in his heart, he knew his decision had been made. Webb told DiMaggio not to worry about the money, and promised him the same $100,000 salary for next year. He offered to have the contract drawn up and sent over for his signature. DiMaggio demurred. It wasn't about the money, he promised. He didn't want to play baseball anymore.

Several weeks later, *Life* magazine published a scouting report on the Yankees that included a sad perspective of DiMaggio's skills. Andy High, a Dodgers scout, who had followed the Yankees for the final month of the season, had compiled most of the report. When the Dodgers didn't win the pennant, their front office presented the scouting report to the Giants in a show of National League unity. After the Giants won the Series opener, manager Leo Durocher raved about the scouting report, saying, "It's great. I never saw a report like it." The report couldn't win the Series for the Giants, but its disclosure embarrassed DiMaggio more than any other player. It read:

- Fielding—he can't stop quickly and throw hard. You can take the extra base on him if he is in motion away from the line of throw. He won't throw on questionable plays and I would challenge him even though he threw a man or so out.

- Speed—he can't run and he won't bunt.

- Hitting vs. right-handed pitcher—his reflexes are very slow and he can't pull a good fastball at all. The fastball is better thrown high but that is not too important as long as it is fast. Throw him nothing but good fastballs and fast curveballs. Don't slow up on him.

- Hitting vs. left-handed pitcher—will pull left-hand pitcher a little more than right-hand pitcher. Pitch him the same. Don't slow up on him. He will go for a bad pitch once in a while with two strikes.

DiMaggio's friends knew that his pride surely would not let him play now that the erosion of his skills had been publicly exposed. And early in December, shortly after his 37th birthday, he phoned Topping, saying that he wanted to come to New York to announce his retirement. But he agreed to Topping's request for another meeting. That's when Topping and Webb played their last card: Manager Casey Stengel's plan to use him on a part-time basis, with DiMaggio determining when he would play. Joe appreciated the offer, but could not agree to be a part-time player.

His retirement was final except for the announcement. On the morning of December 12, at the club's Fifth Avenue office suite in the Squibb Tower, the newsmen were handed a statement announcing Joe DiMaggio's retirement. Joe was there, of course, with Topping, Webb, and Stengel alongside him. "I can no longer produce for my ball club, my manager, my teammates, and my fans the sort of baseball their loyalty to me deserves," said a tearful DiMaggio. "Until yesterday," Webb told DiMag, "we had still hoped you would stay. But, since you didn't change your mind, it's a sad day, not only for the Yankees, but for all baseball as well." When the questions began, one newspaperman naturally asked, "Joe, why are you quitting?" "I no longer have it," he replied.

Mickey Mantle and Casey Stengel in the dugout at Fenway Park. "Who's your center fielder now?" a reporter asked Stengel when Joe DiMaggio retired. "The kid. Mickey Mantle." COURTESY OF THE LESLIE JONES COLLECTION, BOSTON PUBLIC LIBRARY

No matter what was said later, his retirement boiled down to that simple explanation.

Over in another corner of the Yankees offices other baseball writers had Casey Stengel surrounded. "Who's your center fielder now?" one wondered. "The kid," the manager said. "Mickey Mantle."

The Yankees were celebrating an anniversary: 50 years in New York, and it was the first season that the team aired their games exclusively on WPIX-TV, a partnership that would last for more than 45 years. The sports world was continuing to open its eyes to the incredible reach of the relatively new medium of television. The year marked college football's first foray into national television. On New Year's Day, Big Ten champion University of Illinois capped a 9-0-1 season with a 40–7 drubbing of Pacific Coast Conference winner Stanford University. NBC-TV telecast the game to the entire nation—a first for college football.

In another first, 1952 was also the first season since 1936 when the Yankees would be without Joe DiMaggio. The Yankees were now faced with a problem that did not seem to have an immediate solution. For almost 30 years there had always been a superstar in the lineup, commanding attention, grabbing the headlines, filling the big ballpark in the Bronx. First it was the Sultan of Swat, then it was the Iron Horse, and then it was the Yankee Clipper. Suddenly, the only possibility in the Yankees universe to extend the lineage of pinstriped icons was a 20-year-old kid from Commerce, Oklahoma. With the Yankee Clipper retired, manager Casey Stengel told his bosses that he wanted to reshape the team around catcher Yogi Berra, the Most Valuable Player in the American League in 1951, pitcher Allie Reynolds, and the manager's special protégé, Mickey Mantle.

General manager George Weiss, now in charge of the Webb-Topping baseball money in place of the departed Larry MacPhail, had tickets that needed to be sold, turnstiles that needed to spin. In Mantle he could imagine a genuine box office star. Weiss told his key organizational men to start spreading the word to the beat writers who cover the team about their new shiny switch-hitting, power-hitting outfield-playing slugger. Managers, coaches, and scouts—everyone in the Yankees front office—were instructed by Weiss to drop a sly mention in the press box, or in a tavern after the game, or on a train to writers as they bounded from city to city. They all recited from the same script: "The Mantle kid is going to be the greatest."

Alas, the reassuring drumbeats did not herald trumpets. Unfortunately, Stengel's Yankees dug a deep hole from the start. The team finished April mired in sixth place in an eight-team league. The season hit rock bottom during an uncharacteristically sloppy 10–6 loss to the Indians in Cleveland on May 13, a game in which the three-time defending champions committed three errors. Bobby Brown started at third base and was 0-for-2. Mantle replaced Brown in the field in the bottom of the fifth with the Indians leading, 7–0; he had two singles in two at-bats. This was the only time Mantle played third in a big-league game. The loss dropped the Yankees 5 1/2 games off the pace, their largest deficit of the season.

New York's march to mediocrity continued through Memorial Day. Reynolds pitched 15 complete games in a row to open magnificently, but Vic Raschi was unable to complete games because of the continuing deterioration of his right knee. As always, or so it seemed of late, Eddie Lopat's arm pained him. The Yankees season seesawed in frustration; the team was not gaining traction. They'd put together a three-game winning streak, and just as quickly suffer a three-game losing skid. Mired in fifth place with an abysmal 18-17 record on May 30, it appeared that the Yankees were ripe for the taking. Not only did they have to make due without the retired DiMaggio, but also, as the Korean conflict intensified, the armed forces were calling to the colors thousands of men, including dozens of major leaguers. The war effort had already called to arms from the Yankees their promising pitcher Tom Morgan, and, for a second straight year, young pitching phenomenon Whitey Ford. In May, infielder Jerry Coleman was called back into military service as a Marines pilot and shipped to Korea. Fellow teammate Bobby Brown was the next to go over there.

Jerry Coleman's nine-year career with the Yankees included four World Series titles and was interrupted by his military service in World War II and the Korean War. He flew Douglas SBD Dauntless divebombers in the Pacific in World War II, and then played three seasons of minor-league ball before making his big-league debut with the Yankees in '49. He batted .275 in his first year and led all second basemen in fielding percentage. He was the Associated Press Rookie of the Year that season. Coleman's best season was 1950, when he was an All-Star and was named MVP of the Yankees' four-game sweep of the Philadelphia Phillies in the World Series. In October 1951, he found out that Marines pilots from World War II were not discharged, but on inactive status, and that he'd be going to Korea for 18 months. Coleman said he took his physical along with Ted Williams, in Jacksonville, Florida, in May. Due to military service, he missed the bulk of the next two seasons. As a lieutenant colonel in the Marines, Coleman flew 120 missions combined in the two wars. He was awarded two Distinguished Flying Crosses, 13 Air Medals and three Navy Citations. While recounting his military career in an interview in 2012, he said: "Your country is bigger than baseball."

Third baseman Bobby Brown, who had earned his medical degree from Tulane University, landed in Korea as the battalion surgeon for the 160th Field Artillery Battalion, 45th Division. He left in July 1953 for a Tokyo Army hospital, where he stayed until April 1954. The Korean War stole his youth, robbed his innocence, and certainly shortened his baseball career. Brown played on four World Series championship teams with the Yankees. But once he left for Korea in 1952, he knew his baseball career was essentially over. He had a career .439 batting average in the World Series when he went to war, but he lost his playing skills. When he returned in 1954, he played in just 29 games. "I still remember my unit landing at Incheon," he said. "It was the first day of the World Series. Don Newcombe was starting for the Dodgers. And I'm in Korea."

Yankees second baseman Jerry Coleman was the only major-league player who saw combat in both World War II and Korea. As a Marine pilot, he flew 120 missions in both wars and earned multple citations, including two Distinguished Flying Crosses. Most of the 100-plus major-league players who were drafted or enlisted remained stateside. NATIONAL BASEBALL HALL OF FAME AND MUSEUM, INC.

More than 100 major-league players were drafted or enlisted, but most of them, like Hall of Famers Whitey Ford, Ernie Banks, and Willie Mays, never saw combat. They remained stateside. However, in 1952, the war nearly took the life of Ted Williams, a Hall of Famer and one of America's legendary baseball players. The "Splendid Splinter," who won six batting titles and hit an amazing .344 in his 19-year career with the Boston Red Sox, was called up from the reserves in May, along with major leaguers such as Jerry Coleman and Cincinnati Reds center fielder Lloyd Merriman. Ted Williams was a pilot in the US Army during World War II, serving with distinction. Before the Korean War ended in 1953, Williams flew 39 combat missions as a Marines pilot. His plane was hit by enemy fire several times, including once when he had to land his flaming F-9 Panther jet on its belly rather than eject—fearing that doing so from a compact cockpit would do permanent damage to his knees. He executed the dangerous maneuver and walked away without serious injury, just moments before the plane exploded. Williams was awarded many medals for his 39 missions but lost some of his hearing because of the gunnery noise. He served with John Glenn, who went on to greater fame as an astronaut and US senator. "Ted flew as my wingman on about half the missions he flew in Korea," said Glenn. By all accounts, Williams was a competent pilot, and if not for baseball, his first love, he may have had a full-time career as a Marines pilot. "I liked flying," Williams said. "It was the second-best thing that ever happened to me."

In the standings of the AL pennant chase, five teams—Boston, Chicago, and surprising Washington, as well as New York and Cleveland—were bunched close together, separated by just 3 1/2 games, with no team a standout. The Philadelphia Athletics caused some trouble, too. The A's had a tiny left-hander, Bobby Shantz, who won 24 games, while first baseman Ferris Fain became the AL's leading hitter with a .327 average. With no team playing well enough to run away with the pennant race, one club needed to separate itself from the rest of the pack. In a June awakening, the Bronx Bombers reeled off 13 wins in 15 games, and jumped four teams in the standings. Yogi Berra began to fill the role of power hitter. In a dozen June games Berra hit 10 home runs, pulling the Yankees into a first-place tie with Cleveland as the Indians hiccupped momentarily.

With Berra beginning to drive in important runs, the Yankees grabbed the lead on June 14, holding on to it dearly. The outfield of Mantle, Hank Bauer, and Gene Woodling fell in line nicely. All were performing to their capabilities and hitting over .300. Woodling was a longtime Stengel favorite. At 5-foot-9 and 195 pounds, he was a stocky outfielder his teammates called Porkie. He crowded the plate and was a difficult batter to strike out. He flourished with the San Francisco Seals of the Pacific Coast League in 1948. Tutored by Lefty O'Doul, the Seals manager, who had been a two-time NL batting champion, Woodling led the league in hitting with a .385 average and was named the *Sporting News* Minor League Player of the Year. More important, he impressed Stengel, who was managing the Oakland Oaks. When Stengel became the Yankees manager in 1949, he got Woodling. In his first season with the Yankees, Woodling shared playing time with Johnny Lindell and Cliff Mapes. Although essentially the regular left fielder after that season, on occasion he found himself a victim of Stengel's platoon system. Woodling was intensely competitive and outspoken, and as such, verbally sparred with his manager over playing time. Teammates recalled him screaming at Stengel when his name was left off the lineup card. Peter Golenbock wrote in *Dynasty*, "During one clubhouse meeting, Stengel said, 'There's one guy in this room who don't talk behind my back.' All the Yankees turned and looked toward Woodling."

Mantle took up the gauntlet in July, batting .322 with 46 hits, 33 RBIs, 28 runs scored, and nine homers for the month's work. In Detroit on July 26, he slammed his first career grand slam. The ball landed in the upper deck in left-center field at Briggs Stadium. Three days later in Chicago, Mickey's second career grand slam home run provided the game-winning margin in a 10–7 slugfest at Comiskey Park. In the days before instant replay, exit velocity, and electronic measuring devices, no player's home runs generated more attention than those hit by The Mick. "The imprint of baseball greatness is upon Mickey Mantle just as surely as the portrait of Thomas Jefferson graces the current three-cent stamp," wrote *Sport* magazine's Harold Rosenthal. The hyperbolic Stengel was calling him the greatest switch-hitter in the history of the game. Fans were calling him the most exciting player not named Willie Mays. Yet for all the accolades, Mickey still toiled under the enormous shadow of his predecessor.

Joe DiMaggio was more than a baseball idol. He was a national celebrity, even in retirement. At his peak, DiMaggio was often saluted in the popular culture. In addition to being serenaded in song as *Joltin' Joe DiMaggio* by Les Brown, DiMaggio was also mentioned in films and Broadway shows; the sailors in *South Pacific* sing that Bloody Mary's skin is "tender as DiMaggio's glove." Ernest Hemingway's novella *The Old Man and the Sea* was published in the fall and included a salute to Joe D when the main character Santiago says, "I would like to take the great DiMaggio fishing; maybe he was as poor as we are and would understand."

Baseball players could now be appreciated in a new way. The Topps Chewing Gum Company released its first complete set of baseball trading cards in the spring. The 1952 Topps collection is famous for its Mantle rookie card, which without question is the most popular and valuable postwar baseball card in existence. This is not Mantle's true rookie card, but it is the first time he appeared on a Topps card. That, among other things, is what makes this card so valuable. Just as is the practice today, this Topps set was released to the public in two series. The initial offering, which coincided with the start of the baseball season, sold out at a furious pace. Youngsters, excited by a fresh start for their local teams, just couldn't get enough of these colorful, well-crafted cards. The Mantle card, however, was included in the second series, but by the time of issue, it was so late in the season that fan interest had already shifted from baseball to football. The packs didn't sell well, and sat in a warehouse for several years—until 1960 when the company disposed of the surplus stock. That made every card in the series a rarity, and demand for the few remaining Mantles sky-rocketed. A '52 Mantle card in mint condition sold for $2.88 million at auction in 2018.

Mickey Mantle's 1952 Topps card is now the most popular and valuable postwar baseball card. TOPPS ® TRADING CARDS USED COURTESY OF THE TOPPS COMPANY, INC.

There was not a day in July of '52 that the Yankees were not on top. Their biggest lead of the season was a 5 1/2-game cushion on July 19. New York had made up 10 games in the standings in just two months' time, and had to do so without their starting second baseman and one of their best starting pitchers, lost to military service. New talent, including the young, pugnacious Billy Martin replacing Jerry Coleman at second base, and veteran pitcher Johnny Sain with 11 wins filling the void for Whitey Ford, were main factors contributing to New York's resilience. Most of all, though, the Yankees had Casey Stengel and his amazing ability to plug a hole with the right substitute or to play mix-and-match with his pitching staff. In 1952 the Yankees had 15 pitchers who worked at least 15 innings—and of course, Yogi Berra had to break them all in.

Billy Martin, a scrapper who was far more valuable to the team than his .267 batting average might indicate, made his presence felt on the Yankees. As a player, he seemed to have as many fights as the newly crowned heavyweight champion Rocky Marciano. Before a game on May 24, the mercurial Martin goaded Red Sox infielder Jimmy Piersall into a fight and then later brawled with Clint Courtney, Tom Lasorda, and Jim Brewer. Battling Billy was his sobriquet, and it was an apt one.

Chicago Cubs Hall of Fame slugger Ernie Banks once quipped that Martin was the only person ever to appear in both the *Baseball Register* and *Ring Magazine*. With fights becoming routine, the story goes that when Phil Rizzuto received a death threat, Stengel suggested he and Martin switch numbers. The shortstop refused, however, because, he said, he'd rather take his chances with a guy with a gun than risk being mistaken for Martin and getting beaned or beat up by an opponent.

The Yankees had to fight off a formidable opponent in the Cleveland Indians, who under second-year manager Al Lopez seemed, at least statistically, to have the stronger team. Cleveland, not New York, led the AL in runs scored, home runs, and slugging percentage. Al Rosen led the league with 105 RBIs, one more than Larry Doby, who led the league in runs scored (104), home runs (32), and slugging percentage (.541). Rosen, Dale Mitchell, and Bobby Avila all hit .300 or better. Three starting pitchers—Early Wynn, Mike Garcia, and Bob Lemon— each won at least 22 games. Larry Doby was the first black player to lead either league in homers, yet ironically, perhaps no one is more remembered for being second. He was the second Negro to play Major League Baseball in the modern era after Jackie Robinson. He was also the second black manager of a major-league club after Frank Robinson.

In 1947, only 11 weeks after Jackie Robinson's big-league debut, Cleveland owner Bill Veeck signed Doby as the AL's first black player. Doby suffered the same indignities as Robinson, but his struggles did not get the media attention Jackie's received. Whether it was being forced to stay in separate hotels or eat in separate restaurants on the road, or not being accepted by some of his teammates, Doby persevered. His first major-league manager Lou Boudreau recalled, "Larry proved to them (the other players) that he was a major leaguer in handling himself in more ways than one—on the field and off the field." The next year Doby became the first black player to hit a home run in the World Series. In 1978, the same man who gave him his shot as a player in the major leagues in 1947, Bill Veeck, hired him to manage his Chicago White Sox.

There were still only three of the eight AL teams employing black players in 1952. But the prominence of the roles filled by the few black players that season was the most significant the league had yet seen. The St. Louis Browns deployed 45-year-old Satchel Paige in his most productive major-league season, in which he won 12 games and became the oldest player selected to an All-Star team.

The second half of the 1952 season proved to be one of the tightest pennant races in AL history. For several weeks, the Yankees and Indians, closer than Siamese twins, were stacked one-two in the standings. The Indians finally caught up on August 22 when Mike Garcia beat the Yankees in the first of a two-game series with the Indians visiting New York, and the two teams were deadlocked. The next day, Vic Raschi hurled the Yankees back into first place with a 1–0 shutout over Early Wynn. The Yankees never had to share first place again. They went 25-7, a torrid .781 pace, after August 22, and they needed every one of those wins, because the Indians went 24-10, but it wasn't good enough to crack the Yankees code. In what had become almost an annual fall ritual, the Yankees were AL champions again, this time by two lengths.

Mantle was the key performer in New York's pennant drive. He batted .362 in the final six weeks of the season to finish the year at .311. He improved with 23 home runs and 87 RBIs. His numbers were not eye-popping like they would be in later seasons, but his productivity placed him at the top of the charts in batting average (third), on-base percentage (third at .394) and slugging percentage (second at .530). The Yankees also received a bravura performance from Berra, who led the team with 30 homers and 98 RBIs. Allie Reynolds had the finest season of his career, finishing 20-8, with a league-leading 2.06 ERA, 160 strikeouts, and six shutouts. He placed third among AL hurlers with a career-high 24 complete games. He also had six saves. Reynolds's exceptional performance earned him a second-place finish in the league MVP voting and his second consecutive selection to the *Sporting News* All-Star Team. Down the stretch, the Big Three of Raschi, Reynolds, and Lopat were close to unbeatable. So was General Dwight D. Eisenhower, the Republican candidate for president of the United States; Ike won a convincing victory over Democratic nominee Adlai Stevenson.

Nationalism was on the rise. The United States won the medal count at the Summer Olympic Games in Helsinki, Finland, but the real story was the presence, for the first time in Olympic history, of a powerful team from the Soviet Union. Reflecting the attitudes of "East versus West" that had been spawned by the Cold War, the Soviet Union decided to participate in the competition, although from a distance. Instead of joining the other athletes in the Olympic Village, the Soviets set up their own camp strictly for Eastern Bloc countries near the Soviet naval base at the Porkkala peninsula, located 19 miles west of Helsinki. All Russian athletes were then chaperoned by Soviet officials everywhere they went in an effort to prevent communication with athletes from the West. The Games became almost a dual meet between the Russians and Americans. The United States surged at the end for a 75–68 medal-count victory. Included among the American medals were 41 golds, 18 more than the Russians could manage. Politics aside, one of the biggest stories was the world-record performance of Bob Mathias in the decathlon. The California native, a winner at age 17 in the 1948 decathlon at the Games in London, amassed 7,887 points to win the event by the largest margin in Olympic history. It was a year of tremendous accomplishment off the field, too. After an eight-year study, scientist Jonas Salk finally developed a vaccine that prevented the crippling disease known as polio. Though he was hailed as a miracle worker and a national hero, Salk remained shy of the public eye. He declined to apply for a patent for the vaccine, saying that he was more concerned with people having access to it than the money it would bring him.

After winning the AL pennant by a whisper-thin two-game margin over the Indians, the Yankees returned for their 18th World Series appearance against their crosstown rivals, the Brooklyn Dodgers. The Bronx Bombers had spoiled the Giants fairytale season the year before and were determined to retain their title as the kings of New York baseball teams. The defending NL champion Giants spent their summer in second place, never in the race. The military had come calling for Giants center fielder Willie Mays, who made no secret he wanted no part of the war, or the Army. "Naturally, I'm not interested in the Army," Mays told the *Birmingham* (Ala.) *News* after being drafted. "But if I have to go, I'll make the best of it." Mays applied for hardship status, saying his mother and nine siblings relied on him for support. It didn't work. Mays, who won NL Rookie of the Year in 1951, reported to duty May 29, 1952. He missed the rest of the season and all of 1953. He missed more than 260 games during his military service, spending those two years playing baseball in the Army at Fort Eustis in Virginia.

Haunted by the pennant race heartbreaks on the last day of the previous two seasons, the Dodgers must have felt an uneasy case of déjà vu when, at the beginning of September, their nine-game lead over the Giants was cut to three in just two weeks. The eerie parallels of 1950 and 1951 would be short-lived, however, as the Dodgers this time held steady to finish in first place by a comfortable 4 1/2 games. It was the first time in five years that the NL pennant was not decided on the last day of the season.

The Brooklyn Dodgers were loaded for bear. Every player on the team was at his prime and enjoying the zenith of his career. Three stars from the Negro Leagues—infielder Jackie Robinson, catcher Roy Campanella, and pitcher Don Newcombe—would eventually be enshrined in the Baseball Hall of Fame, as would shortstop Pee Wee Reese and center fielder Duke Snider. First baseman Gil Hodges, third baseman Billy Cox, and outfielders Carl Furillo and Andy Pafko also were performing exceptionally at the time.

The formidable Brooklyn starting pitching staff featured Carl Erskine, Billy Loes, and 37-year-old spitballer Preacher Roe. Erskine, known as Oisk in the borough of Brooklyn, was 14-6 with a 2.70 ERA, including the first of his two career no-hitters, June 19, against the Cubs. Only a four-pitch walk in the third inning to his opposing pitcher, Willie Ramsdell, prevented him from pitching a perfect game.

The Dodgers were without their mound workhorse Don Newcombe, also drafted into the Army. Newcombe pitched in the Negro Leagues before breaking in with Brooklyn in 1949. He led the Dodgers to the pennant with 17 victories, winning the NL Rookie of the Year Award. And he kept getting better; he won 19 games in 1950 and 20 games in '51. Then he was drafted. Newk missed two seasons, and when he returned, he went just 9-8 with a 4.55 ERA in 1954.

Charles Dillon Stengel had acquired the nickname Casey because he was from Kansas City (or K.C.). Because Casey would achieve such success as a Yankees manager, many people don't realize he had a 14-year playing career from 1912 to 1925. In his years as an outfielder with the Brooklyn Dodgers, Stengel learned to play the tricky caroms off the Ebbets Field outfield wall. Before the opening game of the 1952 World Series between the Yankees and Dodgers, Stengel took Mickey Mantle into the Ebbets Field outfield to pass along some tips on playing the oddly angled concrete wall. The young center fielder was shocked to learn that Casey had roamed this very outfield as a player some 35 years earlier. "You mean *you* once played here?" Mantle asked. Stengel commented later, "The kid thinks I was 60 years old when I was born."

Casey had been a fair major-league ballplayer. In his first game with the Brooklyn Dodgers in 1912 he got four hits in the game. "The writers promptly declared they had seen the new Ty Cobb," said Stengel. "It took me only a few days to correct that impression." His most memorable moments on the field occurred while playing for the New York Giants in the 1923 World Series against the Yankees. Stengel won the opening game with an inside-the-park home run with two outs in the ninth inning, the first Series homer in new Yankee Stadium. Then he won Game 3 with a seventh-inning home run into the right field stands at Yankee Stadium for a thrilling 1–0 victory. Thirty years later, managing the Yankees, Stengel had a chance to equal a record by winning four World Series in a row. Only the Joe McCarthy–led Yankees from 1936 to 1939 had accomplished the feat.

The 1952 World Series opened at Ebbets Field in Brooklyn, one of the most iconic ballparks ever built. Constructed on a former garbage dump in Brooklyn, in an area of Flatbush that was called Pigtown, Ebbets Field was a small ballpark, tightly squeezed into the urban street grid. In fact, the team name *Dodgers* referred to the way their fans had to dodge trolley cars to get to the stadium. There was very little foul territory in Ebbets Field, so fans got to see up-close action. The right and left field walls became plastered with advertisements, the most famous being the Schaefer beer ad that gave the official scorer's ruling on hits and errors. Below this placard was an Abe Stark "Hit Sign, Win Suit" advertisement.

Joe Black toed the rubber in Brooklyn for the series opener. An African-American Dodgers prospect, he was summoned to the big club in the absence of Don Newcombe, and quickly established himself as the team's ace reliever. The 28-year-old rookie pitcher had performed very well during his first year in the big leagues, posting a 15-4 record and a 2.15 ERA that barely missed qualifying for the league lead. With just two career starts under his belt, manager Charlie Dressen sent Black to the mound with the task of shutting down New York. Black did what was asked of him, allowing two runs on six hits and pitching a complete game to earn the 4–2 win, the first by a black pitcher in World Series history. Robinson, Snider, and Reese each homered for Brooklyn. Not to be outdone, the Yankees came out swinging in Game 2. Billy Martin put the Dodgers back in their place with a three-run blast and an RBI single that paced the Yankees to a 7–1 decision. That more than backed up Vic Raschi's smooth three-hitter while going the distance.

The Dodgers owned a slim 3–2 lead after eight innings of Game 3 at Yankee Stadium, and then tallied another pair of runs when Reese and Robinson were able to score on Yogi Berra's passed ball in the top of the ninth. Those runs proved important when Yankees pinch-hitter Johnny Mize homered into the left field stands in the bottom of the frame, making the final score 5–3. Reynolds and Black came back to the mound on two days rest to start Game 4. This time it was all Reynolds, as the Yankees ace tossed a complete-game shutout with 10 strikeouts to beat Black and the Dodgers, 2–0. Both teams collected just four hits, but the Yankees made theirs count. Mize, this time starting at first base and batting cleanup, hit his second home run of the series in the fourth, and New York tacked on an insurance run in the eighth to square the series at two games apiece.

In the pivotal fifth game Carl Erskine experienced one of the more phenomenal—and unlikely—pitching efforts by any starting pitcher ever in a World Series. The Dodgers were leading, 4–0, when suddenly the Yankees, held to just one hit to that point, erupted for five runs off Erskine in the bottom of the fifth, punctuated by a Johnny Mize three-run homer to deep right field. Right after the homer, Erskine's manager Charlie Dressen paid him a visit on the mound. Erskine assumed his day was done. "It's the fifth game, on the fifth of October and this is [my] fifth wedding anniversary," Erskine related. "Now it's the fifth inning and I've just given up five runs."

Instead of asking for the ball, Dressen wanted to know what his pitcher's plans were for after the game. According to Erskine, his manager said, "I know it's your anniversary. Got any plans for dinner with Betty?" Erskine replied that they had reservations at a popular restaurant. "Well," said Dressen. "Get this game over with, so you don't keep her waiting."

That was it. The reprieved Erskine then went on to retire the next 19 batters in a row. Duke Snider was the hero when his RBI double in the 11th inning off relief pitcher Johnny Sain put the Dodgers ahead for good. Erskine proceeded to retire the Yankees in order in the bottom of the inning, including Yogi Berra on a game-ending strikeout. (For the record, the time of game was three hours even, which meant Carl and Betty Erskine easily made their seven o'clock dinner reservation.) It was only later during the dessert course that a patron pointed out to Erskine that he had held the Yankees hitless for nine of the 11 innings for a 6–5 complete-game victory.

The Dodgers had a three-games-to-two World Series lead over the New York Yankees and there was reason to anticipate that Brooklyn would soon have its first championship flag to fly with all those NL pennants. The ever-raucous fans of Brooklyn, packed into the friendly bleachers of cozy Ebbets Field for Game 6, were more vocal and euphoric than ever. Especially Hilda Chester, otherwise known as "Howlin' Hilda," seated in her usual spot in the center field bleachers where she regularly and loudly yelled at the opposing players, her booming voice echoing throughout the stadium. She was as much a part of Dodgers lore as Jackie, Pee Wee, and the Duke. Bill Gallo of the *New York Daily News* called her "the most loyal and greatest fan to pass through the turnstiles of the Flatbush ballpark." The *Los Angeles Times* cited her as "perhaps the greatest heckler of all time" who would "scream like a fishmonger at players and managers, or lead fans in snake dances through the aisles."

Duke Snider, enjoying an amazing Series, smashed a pair of solo homers off Game 6 starter Raschi, but Snider's teammates weren't as effective. Raschi pitched into the eighth inning and collected a Series-tying 3–2 win with some relief help from Reynolds, who thought nothing of relieving on days he didn't start and fired bullets for an inning-plus to hold off a late Brooklyn rally to earn the save. For the Yankees, Berra and Mantle both homered, and Raschi helped himself with an RBI single. That forced a decisive Game 7.

Crafty left-hander Eddie Lopat, whose fastball couldn't break a pane of glass, started the winner-take-all-game for the Yankees. The veteran, bothered by shoulder problems, had won only 10 games for the Yanks in '52 (after going 21-9 in '51), while Joe Black got his third start in seven days for the Dodgers. Mickey Mantle homered in the sixth inning of Game 7 to break a tie and the Yankees scored another run on Mantle's RBI single in the seventh to extend their lead over Brooklyn. When Lopat ran into trouble in the fourth inning, Stengel called on an equally exhausted Reynolds again, and he worked three more innings, leaving in the top of the seventh with a 4–2 lead, courtesy of Mantle.

The fans at Ebbets Field grew restless. It was up to Vic Raschi and his weary arm to keep the Dodgers at bay in the bottom half of the seventh, but after having started the previous game he had little left. The Dodgers fought back, loading the bases on a pair of walks and a single, with just one out. "They're FOB," said broadcaster Red Barber, in his familiar style—"Full of Brooks" (Brooklyn Dodgers). Stengel went to the mound and waved for reliever Bob Kuzava to relieve Raschi.

Bob Kuzava, making his first appearance of the postseason, would have to face the lefty-swinging slugger Duke Snider, who already had 10 hits in the series. The count went to three balls and two strikes on Snider. Kuzava, a lefty who could get the ball up to the plate in the high 90s, but always had a little control trouble, threw a high fastball that Snider chased out of the strike zone, sending a weak popup to Joe Collins at first. Two outs. The bases were still loaded. The Yankees were clinging to a two-run lead. The Series was still hanging in the balance. Jackie Robinson, one of the game's greatest clutch hitters, came up to bat with 33,195 fans screaming for their lives. The count ran full. Kuzava went to his best pitch and fired a fastball just off the plate and about shoulder high. The baserunners took off with the pitch. Robinson swung and hit a seemingly innocent little popup on the infield. But as Kuzava stood transfixed on the mound and the runners circled the bases at full speed, first baseman Joe Collins searched frantically for a ball he had lost in the sun. Third baseman Gil McDougald and Phil Rizzuto at shortstop were too far away to catch it. Berra never took off his mask at home plate to look for it.

It appeared as if the ball might fall safely to the ground—with disastrous results for the Yankees. Recognizing the dilemma, second baseman Billy Martin darted to the rescue for New York. He raced across the diamond, his hat now gone from his head, and speared the ball at the last moment, making a game-saving knee-high catch between the pitcher's mound and first base for the final out of the inning. Most of the Yankees pounded Martin on the back in congratulations as he ran to the bench. He couldn't understand all the fuss. Being patted on the back for catching a popup. Of all the plays Yankees manager Casey Stengel bragged about, his favorite was the gutsy, breathtaking catch turned in by Martin at Ebbets Field. "He made the catch on Robinson and you could look it up. Nobody else wanted to get it," Stengel said years later. "The rest of them (other Yankees infielders) all stood out there like statues when the ball went up. Only the little bantam second baseman had the sense to catch it."

There have been so many dramatic plays in Yankees World Series history, so many miraculous defensive gems, so many extraordinary efforts by the players in Yankees pinstripes. But none match Billy Martin's catch. Their rally snuffed out, that was it for the Dodgers. Thanks to Martin's play of the series, Kuzava got out of the inning and got Brooklyn out without much trouble in the eighth and ninth to save it. The Yankees were champions of baseball for the fourth consecutive season under Stengel's leadership. "It's déjà vu all over again," said Berra. The Dodgers were denied a championship for the sixth time in as many tries, the last four to the Yankees. Gene Woodling, the Yankees left fielder, led all regulars with a .348 batting average. Mize, who had hit only four home runs during the regular season, hit three against the Dodgers—and was robbed of a fourth by Brooklyn right fielder Carl Furillo, who made a leaping catch above the fence in the 11th inning to preserve a Dodger win for Oisk. Duke Snider went wild at the plate. He batted .345 and hit four home runs and had eight RBIs.

Snider wore number 4 in Dodgers blue, and was often regarded as the third-best center fielder in New York—behind Mays and Mantle—during what many fans considered the city's golden era of baseball. Ebbets Field was filled with stars such as Reese, Campanella, and Hodges, yet it is Snider's name that refrains in the ballpark favorite song "Talkin' Baseball" by Terry Cashman. ("Willie, Mickey, and the Duke," the popular song goes.) Snider, who always wore his emotions on his sleeve, had a love-hate relationship with Ebbets Field fans. Any home run in a key spot and he would strut his stuff as the Duke of Flatbush. Any strikeout in a clutch situation and he would sulk on his walk back to the dugout as Brooklyn fans booed him. It was all part of the love affair between the borough of Brooklyn and "Dem Bums" who lived in the local neighborhoods.

Gil Hodges hit 32 home runs and drove in 102 runs during the regular season, but went hitless in 21 Series at-bats. It's a measure of his overwhelming popularity and the respect he earned as a player that a priest in Brooklyn famously asked his congregation to pray for Hodges to get a hit. In his classic *The Boys of Summer*, author Roger Kahn reported, "More than 30 people a day wrote to Hodges. Packages arrived with rosary beads, rabbits' feet, mezuzahs, scapulars."

The Dodgers' downfall was a paltry .215 team batting average. The Yankees hit only slightly better, at .216, but popped 10 homers. Two were the result of swings by Mickey Mantle. Improving on his regular-season play, The Mick batted .345 with a double, triple, and two home runs. He returned to Commerce, Oklahoma, a hero. A post–World Series parade given in Mickey's honor drew three times the town's population. With The Mick coming into his own, his ascension in the Yankees pantheon was nearing completion. As Lou Gehrig took the torch from Babe Ruth, as Joe DiMaggio took it from Gehrig, Mickey Mantle now grabbed it from DiMaggio. And so in 1952 one Yankees era ended as another was about to begin. Fans were beginning to think that maybe the Mantle kid would be the greatest.

1953: THE BEAT GOES ON

Mickey Mantle arrived at spring training with unbridled confidence as the unquestioned heir to Joe DiMaggio's kingdom. The 21-year-old Mantle, who had finished third in the Most Valuable Player Award voting in '52, only his second year in the majors, was already hands down everybody's favorite player. "He is absolutely the greatest looking kid I've ever seen in the big leagues," said Detroit Tigers infielder Johnny Pesky. "He does everything the way it should be done." In an exhibition game in Pittsburgh, Mantle hit a left-handed home run that traveled 450 feet onto the roof at Forbes Field. Three days later, at Ebbets Field in Brooklyn, the public address announcer informed the crowd, including the new papa as he approached home plate to take his turn at bat, "Mickey doesn't know it yet, but he has just become the father of an eight-pound, 12-ounce baby boy." Mickey Mantle Jr., whose given middle name was Elvin in memory of the Yankees slugger's recently deceased dad, was the first of four children, all sons, with wife Merlyn.

The Mick swung a potent bat. Four days into the season, in an amazing show of raw power, he blasted an incredible home run that cleared the 50-foot outer wall at Washington's Griffith Stadium and came to rest in the backyard of a house, 565 feet away from home plate. It was possibly the longest ball ever hit. Batting right-handed against Senators lefty Chuck Stobbs with two out and Yogi Berra on first base in the fifth inning of an April 17 game, Mantle sent a massive shot toward left-center field. The ball cleared the bleacher fence, 391 feet from the plate, glanced off a football scoreboard that sat atop the

50-foot outer fence, and bounded out of sight. The ball traveled 460 feet in the air and there's no telling how much farther it might have gone had it cleared the scoreboard. It marked the first time a ball had ever been hit completely out of Griffith Stadium on the fly to left field. The Yankees went on to defeat the Senators, 7–3. This blow was responsible for the expression "tape-measure home run" because the Yankees publicity director, Red Patterson, immediately left the press box, found himself a tape measure, and paced off the distance to the spot where witnesses said the ball came down. Mantle and perhaps others probably have hit longer home runs. That was certainly the view of Stobbs. "He hit 'em pretty far against a lot of people," said Stobbs. "The only reason they remember this one is because they marked the spot on the beer sign where the ball left the park, but Bucky Harris [the Senators manager] later made them take the marker down." Added Stobbs: "I got Mantle out pretty good later on. I think he was two for twenty-five off me one year, but nobody ever talks about that."

Fans across the country could now witness Mantle's long-distance feats. For the first time, Major League Baseball was nationally televising games on a weekly basis. ABC-TV began airing the *Game of the Week* but with a hitch: The games couldn't be shown within 50 miles of markets where major-league teams resided, for fear by owners that people in those areas would be more likely to tune in than to go to the nearby ballpark. Viewers allowed to watch the games heard Buddy Blattner announcing alongside the colorful former St. Louis Cardinals pitching star Dizzy Dean. Blattner was the dependable straight man of the broadcast duo. The outrageous Dean, a Hall of Fame pitcher for the notorious Gashouse Gang Cards in the 1930s, could be depended upon to mangle the English language. He resorted to such country colloquialisms as "he slud into third base," and often broke into a song with his rendition of "The Wabash Cannonball" during lulls in the on-field action.

While some people viewed the world only in terms of black and white, almost everyone began viewing it in black and white—on television. The exciting new medium quickly moved from luxury to necessity. And its growing influence on sports could not be overstated. For the first time, images of American sports heroes in action were not just in the fans' imaginations, static newspaper photos, or grainy newsreel footage. Fans could now see their favorite stars live on national television. The impact of the little cathode ray tube inside the small screen already was being felt by American sports fans as the new decade dawned. Due to crude equipment and limited by a single camera operator, sports telecasting had been confined to the tight, easy-to-follow action of arena sports such as boxing and wrestling. But that didn't stop programmers from experimenting with the more active games played outdoors.

People may have liked Ike, but they absolutely loved Lucy. The CBS-TV sitcom *I Love Lucy* starring real-life spouses Lucille Ball and Desi Arnaz was America's number one television show. Eisenhower's presidential inauguration on January 20, 1953, drew 29 million viewers, but when Lucy gave birth to Little Ricky in an episode broadcast the previous night, 44 million viewers (72 percent of all American homes with a TV) tuned in to watch. As the Cold War tensions between the United States and the Soviet Union intensified, anti-communist hysteria was on the rise. The perceived threat posed by communists in the United States became known as the Red Scare, and communists in the United States became known as "Reds" for their allegiance to the red Soviet flag. It was in this context that the Cincinnati Reds changed their name to Redlegs to avoid the social stigma of being associated with the nickname given to America's archenemy. It's not that anybody actually thought a newspaper headline in the sports section reading, "Reds Bomb St. Louis," might spread pandemonium; it was just a sign of the times. The Cincinnati ballclub gave no official explanation for the change, but the team did revert back to the name Reds in 1959.

The omnipotent Yankees were still the same old Yankees, but this year, the team was better than ever. Whitey Ford returned from the service to join the Big Three of Allie Reynolds, Vic Raschi, and Eddie Lopat, forming a Big Four starting rotation of two righties and two

Whitey Ford, Mickey Mantle, and Billy Martin were key pieces of the Yankees machine in 1953, and running buddies off the field. NATIONAL BASEBALL HALL OF FAME AND MUSEUM, INC.

lefties. Manager Casey Stengel had Joe Collins at first, Billy Martin at second, Phil Rizzuto at short, and Gil McDougald at third. Mantle, Hank Bauer, Gene Woodling, and Irv Noren were the outfielders, and Yogi Berra was the catcher. The 40-year-old wonder Johnny Mize, who still knew how to swing a dangerous bat, was a pinch-hitter with pop off the bench. Pastime pursuits, however, seemed a quaint diversion when compared to the world's front-page news. The United States detonated a 32-kiloton nuclear bomb, at the time the most destructive pure fission weapon ever designed, setting off a huge mushroom cloud over the desert at the Yucca Flats Nevada test site. By summer, the Cold War shifted into overdrive with the public acknowledgement by the Soviet Union that it had successfully tested its first hydrogen bomb. Suddenly, the world situation became even more frightening.

The American public passionately embraced TV as a welcome escape from the troubled world around them. It was the Golden Age of television and radio personalities were making the transition to the small screen. Arthur Godfrey. Jack Benny. George Burns and Gracie Allen. There was *Dragnet*, *The Life of Riley*, and *Texaco Star Theater* with Uncle Miltie, Milton Berle. The first issue of *TV Guide* magazine hit newsstands in 10 cities in April with a circulation of 1.56 million subscribers. The magazine would help folks keep track of an ever-growing number of popular programs, like *Your Show of Shows* with Sid Caesar and Imogene Coca.

The Bronx Bombers planted their first-place flag on April 21 and stayed on top through the long hot summer. The Boston Red Sox were never seriously in contention, but they got some good news when the military released Ted Williams from active duty after flying 39 missions as a Marine Corps captain in Korea. After three years of bloody battle, the conflict in Korea finally had ended. The war cost the lives of millions of Koreans and Chinese, as well as over 50,000 Americans. It had been a frustrating war for Americans, who were used to forcing the unconditional surrender of their enemies. Returning prisoners of war brought home stories of communist brainwashing, and of physical and emotional atrocities related to their torture.

The 34-year-old Williams returned to baseball action on August 6. He had been out of baseball since heading into the Corps after only six games in 1952. He left Boston fans an indelible memory on April 30 by hitting a game-winning home run in his last big-league game before shipping out. In his first appearance of the '53 season, Williams popped up to the first baseman as a pinch-hitter in the ninth inning of an 8–7 loss to the St. Louis Browns at Fenway Park. In his second appearance three days later, he electrified the Fenway faithful by pinch-hitting a home run. It was another week before he was ready to take the field, but when he did, he went on a hot streak that lasted until the end of the season. He finished the year with a .407 batting average and 13 home runs in only 91 at-bats.

Some 6,300 miles away from Korea, the Braves, charter members of the National League and a fixture in Boston for 77 years, opened the 1953 season in a new home—County Stadium in Milwaukee. The franchise shift was the first in major-league baseball since 1903, when Baltimore of the fledgling American League moved to New York and became the Highlanders (later to be called Yankees). The shift was a result of sagging attendance and lost revenue in recent years. In Boston, Lou Perini had witnessed a stunning fall from grace for his Braves. In four years, the team deteriorated from NL champions to a second-division club, and its attendance plunged from 1.5 million to a scant 280,000. Perini reported a loss of $700,000 and claimed that Boston had become a one-team city since the arrival of television.

Competing head-to-head with the prestigious Red Sox was a task Perini wanted nothing more to do with. He petitioned NL owners to okay the move to Milwaukee and received unanimous approval on March 18. The move on short notice created minor problems in scheduling and travel arrangements, but the biggest obstacle was getting permission from the minor-league Milwaukee Brewers of the American Association. The Brewers, who had played in Milwaukee for more than half a century, accepted a cash payment for their territorial rights and agreed to move to Toledo, Ohio. The Braves played their first home game in County Stadium, a new $5 million facility, on April 14. More than 36,000 fans showed up to watch the Braves take on the Cardinals of St. Louis, at the time the only major-league city west of the Mississippi River. The Braves defeated the Cardinals, 3–2, in 10 innings. Rookie center fielder Billy Bruton was the hero. He hit a game-ending home run to make a winner of Warren Spahn, who went the distance. It was Bruton's only home run of the season. The fans were so excited that during the game they cheered everything and anything. They even went nuts over a simple pop foul. County Stadium was so crazy the *Wisconsin State Journal* referred to it as "an insane asylum with bases."

It took the Milwaukee Braves just 13 home games to surpass the total gate of the 1952 Boston team. The fans kept on coming, and coming, and coming. By season's end, the Braves would set a National League attendance record of more than 1.8 million fans—more than twice the total of every other NL team except Brooklyn, a distant second at 1.1 million. A year later, Milwaukee became the first NL team to eclipse the two million mark, a figure that held steady in each of the next three seasons. While other teams struggled to draw one million fans for an entire season, the Braves regularly tallied more than that many at the turnstiles by the All-Star Game. Envious baseball owners elsewhere sat up and took notice. For half a century, Major League Baseball's geographical landscape was unchanged. The same 16 teams representing the same 10 Northeast cities, all played ball and maintained the status quo. But postwar America was on the fast track. Air travel, television, the automobile, and the citizenry's flock to the suburbs were quickly transforming the United States into a smaller, more accessible, and more affordable society. Aging ballparks were decaying along with the inner cities that housed them. Emerging markets boomed and made pitches to bring major-league baseball to their cities. By year's end it would be the turn of the St. Louis Browns. Following the 1953 season in which the Browns lost 100 games and drew less than 300,000 fans, the owners could not compete with the Cardinals any longer and moved the franchise to Baltimore, to become known as the Orioles.

It was a new era for baseball, and for a spinoff, plastic version of the sport. A brand new game called Wiffle Ball, invented by David N. Mullany at his home in Fairfield, Connecticut, was introduced and sold in stores, changing backyard play forever. The perforated plastic ball was easy to make curve and even harder to hit. The frozen foods company Ore-Ida, finally figuring out what do with the leftovers from its french fries, offered a new product called Tater Tots found in your grocers' freezer. Knopf published *Go Tell It on the Mountain* by James Baldwin, Patti Page reached number one singing "(How Much Is) That Doggie in the Window," and J. Fred Muggs, a chimpanzee, became a regular on NBC-TV's *Today Show*.

The world was changing in other ways, as well. A glossy new magazine called *Playboy* that included nude photos published its first issue with Marilyn Monroe on the undated cover, because rookie publisher Hugh Hefner feared there would not be a second issue. He needn't have worried. Hef's magazine became a worldwide empire. More than that, *Playboy* challenged social conventions about men, women, sex, and nudity, and helped galvanize attitudes about civil liberties and civil rights.

Edmund Hillary and Tenzing Norgay became the first mountaineers to reach the top of Mount Everest, when they arrived at the summit a whopping 29,035 feet above sea level—the highest point on earth—on May 29. Hillary, from New Zealand, and his Nepalese Sherpa guide, were part of an Everest expedition organized by John Hunt of Great Britain. Word of the pair's achievement reached Queen Elizabeth II on the eve of her coronation, to which Hillary and Norgay said they gave the queen a "world-shaking coronation present," and they were right.

The Yankees, already on top of the baseball world, reached new heights. They got out of the gate at a blistering 41-11 pace, which included an 18-game winning streak, and mounted a 10-game lead over the second-place Cleveland Indians before school let out for summer. Mantle hit in 16 straight games and was leading the league with a .340 batting average to fuel the torrid pace. The team had it all—dominant pitching, timely hitting, solid defense—and there were plenty of heroes to go around. Collins beat the White Sox with a ninth-inning home run on June 2; Bauer made an acrobatic diving catch to halt a Tigers rally for the final out on June 9; and in a Cleveland doubleheader before 74,708 spectators on June 14, Berra homered to win the first game and tripled in the winning run of the nightcap. Ford and Lopat each had 7-0 records, and Reynolds was credited with seven saves in seven relief appearances.

Ford started New York on another winning streak in early August by collecting four hits and striking out eight in an 11–3 win over the St. Louis Browns at the Stadium. The Yanks then swept three games from the Detroit Tigers, but the Chicago White Sox trailed New York by just five games when they came to the Bronx on August 7 for a crucial four-game series. With the Yanks trailing, 1–0, in the first game, Mantle came up with two men on, slammed a ball into the gap in left-center, and never stopped running until he scored an inside-the-park home run. Yogi Berra and Billy Martin added homers as Eddie Lopat beat the Sox, 6–1. Then the Yanks delivered the knockout blow in an August 8 doubleheader. The first game was a tight pitching duel between Ford and Cuban right-hander Sandy Consuegra. The game played before 68,529 Ladies Day fans remained scoreless when the Yankees batted in the bottom of the ninth. After a walk to Woodling and a sacrifice bunt by Martin, Stengel sent Mize up to hit for Ford. Big Jawn came through with a single to left to win it for the Yanks, 1–0, and give Ford his 13th win of the season. "(Ford) is always around the plate. He's so easy to catch I could do it sitting in a rocking chair," said Berra.

Although Ford allowed just five hits in recording his third shutout of the campaign, New York left-hander Bob Kuzava trumped him by pitching an even better game in the nightcap. Kuzava pitched a one-hit shutout—losing the no-hitter with one out in the ninth on a double by Bob Boyd—and the White Sox were suddenly eight games back. The only bad news for New York was that Mantle had injured his right knee making a fine play in the first game and would be out indefinitely. Even with Mantle sidelined, the Yankees unloaded on Washington pitching for 28 hits in Ford's next start and led, 22–0, after seven innings. Whitey had collected four hits for the second time in 10 days and had allowed just three, but Casey decided to give him the rest of the day off. It appeared the Yanks would set a major-league record for the most lopsided shutout win, but rookie left-hander Steve Kraly (making just his second major-league appearance) gave up a run and the Yanks had to settle for a 22–1 win. "I always thought that record would

WHITEY FORD
pitcher NEW YORK YANKEES

After two years in the service, Whitey Ford returned to the Yankees in 1953 and didn't miss a beat. He pitched more than 200 innings and compiled an 18-6 record. TOPPS ® TRADING CARDS USED COURTESY OF THE TOPPS COMPANY, INC.

stand until it was broken," said Berra. Of their 30 August games, the Yanks won 20, and behind consistent pitching and clutch hitting, they forged to a lead they would not relinquish. On September 1, they beat Chicago, 3–2, on a homer by Mantle, who had returned to the lineup wearing a brace on his injured knee. The Yankees record improved to 87-43 and their lead over the White Sox ballooned to 9 1/2 games. Chicago, and the rest of the American League, was finished for the season.

The Yankees maintained first place to the wire, and glided to an early clinching date on September 14. Stengel's platooning once again did the job. Woodling (his on-base percentage of .429 ranked best in the league), Mantle, Bauer, and Noren comprised the outfield, yet none played more than 133 games, thanks to Stengel shuffling the deck. Eight different men played shortstop at one time or another, and Mize appeared in 66 games as a pinch-hitter, without so much as picking up his first baseman's mitt. The regular starters provided a balanced attack. Catcher Yogi Berra (who hit .296) and Mantle (who batted .295) both combined for 200 RBIs and Gene Woodling (.306) and Hank Bauer (.304) led the lineup in hitting. Billy Martin, setting career highs with 15 homers and 75 RBIs, became a rock in his second year starting at second base. Few came rougher than Martin, who cemented his reputation as a big-time brawler by punching out St. Louis Browns catcher Clint Courtney for the second time in as many seasons. The tough guy persona was celebrated on the big screen, too. Black leather jackets and blue jeans became a popular fashion statement thanks to *The Wild One* starring Marlon Brando. Brando's character, a biker named Johnny, is asked, "What are you rebelling against?" His reply: "What have you got?" After the film's release, motorcycle sales skyrocketed.

The summer of '53 was the height of the Red Scare. Paranoia against communism was reaching absurd levels, and the US Department of Justice was well on its toes. Charlie Chaplin and his family were sailing on the *Queen Elizabeth* to attend the London premiere of his film *Limelight* when he was informed that he would be arrested upon returning to America. The US attorney general rescinded Chaplin's re-entry permit based on suspicion of communist inclinations and announced that Chaplin would have to answer questions about his political views and moral behavior before being allowed to re-enter the country. Having had enough, Chaplin chose to remain in Europe, and said he would never return to the United States, even if Jesus Christ were the president. He settled with his family in Switzerland and remained there until his death, another victim of the Cold War.

The Yankees machine rolled through the American League schedule *Blitzkrieg*-style like the German Panzer tank forces. Their offense ranked first among the eight AL teams in batting average, on-base percentage, slugging percentage, total bases, runs scored, and walks, and second in home runs. But the major strength of the team was pitching, as evidenced by the staff's 16 shutouts on the season, also best in the circuit. Whitey Ford was back from his stint in the military and showed no rust, emerging as the team ace with an 18-6 record in his first full year as a starter. Fellow lefty Eddie Lopat posted a 16-4 record for a .800 winning percentage that was best in the majors, to go along with a 2.42 ERA that placed second to Warren Spahn. Johnny Sain, 14-7, pitched brilliantly, and Allie Reynolds, who won 13 games despite a back injury that limited his effectiveness, gradually took on the role of closer as he led the Yankees with 13 saves. Vic Raschi, fighting an arthritic knee, also won 13 games and didn't drop consecutive decisions all year. A good-hitting pitcher, he set a record for pitchers on August 4 when he knocked in seven runs in a game, beating Detroit, 15–0.

Stronger than the year before, the '53 Yankees won the pennant easily, finishing in front of the Indians by 8 1/2 games. Cleveland's Al Rosen (.336 average, 43 home runs, 145 RBIs) became the first third baseman in AL history to earn the Most Valuable Player Award. But even Rosen's spectacular effort came with its own disappointment. Needing a hit in his final at-bat of the season to win the batting title and the Triple Crown, Rosen appeared to beat out a grounder to third, but missed stepping on first base. He wound up finishing one point behind the .337 average posted by Washington's Mickey Vernon. Had he been safe, Rosen would have won the batting title by one-tenth of a point, but Rosen wouldn't let his manager, Al Lopez, argue the call. "I was out Al," he said. "I missed the bag."

Meanwhile, in the National League, the Brooklyn Dodgers were on a roll. Manager Charlie Dressen's team won 105 regular-season games and coasted to the NL pennant by a comfortable 13 lengths over the second-place Milwaukee Braves. Brooklyn zoomed after the All-Star break, never to lose more than two in a row the rest of the season, on its way to a 105-49 record, the best in Dodgers franchise history. In '53 the Dodgers may have fielded their best team yet. They hit 208 homers and scored 955 runs, the most by any team in the league since 1930, and they outscored the second best-hitting team that year by 187 runs, the largest gap between the top two teams since 1874.

Leading the titanic assault was the catcher Roy Campanella with a .312 batting average, 41 homers, and league-leading 142 RBIs, for which he was named the NL's Most Valuable Player. Campy was buoyed by center fielder Duke Snider with a .336 batting average, 42 homers, 126 RBIs, and a league-leading 132 runs scored. They became the first duo from any NL team to each hit over 40 homers in the same season. First baseman Gil Hodges batted .302 and added 31 round-trippers to go along with 122 RBIs. Outfielder Carl Furillo earned the league batting title at .344. Jackie Robinson, now mostly an outfielder and third baseman, hit .329, and Jim "Junior" Gilliam, Robinson's replacement at second base, hit .278, scored 125 runs, and led the league with 17 triples, earning himself the league's Rookie of the Year Award. On the mound, Carl Erskine was 20-6 and capably stepped in as the ace in the absence of Don Newcombe, wrapping up his two-year tour of duty with the armed forces in Korea. Russ Meyer won 15, and Billy Loes 14. Clem Labine won 10 games in relief, 11 overall. Preacher Roe was 11-3, giving him a record for the past three years of 44-8, a winning percentage of .846. And rookie Johnny Podres won nine games against just four losses. With Billy Cox at third, Pee Wee Reese at short, Gilliam at second, and Hodges at first, the Dodgers had the best infield defense in all of baseball.

The Yankees and the Dodgers won their pennants handily and were set to battle again in their second straight Subway Series. The hard-hitting team from Brooklyn was feeling pretty good about their chances. They were loaded with offense, pitching, and defense, and if they were ever going to beat the hated New York Yankees, this was the year. Had a few games gone their way in 1950 and '51, Brooklyn would very well have been playing in its fifth straight World Series. The Yankees needed no such luck. Casey's teams had tied the McCarthy-led Yankees record of four straight World Series triumphs in the 1930s. Now that they had tied the record, Stengel's Yankees would set out to do what had never been done—capture the pennant and the World Series for the fifth time in a row.

The first World Series between the American League and National League was played in 1903. Cy Young and the Boston Pilgrims beat Honus Wagner and the Pittsburgh Pirates five games to three. Cy Young came to Yankee Stadium on September 30, 1953, to throw out the ceremonial opening pitch of the Fall Classic, commemorating the golden anniversary of the first World Series. He was 86 years old. Honus Wagner, legendary shortstop on the Pirates, was invited, but he was too ill to travel from his home in Carnegie, Pennsylvania.

Game 1 of the '53 Series began as Game 7 in '52 had ended—with Billy Martin landing a punch right to the Dodgers' gut. The second baseman socked a three-run triple in the first inning and went on to collect three more hits in the 9–5 opening victory. Joe Collins and Yogi Berra belted homers for New York, and Berra performed the remarkable feat of throwing out two Dodgers runners at third base on successive sacrifice bunt attempts. Jim Gilliam, Gil Hodges, and George "Shotgun" Shuba—best known as the Montreal Royals teammate who shook Jackie Robinson's hand after the rookie had homered—went deep for the Dodgers. Shuba's shot was the first pinch homer by an NL player in World Series history, but the feat did little to numb the pain felt by Martin's big hits. Martin continued to vex Dodgers pitchers in Game 2 by adding a game-tying, bases-empty homer in the seventh. Mantle added to his ever-growing World Series heroics with a two-run drive that broke a 2-all tie in the eighth inning and nailed down Eddie Lopat's 4–2 win over Preacher Roe.

The Yankees won the first two games at Yankee Stadium in the Bronx, and then the scene shifted to Brooklyn, where 35,270 packed Ebbets Field. The sounds from Gladys Gooding, baseball's first full-time organist, could be heard throughout the park. (Gooding, who for years played the organ at RKO and Loews Theaters before coming to Ebbets Field—and later Madison Square Garden—is the answer to a trivia question about being the only person who ever played for the Dodgers, the Rangers, and the Knicks.) Carl Erskine, who did not get past the first inning in the opener at the Stadium, came back for the third game against Vic Raschi, an eight-year veteran. About the only thing you could say about Erskine's quick KO in Game 1, was that he was well rested for his Game 3 start three days later. In outdueling Raschi, Erskine turned in one of the most dominant starts in World Series history, breaking the 24-year-old Series record by striking out 14 batters, including Mickey Mantle and Joe Collins four times each. Despite the dominating pitching performance, the game was in doubt until the bottom of the eighth when Roy Campanella deposited a

Raschi pitch into the left field stands to break a tie and clinch a 3–2 Dodgers victory.

Whitey Ford got the Game 4 call for the Yankees, pitted against the enigmatic Billy Loes, two years Ford's junior. Ford and Loes knew each other from the old neighborhood; the two had grown up together in Astoria, New York. Loes was a zany character and distinguished himself as such in the 1952 World Series. When asked how the Dodgers would fare, he predicted the Yankees would win in seven, but claimed to have been misquoted, as saying the Yankees would win in six. During the sixth game that year, he became the first pitcher in World Series history to commit a balk. In the seventh inning, he was beginning his windup when the ball dropped from his hand. "Too much spit on it," he said later. Then a groundball hit by Yankees pitcher Vic Raschi bounced off his leg for a single, allowing a run to score. Afterward, asked why he had fumbled the grounder, he replied seriously, "I lost it in the sun."

Game 4 of the '53 Series was played on a beautiful summer afternoon. Ford lasted one inning. He was greeted rudely by Brooklyn's three-run outburst in the inning. Duke Snider acted as a one-man wrecking crew, as he whacked two doubles and a home run to drive in four runs. The Dodgers tied the series at two games each with a 7–3 win. Loes pitched eight innings before giving way to Clem Labine. In the ninth, the Yankees had the bases loaded with two outs when Mantle singled to left field for the final New York run. But the always-aggressive Martin didn't stop at third on the single. He charged for home and backup outfielder Don Thompson, playing left field in place of Jackie Robinson, gunned Martin down at the plate for the final out of the game. With the series tied at two games apiece and the two teams evenly matched, the third inning in Game 5 proved critical for the Dodgers; Gil Hodges's two-out error opened the floodgates for the Yankees, who scored five runs and took control of the Series. Mantle, still playing on weak legs, blasted a grand slam home run into the upper deck of the left field stands, giving the Yanks a 6–1 lead they would not relinquish. Prior to the grand slam, Yankees batters had complained about a blinding glare coming from center field. The glare was traced to a man in an apartment across the street from Ebbets Field who was using a mirror to distract the hitters. A tarpaulin was quickly erected to block the reflection and the game resumed. Stengel had started journeyman Jim "Hot Rod" McDonald in the game. Though he allowed 12 hits, he surprisingly lasted into the eighth inning, earning a World Series win to go with his 24 lifetime big-league victories. The Yankees hit four homers in an 11–7 win to take a three-games-to-two Series lead.

Back at Yankee Stadium the next day, Ford started the potential clinching game for the Yankees' fifth consecutive world championship. This time, things turned out differently for Ford. Erskine tried to come back for Brooklyn on two days rest, but didn't have much left in the tank. The Yankees had a 3–0 lead after two innings. The Dodgers didn't score off Ford until the sixth. He worked a scoreless seventh and then Stengel brought in Allie Reynolds to pitch the eighth. Ford had pitched seven innings, allowing one run, six hits, one walk, and struck out seven. It was a move as startling as any in Casey's brilliant managerial career. With Reynolds on the mound, New York had plenty of confidence. He retired the side in the eighth, but then the Dodgers made things interesting. In danger of elimination, Brooklyn came to bat in the top of the ninth inning with the Yankees leading, 3–1. After Duke Snider drew a one-out walk, Carl Furillo slammed a dramatic two-run home run off Reynolds into the right field stands, and the contest was tied at three runs apiece. Stengel's move had backfired. The Yankees, however, would not be denied.

In the bottom of the ninth, Hank Bauer led off with a walk, and moved to second base on Mantle's infield single, bringing Billy Martin to the plate. Brooklyn's ace relief pitcher Clem Labine wanted Martin to hit a groundball that could be turned into an inning-ending double play. Labine's sinkerball was his best pitch and he specialized in getting out of jams with a groundball when he needed it. At a muscular 6-foot and 202 pounds, Bauer was a strong runner at second, and if there was a close play at the plate, would do whatever it takes to get in safely. He played baseball with a fullback's ferocity. "When Hank came down the base path, the whole earth trembled," said Johnny Pesky, shortstop for the Boston Red Sox. With the count one ball and one strike, Labine threw a sinking fastball at the knees and a little off the plate. Martin swung and knocked a single to center. Bauer came chugging around third, jumped on the dish, and scored easily the winning run, giving the Yankees their fifth straight World Series triumph. Martin was the hero for the Yankees for the second World Series in a row. Stengel hugged Martin in the Yankees clubhouse after the game and shouted to the press, "My boy did it!" It was probably Stengel's happiest moment in a baseball uniform.

Billy Martin, who made the clutch shoe-top catch to shut down the Brooklyn Dodgers and save the day for the Yankees in the seventh game of the 1952 World Series, slayed the Dodgers with his bat this time. The team's weakest hitter during the regular season, Martin went wild against the Dodgers' pitching staff. The Yankees' aggressive second baseman had a Series high .500 average with 12 hits, including a double, two triples, two home runs, and eight RBIs. He started the series with a three-run triple in the first inning of the first game and finished with a game-winning single in the bottom of the ninth inning of the last game to secure a 4–3 victory for a historic Yankees championship, the team's fifth in a row. The 1953 championship put Stengel's first five Yankees teams in a class by themselves. "I never could have done it without my players," the manager once said of his October success. Martin was one such player. The 165-pound second baseman seemed to save his big hits for big games and was an especially productive October player. There was always a Jerry Coleman—and later a Bobby Richardson—around to challenge Martin for his second base job, but few Yankees could ever challenge him for his Fall Classic showings. Asked why he thought so highly of Martin as a player, Stengel replied, "If liking a kid who will never let you down in the clutch is favoritism, then I plead guilty."

1954: STAYING POWER

By winning his fifth World Series in a row, Casey Stengel eclipsed the extraordinary exploits of Joe McCarthy, who had piloted the 1936–1939 Yankees to four consecutive championships. A nucleus of nine of the players on the '53 team had been with Casey for all five championships: Hank Bauer, Yogi Berra, Eddie Lopat, Johnny Mize, Vic Raschi, Allie Reynolds, Phil Rizzuto, backup catcher Charlie Silvera, and Gene Woodling. Mickey Mantle and Billy Martin had each played in the last three.

Over the years many people have said that Stengel's contribution to the Yankees has been overrated—that with the talent he had at his disposal, all he ever had to do was fill out the lineup card and then sit back and watch. They point to his mediocre managing record with other teams as evidence. While there were certainly some years when the Yanks were so much better than everybody else that it didn't take a genius to manage them, 1953 was not one of those years.

The 1953 Yankees did not have the best talent in baseball; with the exception of Mantle, Berra, and Whitey Ford, they were a mix of aging veterans and overachievers like Martin, Bauer, and Woodling, players who squeezed every ounce of effort and performance out of their average natural ability. In terms of talent, they were no match for the '27 Murderers' Row Yankees of Babe Ruth, Lou Gehrig, Tony Lazzeri, and Earle Combs; or the '36 Yankees of Gehrig, Joe DiMaggio, Bill Dickey, Lefty Gomez, and Red Ruffing. But what they lacked in talent, the '53 Yankees made up for with heart. No one will ever claim that this Yankees team was the greatest of all time, but it remains the only one in baseball's long history to win five straight World Series. In the four major professional sports, only the Montreal Canadiens in ice hockey and the Boston Celtics in basketball have ever won five or more consecutive world championships.

Following the 1953 season, Whitey Ford was happy to get his second World Series ring and even happier to get his World Series check for over $8,000—an amount nearly equal to what he had been paid for the entire regular season. (He reportedly used the money for a down payment on a home in Glen Cove, on Long Island.) A number of Yankees stars held out prior to the 1954 season, including Mantle, Rizzuto, and all four of the team's starting pitchers. Lopat signed first for $27,500, and then Reynolds signed for $40,000, matching Raschi's 1953 salary as the highest salary ever paid to a Yankees pitcher at the time. The team's general manager George Weiss then shocked Yankees fans by selling Raschi, his longtime ace, to the Cardinals because the pitcher refused to accept a 25 percent cut from his 1953 salary.

Vic Raschi had been 120-50 in eight seasons with the Yankees and had helped them win six titles. During the Yankees unprecedented streak of five straight World Series titles between 1949 and 1953, his record was 92-40—an average of 18 wins a season and a winning percentage of .697. But when he won only 13 games (against six losses) on a painful right knee in '53, Weiss sent Raschi a contract calling for a pay cut. Raschi ignored the offer. Weiss thought Raschi had become expendable with the return of the young Ford from military service. A short time before pitchers and catchers were to report to training camp, Weiss sold Raschi to St. Louis for $85,000. When Raschi arrived in St. Petersburg, Florida, to continue negotiations, a newspaperman informed him of the sale. Weiss hadn't even bothered to call to tell him. Raschi went to see the general manager and said simply, "Mr. Weiss, you have a very short memory."

George Weiss had a reputation as a tough negotiator with his players. In this era before free agency, a player was effectively bound to his team for life, or until the team wanted to trade or release him. Taking over the Yankees general manager job at the age of 53, after 16 years as farm director, Weiss dressed and acted like a corporate titan. He was often seen as cold, calculating, and unemotional to those outside the executive suite, making a conscious effort to keep his distance from the players whose careers he determined. Weiss's hard line on Raschi sent a message to the other holdouts. Rizzuto fell in line three days later, signing for $40,000, and the following day Mantle and Ford signed contracts for $21,000 and $16,250, respectively.

Although he never threw a pitch or swung a bat, Weiss deserves much of the credit for the Yankees' sustained run of excellence. In 1932, at 37, he was hired by Yankees owner Jacob Ruppert to run the team's minor-league system. Over the next several years, Weiss's farm program graduated a slew of players who would become mainstays for the Yankees dynasty from 1936 to 1943. When he was named general manager of the Yankees, they were already established as baseball's preeminent organization. Yet the team Weiss inherited, like all the immediate postwar teams, was one in transition. From 1944 to 1948, five different American League teams had won the pennant. The Yankees had struggled in 1946, finishing a distant third, but had come back to win in 1947 under new manager Bucky Harris. When the Yankees slumped back to third in 1948, Weiss dumped Harris, who had been hired by Larry MacPhail. Weiss wanted his own man in charge on the field, and then surprised the baseball community by hiring Casey Stengel, his friend for many years.

The five-year period from 1949 to 1953 had been a time of transition for the Yankees. The 1949 team that beat the Dodgers in the World Series had been built around DiMaggio, Henrich, Rizzuto, Berra, and pitchers Raschi, Reynolds, and Lopat. By 1953, DiMaggio and Henrich were gone and the others (with the exception of Berra) were nearing the end of the line. The torch had been passed to the next generation of Yankees stars, headed by Mantle and Ford. They fully expected to win their sixth straight World Series in 1954.

When Joe DiMaggio and Marilyn Monroe began their courtship in 1952, the public was captivated. It was a storybook romance between a legendary baseball hero and the biggest, most alluring star on the screen. On January 14, 1954, the two were married in a civil ceremony in San Francisco, DiMaggio's hometown. Only one of his former teammates, Lefty O'Doul, attended. The marriage never had a chance, though. DiMaggio, who retired after the 1951 season, was a quiet and reserved man, and preferred to remain out of the public eye. He wanted a family. Monroe attracted attention wherever she went. She wanted a career. Less than nine months after their marriage, she filed for divorce and the marriage ended in October 1954, just 274 days after the wedding. It was apparent from the start that the two were not suited as husband and wife. While they were on their honeymoon in Japan, Monroe was asked to detour to Korea to entertain the American troops. DiMaggio didn't like the idea, but Monroe went. When she returned, she was ecstatic. "Joe, you've never heard such cheering," she said. To which DiMaggio, who had been adored by tens of thousands of fans every time he stepped to the plate at Yankee Stadium, replied, "Yes, I have."

The look of Brylcreem, a hair-styling product popular with military pilots during World War II, stuck in the 1950s and was a hit with slick advertising executives who agreed that, "A little dab'll do ya." Major League Baseball was fine-tuning its look, too. It seems quaint by today's standards, but players used to leave their gloves on the field when their team went up to bat. Major League Baseball banned the practice prior to the 1954 season, instituting Rule Number 3.10, requiring that "members of the offensive team shall carry all gloves and other equipment off the field and to the dugout while their team is at bat. No equipment shall be left lying on the field, either in fair or foul territory."

According to the commissioner's office, what did the tradition in was how unsafe it was to have a foreign object on the field. Cynics, however, pointed out that gloves idly lying on the field looked bad on television, a new medium with a growing influence on the sport. The new rule was unpopular with many players. Richie Ashburn, the Hall of Fame center fielder for the Philadelphia Phillies, complained about not being allowed to leave his glove on the field anymore, saying, "If it's beauty they are striving for in the parks, why don't they plant some flowers?"

On sun-drenched spring training fields in St. Petersburg, Florida, three young players from the Yankees farm system made big impressions. Elston Howard first attracted notice because of his race. Then he quickly attracted more notice for his ability to hit the cover off a baseball. Howard had been the first black player signed by the Yankees organization. Though he was sent back to the minor leagues for seasoning, it was clear Howard would be back. Also drawing rave reviews from manager Casey Stengel was 24-year-old right-hander Bob Grim, who would take Raschi's spot in the rotation. Bill Skowron, 23, a powerfully built right-handed first baseman, had been discovered on the campus of Purdue University. The two-sport star played freshman baseball and football for legendary Hall of Fame football coach Hank Stram. When Skowron signed with the Yankees in 1950, Purdue varsity football coach Stu Holcomb, later the general manager of the Chicago White Sox, accused the Yankees of thievery because Skowron was going to be the starting halfback on his Boilermakers team.

The Yankees limped out of the gate in April and landed with a thud in May, three games out of sixth place in an eight-team league. A feeling of disenchantment ran through the Yankees clubhouse. The spring sale of Raschi created a furor among his teammates, making some of the other Yankees veterans leery and cynical. Whitey Ford reported to spring training out of shape and overweight. Stengel was clearly unhappy. In addition, the club was without the steadying influence of Johnny Mize, who retired to work in the orange groves near his offseason home in Deland, Florida. To replace Mize, Weiss acquired St. Louis Cardinals star outfielder Enos "Country" Slaughter for three minor-league prospects. Slaughter was 38 years old, and highly decorated. He had been selected for eight straight All-Star Games from 1946 to 1953, and of all active players, only Stan Musial had more career hits, and only Ted Williams had driven in more runs. "One of the greatest," remarked Stengel. "He will do anything to beat you."

The St. Louis Browns had moved to Maryland and were now playing as the Baltimore Orioles. A crowd of 46,354 watched the Orioles beat the Chicago White Sox, 3–1, in the first game at Baltimore's Memorial Stadium. On April 23, while pitching with the Cardinals at St. Louis's Sportsman's Park, the former Yankees ace Vic Raschi gave up the first of Henry Aaron's 755 career home runs. Aaron, Major League Baseball's future home run king, had also notched his first career hit off Raschi eight days earlier. Raschi won his first five starts with the Cardinals, but he ended the year with an 8-9 record and retired in 1955 after being traded to the Kansas City A's during the season.

Aaron's star rose because another star had fallen. Before the start of the 1954 season, the Milwaukee Braves were involved in a multi-player deal with the New York Giants that sent Bobby Thomson to the Braves. Thomson was a terrific slugger for the Giants but was most notably known for his home run against the Brooklyn Dodgers to decide the 1951 National League pennant. Just acquired from the Giants that off-season, Thomson would fracture his ankle in three places while sliding into second base during an exhibition game on March 13 against the Yankees. It would take Thomson five months to recover. With Thomson sidelined, the Braves needed an answer to fill their outfield hole, and inserted into the lineup a promising 20-year-old prospect from Mobile, Alabama, named Henry Aaron. The next day, Aaron suited up to play left field wearing the Milwaukee Braves jersey. Even though it was an exhibition game, Aaron came out swinging; he had three hits, including a home run, against the Red Sox. The Braves knew they had found someone special.

Watching Yankees games on television and listening to them on radio was a joy. Red Barber, who had resigned as Brooklyn Dodgers broadcaster over a salary dispute, now teamed up with Mel Allen on Yankees broadcasts. From his beloved perch in the "Catbird Seat," Barber established hallmarks of excellence in baseball broadcasting, impressing listeners as a down-to-earth man who not only informed but also entertained with folksy colloquialisms such as "pea patch" and "rhubarb" which gave his broadcasts a distinctive flavor. A native of Columbus, Mississippi, Barber launched his distinguished major-league announcing career in Cincinnati in 1934. He remained with the Reds through 1938. Brought to Brooklyn by Larry MacPhail in 1939, Barber served as the "Voice of the Dodgers" for 15 years before transferring to the New York Yankees for an additional 13 seasons behind the mike. Superficially the two play-by-play giants got along, but Red later admitted to a reporter, "Mel interrupted me on-air."

Americans were spending more time watching television. The Swanson frozen food company contributed to an American food revolution by selling its first TV Dinner. Swanson didn't actually invent the frozen dinner. That can be credited to (or blamed on) Clarence Birdseye, who in 1923 invented a system of packing and flash freezing waxed cardboard boxes of fresh foods. But it was Swanson's packaging—the compartments for individual servings—that helped transform its frozen TV Dinner meals into a cultural icon. Priced at 89 cents, customers feasted on turkey with cornbread stuffing, sweet potatoes and buttered peas right in front of their television screens. By year's end, Americans had bought 25 million of them, proving that Americans had two passions—they loved timesaving modern conveniences and they loved their newest form of entertainment, the television.

Third baseman Bobby Brown was scheduled to retire from baseball on June 30, at the age of 29, to begin his hospital internship. He had spent parts of eight seasons in New York, but he felt the calling to become a full-time doctor, a decision he never regretted. Brown had graduated from Stanford University in 1946 and was set to attend medical school at Tulane when the Yankees scooped him up with a signing bonus of more than $50,000, outrageously high at the time. He convinced the dean at Tulane that he could play ball and still go to medical school. He did both exceptionally well. He spent the summer with the Newark Bears, the Yanks top farm team, where he hit .341. Jackie Robinson hit .349 for the Montreal Royals, edging Brown for the batting title. Because of his great season with the Bears, Brown was called up to New York after the International League season ended. The 6-foot-1, 180-pound infielder made his big-league debut on September 22, 1946, playing shortstop and batting third in the second game of a Yankee Stadium doubleheader against Philadelphia. He got his first big-league hit in that game, as did his roommate Yogi Berra, also making his debut. Bobby appeared in seven games, going 8-for-24.

In 1947, Brown batted .300 in 69 games, and then played an important role in the Yankees' seven-game World Series win against the Brooklyn Dodgers. The Yankees used the 22-year-old, left-handed-hitting Brown as a pinch-hitter four times, and four times he came through: two doubles, a single, and a walk. His fourth-inning double in Game 7 tied the score at 2 and sent the eventual series-winning run to third base. Between 1948 and 1951, Bobby averaged 104 games played per season, platooning with Billy Johnson (1948 to 1950) and Gil McDougald (1951) at third base. He was a steady contributor to the Yankees lineup. During this four-year span, Brown collected 364 hits in his limited time, sporting a .281 batting average.

Juggling baseball and medical school, Brown had no choice but to skip spring training every year and start the season cold. He loved both pursuits too much to give up either, and back then, baseball didn't dwarf a doctor's salary. "I could have been a better player if I wasn't in med school, but I'd have been a better student, too, if I wasn't playing ball," he said. A famous apocryphal story that Brown swears is true concerns the time when Brown's road roommate was catcher Yogi Berra, who had little formal education. The two were reading in their hotel room one night—Berra a comic book and Brown his copy of *Boyd's Pathology*. Berra came to the end of his comic, tossed it aside, and asked Brown, "So, how did yours turn out?"

It was clear that Brown was an exceptional hitter under pressure. In the 1949 World Series, he had six hits in 12 at-bats, including a double and two triples, and he drove in five runs. Then in 1950, when the Yankees swept the Phillies in the Series, Bobby went 4-for-12, with a double and a triple. The next season brought a fourth trip to the World

Series for Brown. In 1951 against the Giants, he had five hits in 14 at-bats with two walks as the Yanks won another title. By the age of 26, Brown had won four world championship rings and had a .439 career batting average (18-for-41) in World Series play.

When the Korean War broke out, Dr. Bobby Brown was sent to Korea to serve with the 45th Division in the US Army and was assigned to the 160th Field Artillery Battalion, heading the battalion aid station. If he hadn't missed the 1952 and 1953 Series to serve in Korea, Brown would have played through the Yankees' five consecutive World Series wins, from 1949 to 1953, a record still standing today. After 19 months of military service in Korea and at Tokyo Army Hospital, Brown returned to the Yankees in May 1954. The Yankees had lost seven of their first 16 games, leading Casey Stengel to exclaim, "Boy, do we need a doctor!" Perhaps the manager wasn't joking. On April 24, 1951, Bobby was shagging fly balls when he was called to the Yankees clubhouse. He was asked to treat Stengel, who was suddenly overcome with nausea. As it turned out, Casey had had a kidney stone.

While at Tokyo Army Hospital, Bobby joined Joe DiMaggio and Lefty O'Doul to give clinics to the Japanese teams who were in spring training. Joe had brought his bride Marilyn Monroe to Japan for their honeymoon. Joe told the press the only doctor who could treat Mrs. DiMaggio was Lieutenant Brown. After baseball, he worked as a cardiologist for 25 years, during which time he also served as interim president of the Texas Rangers for six months in 1974. In 1984, he left cardiology to become president of the American League, a position he held for 10 years.

Certain numbers are magical in sports: 3,000 hits, 20 wins, 1,000 yards rushing, and a four-minute mile. For a long time, no one thought that last mark was attainable. But on May 7, Oxford University medical student Roger Bannister broke the tape in three minutes and 59.4 seconds on his home track in England. "Naturally I wanted to have a try at it," said Bannister, who decided just minutes before the race to push for the mark. That's because the sun came out shortly before race time, and the day's wind and cold rain ceased. Many people believed American miler Wes Santee would be the first to break the four-minute mark in the mile. As it turned out, not only did Bannister beat everyone, the first American to accomplish the feat was Don Bowden, who didn't do it until 1957. Just in case there were any doubts surrounding Bannister's feat, surveyors took to the track after the race and validated the distance. In fact, they found that four laps around the Oxford track came out to one mile—plus half an inch!

The year was ripe with remarkable achievements. Babe Didrikson Zaharias experienced perhaps her greatest triumph when she won the US Women's Open in golf at Salem Country Club in Peabody, Massachusetts, in July. Zaharias won by a whopping 12 strokes. "The Babe has now completely outclassed all her challengers," Al Laney wrote in the *New York Herald Tribune*. It was not simply the margin of victory that Laney referred to, nor was that what made the win her greatest and made it an inspiration to legions of sports fans. It was because Zaharias's victory came despite a fight with cancer that had required surgery only a year earlier. The grueling 72 holes of the Open, including 36 on the last day, finally began to catch up to Zaharias at the end. Still, she finished with a four-day total of 291—well ahead of all her competitors.

There may never have been a greater female athlete than the Babe, who could do just about anything she wanted to on a playing field. When she was 18, Babe won two gold medals and one silver medal in track and field at the 1932 Olympics in Los Angeles. She also was a star in basketball, tennis, bowling, and volleyball, and she once pitched an inning in a major-league baseball spring training game. Another time, she reportedly struck out Joe DiMaggio in an exhibition. In the end, Zaharias succumbed to cancer. She was just 42 when she died in 1956. She remains the greatest all-around female athlete in history.

Men and women had more disposable income during the prosperity following World War II. The rapidly expanding consumer culture funneled more money into sports than ever before. Sports soon would be not so much a diversion but an integral part of everyday life. The growing market spawned the birth of *Sports Illustrated.* The cover of the first magazine featured Milwaukee Braves slugger Eddie Mathews taking a mighty swing. Cover price: 25 cents. The literate newsmagazine defined and chronicled much of what is important about sports, and it would have a dramatic influence on public perceptions that sports was not a juvenile triviality but instead an important part of the culture. The rise of sports on TV helped *SI*, but the converse is also true. Many of the events that became central to the American sports experience were aided by coverage in the magazine. Today, despite the changing tastes of consumerism, *Sports Illustrated* remains the most widely circulated national sports magazine (though the cover price is no longer 25 cents). The Braves finished third in the NL in '54 with an 89-65 record. The *SI* cover boy Eddie Mathews had his second consecutive 40-home-run season. Henry Aaron batted .280 with 27 doubles, 13 home runs, and 69 RBIs. It would take the Braves a few years after Aaron's arrival to put it all together and reach the postseason, and when they finally did, the Yankees would be waiting.

The Korean conflict had ended in the summer of '53, and though most of the boys had come home, the intense Cold War nuclear arms race was worsening. The United States had detonated a horrifying hydrogen bomb on Bikini Atoll in the Pacific Ocean that was a thousand times more powerful than the devastating atomic bomb dropped on Hiroshima. The world was in turmoil, and the Yankees, after an unprecedented five straight world championships, were too. Whitey Ford got off to a slow start as he worked diligently to get himself in shape. He took the mound to face Frank Sullivan, making his first start in a Red Sox uniform in Yankee Stadium on May 21 before 30,119 partisan New York fans. Sullivan threw a complete-game, 6–3 victory at the Bronx Bombers and beat Ford in the process. Boston scored all its runs in a big sixth-inning uprising that included a three-run home run by ill-fated 24-year-old first baseman Harry Agganis, a rising star. Agganis became gravely ill early the next season and was hospitalized with pneumonia. He rejoined the Red Sox for a short time before returning to the hospital with a viral infection. After showing some signs of recovery, Agganis died of a pulmonary embolism on June 27. Agganis's sudden death is considered one of the greatest tragedies to hit Boston's sporting community.

Two starts later, when Ford lost a heartbreaking game, 1–0, on an unearned run to the Washington Senators at Yankee Stadium on Memorial Day, his record fell to two wins against four losses, and the Yankees dropped into third place behind the White Sox and Indians. After Ford allowed five runs over two innings in a 7–4 loss to Washington on July 2, his record was still only six up and six down, and New York was still no better than 4 1/2 games out. It turned out that Ford was tipping his pitches and had his mechanics out of whack. Once corrected, Ford pitched like an All-Star for the rest of the year. On July 16 he defeated the Baltimore Orioles, 3–2, with a complete-game seven-hitter as the Yankees won their 11th game in a row and closed to a half-game back of the Indians. Mickey Mantle had fully recovered from his knee surgery and was no longer hampered by the bulky leather and metal brace that made it difficult to bat left-handed. By midsummer, he was the most productive hitter in the league, and a threat to win the Triple Crown. As late as July 27, Mantle was leading the league in home runs with 20 and was tied for the RBI lead at 74 with Chicago's Minnie Minoso. He was third with a .323 batting average behind his Yankees teammate Irv Noren and Cleveland's Bobby Avila. Sparked by Mantle and catcher Yogi Berra, the team stayed close on the heels of the hard-charging Indians into the dog days of August. Berra was hitting well in the clutch and driving in runs at a personal-record pace. He had won the Most Valuable Player Award in 1951 and was a runner-up and fourth-place vote getter in the next two years. He was in the running for the award again. Hank Bauer, batting leadoff and hitting around .300, was also having another excellent year.

Though the Yankees were winning more games than they had ever won before under Stengel, the Cleveland Indians were also winning big. Cleveland reeled off winning streaks of six, 11, nine, eight, nine, and 11 games in a row. They were playing at a pace that if maintained would break the major-league record for games won in a season, 116, a record set by the 1906 Chicago Cubs. The team gave no quarter. The Cleveland players were a tight, close-knit bunch of men looking out for one another. The Indians pitching staff was not averse to knocking down opposing hitters to protect their own teammates—two of whom were black (Larry Doby and Al Smith) and another Jewish (Al Rosen)—who were being thrown at by other AL clubs that were slow to tolerate the changing and more enlightened times. In a political move that captured the zeitgeist of the decade, the Pledge of Allegiance, a non-sectarian American vow, was amended to add the words "under God" within the phrase "one nation indivisible." President Dwight D. Eisenhower signed the bill into law on June 14, Flag Day. The Cold War was gaining steam, and Eisenhower was fighting communism across the globe. Two years later, on Flag Day again, Eisenhower also made "In God We Trust" our nation's official motto. Belief in God was something communists did not support.

American prosperity was on the rise. The Dow Jones Industrial Average closed at an all-time high of 382.74. The Yankees had their own blue-chip stocks. Mantle finished the year with a .300 batting average, 27 home runs, 102 RBIs, and a league-leading 129 runs scored. Berra continued to shine offensively; he hit .307, with 22 homers, and 125 RBIs, winning the MVP Award for a second time. At first base Stengel platooned Joe Collins, Eddie Robinson, and Bill "Moose" Skowron, the rookie home run threat. Among the three first basemen, the position supplied 22 home runs and 114 RBIs. Skowron batted .340 as a part-time player and looked very impressive. Gil McDougald played all around the infield—second, third, and shortstop—whenever and wherever Stengel needed him. During the 1950s, the versatile McDougald was probably the third most valuable player on the Yankees roster behind Mantle and Berra. Ford's resurgent second half 10-2 mark gave him a 16-8 record for the year. His 2.82 earned run average was among the best in the league. Although healthy all year, he made only 28 starts as Stengel continued to pitch him only every fifth, sixth, or even seventh day. That practice cost Ford five to eight starts a year and made it difficult for him to win 20 games in a season.

All hailed the Cleveland Indians pitching staff. The team's 2.78 earned run average was the lowest of any AL team since the Dead Ball Era. The starting rotation was led by Bob Lemon and Early Wynn with 23 wins apiece to share the league lead. Teammate Mike Garcia topped the league with a 2.64 ERA while winning 19 of 27 decisions. Hard-throwing Bob Feller won 13 games, losing only three. Two rookies headed the Cleveland bullpen, left-hander Don Mossi and right-hander Ray Narleski, combining to save 20 games. Hal Newhouser, a former two-time MVP who'd been released by the Tigers, chipped in with seven wins and seven saves in 25 relief appearances.

Cleveland had plenty of muscle at the plate, too. They were tops in home runs with 156, including a league-leading 32 dingers by outfielder Larry Doby. Second baseman Bobby Avila hit for an American League–best .341 batting average. (Yankees outfielder Irv Noren was hitting around .350 until September, when he slumped about 30 points to lose the batting title to Avila.) Third baseman Al Rosen, the reigning MVP, busted a finger on defense and played hurt for most of the year, but his offensive numbers of a .300 batting average, 24 homers, and 102 RBIs are more than respectable. First baseman Vic Wertz, acquired in a midseason trade with the Baltimore Orioles, showed a little pop by clubbing 14 homers in 94 games.

Meanwhile, in the middle of the season, Douglass Wallop published a novel called *The Year the Yankees Lost the Pennant*. It later became the hit musical *Damn Yankees*. Stengel was given a copy, but claimed to never read it. The Faustian story was about a fictional 1958 season in which Joe Boyd, a middle-aged salesman and lifelong fan of those perennial losers, the Washington Senators, sells his soul to the devil in order to keep the hated, all-conquering Yankees from winning their 10th straight AL pennant and world championship. Wallop was a diehard Senators fan and clearly feared the Yankees streak of five straight world championships from 1949 to 1953 was destined to go on forever unless some not-so-divine intervention could find a way to stop them. As the book moved steadily up the bestseller list, the real-life Yankees appeared to be also-rans to the Indians. In early September, when the Yankees won the last two of a three-game series over the Tribe at Yankee Stadium to reduce the Cleveland lead to 3 1/2 games, a hint of optimism returned to Stengel's clubhouse. He was certain that the momentum had finally turned in his club's favor. No such luck; the Indians won seven of its next nine to increase the Yankees' deficit to 6 1/2 games.

The Yankees arrived in Cleveland for a showdown on Sunday, September 12, needing a doubleheader sweep in their final meeting with the Indians to have any shot for the pennant. Into Municipal Stadium flocked 86,563 fans, the largest regular-season crowd in major-league history. They came to watch the downfall of the Yankees Empire. Indeed, to conquer the Yankees would be to conquer Everest. After five years of unsuccessfully chasing New York, the Indians faithful would finally reach the mountaintop. The Yankees dropped both games to the home team, 4–1 and 3–2, thus unofficially but effectively signaling the end of their quest for a sixth American League flag in a row. The dual losses boosted the Tribe's lead to 8 1/2 games with just two weeks left in the regular season. The Al Lopez–led Indians clinched the pennant just three games later, and with the Yankees relegated to second place on the last day of the season, Casey Stengel fielded a lineup of familiar names in unfamiliar positions. In an 8–6 loss to the Philadelphia Athletics at the ballpark in the Bronx, Yogi Berra played his only career game at third base, handling two chances without a miscue, shortstop Mickey Mantle flawlessly fielded eight grounders, and Bill Skowron made just one error in his eight opportunities at second base.

This was the last game for the Philadelphia A's, a charter member of the American League under the direction of Connie Mack. The Athletics franchise, winners of nine pennants and five World Series in their proud history, had fallen on hard times recently and were losing the battle of Philadelphia to the National League's Phillies. After spending the first 54 years of their existence in the City of Brotherly Love, the A's were relocating to Kansas City under the new ownership of Arnold Johnson, the 47-year-old Chicago industrialist who had recently bought the Athletics from the Mack family. There had been some opposition to Johnson among AL owners because of his close association with New York Yankees co-owner Dan Topping and his minority ownership of Yankee Stadium, which Johnson, after much legal wrangling, agreed to sell. The A's would open the next season in Kansas City's Municipal Stadium, which had been the home of the Kansas City Blues, a Yankees farm team that Topping relocated to Denver, Colorado. The franchise transfer was the third in major-league baseball in 20 months, following the St. Louis Browns move to Baltimore, and the Boston Braves to Milwaukee.

NBC-TV's *The Tonight Show* aired for the first time; guests included comedian Wally Cox and New York Giants star Willie Mays. The host, Steve Allen, announced to the audience on its debut that "this show is gonna go on forever." Back then, the show ran from 11:15 p.m. to 1:00 a.m., and no one had expectations for success. More than 60 years later, it's the world's longest-running talk show. Americans were spending more and more time in front of their TV sets, though it would still be another decade before Newton Minow, chairman of the Federal Communications Commission, dubbed television a "vast wasteland" and criticized network broadcasters for not doing more to serve the public interest.

The New York Yankees won 103 games during the regular season, but for once the pinstripers weren't good enough. While 103 victories usually will win a pennant, New York finished a distant eight games behind the Cleveland Indians, who had what was then the best regular-season record in American League history: 111 wins and only 43 losses. They broke the record held by the 1927 Yankees, whose record was 110-44. The Indians' .721 winning percentage is still the best in the AL's 115-year history. (Although the 1998 Yankees, with 114 wins, and the 2001 Seattle Mariners, with 116, would win more games, they both lacked a better winning percentage as a result of playing eight extra games.)

The Yankees' five-year streak as world champions finally came to an end. After the season, a despondent Stengel blamed himself as much as anyone for not winning the pennant despite Cleveland's awesome winning percentage. "I was surprised that I lost it," said Casey. "Until after those last two games in Cleveland I didn't expect to lose it. The fault was carelessness in all parts including myself. I kept saying, 'We'll catch 'em next week.'" Despite a second-place finish, there were positive advances, the most promising one being the unexpected development of the young pitcher Bob Grim, a New York boy who won the 1954 AL Rookie of the Year Award voting in a landslide. The right-hander won 20 games, lost six, and had a 3.26 ERA. Grim started 20 games and made 17 relief appearances. Eight of his wins came in relief. He was only the second rookie ever to win 20 games in a season. In 1910, Russ Ford of the New York Highlanders (forebears of the Yankees) won 26 games in his rookie campaign. At 6-foot-1 and 175 pounds, Grim was a big pitcher with an easy motion. He threw a flaming fastball and a quick-darting slider, simply rearing back and firing the ball in hopes the batter would swing and miss. He was extremely difficult to hit when his fastball was tailing and his slider was breaking. The Yankees felt that Grim would be a great one, taking his place with Raschi, Reynolds, Chandler, and Ruffing as right-handed pitching stars.

The 1950s were a time when America was still moving slowly toward change. Among the most noteworthy highlights was the gradual racial integration of the playing fields. Althea Gibson, at age 23 in 1950, broke the color barrier at Forest Hills and became the first African American to play in the US Open tennis tournament. Still, it was a sign of the times that the University of San Francisco's unbeaten 1951 football team was not invited to a postseason bowl game because the squad included black players. Racial segregation—known as Jim Crow laws—was alive and well. Blacks were barred from sharing the same buses, schools, and other public facilities as whites. After hearing Thurgood Marshall (who would eventually be appointed to the Supreme Court) argue the case known as *Brown v. Board of Education*, the US Supreme Court unanimously ruled that segregation of the races be outlawed in America's public schools. The landmark decision, issued on May 17, 1954, was a first step in mandating racial equality, sparking the civil rights movement.

On the diamond, 1954 was a triumphant watershed season for black players, and in a larger sense, for baseball and the country as a whole. Larry Doby's Indians dethroned the dynastic Yankees, a team that represented white supremacy in the game, and went on to play Willie Mays's Giants in the first World Series that featured players of color on both teams. While Doby was the dominant player in the American League, Mays emerged as the preeminent player in the National League, with a flair and boyish innocence that all fans, black and white, quickly came to embrace. In the spring of 1954, little notice was paid to Leo Durocher's team, the New York Giants, coming off a substandard fifth-place showing from the year before. The team was handicapped by the yearlong absence of Willie Mays, still doing time in the Army. Mays returned in 1954 with a breakout performance. In his first game back after two years in the Army, Mays blasted a game-winning two-run homer against Brooklyn. By season's end, the 23-year-old slammed 41 homers, knocked in 110 runs, and won the batting title at .345 with three hits on the season's final day to fend off teammate Don Mueller (.342) and Brooklyn's Duke Snider (.341). Ignited by Mays, the Giants grabbed first place in June—winning 24 of 28 games in the month—sailed through the summer and never relinquished the lead.

The Cleveland Indians, on the heels of the record 111 wins during the regular season, were heavily favored to beat the New York Giants in the World Series. As it turned out, the October Series was a rout—but not by the Indians. The Giants swept in four games. For all intents and purposes, the Series was over on the first day, September 29. Dusty Rhodes's pinch-hit, pop fly landed just over the 297-foot wall down the right field line to give New York a 5–2 win in 10 innings. But that wasn't what turned the Series the Giants way. Instead, it was a brilliant play by center fielder Willie Mays in the top of the eighth inning. Mays was playing in just his third big-league season, and it already was clear that his talents were extraordinary. He could run, hit, and hit for power. But the signature play of this Series—indeed, the signature play of his career—came from his glove. With the score tied at 2, the Indians put their first two runners on base to lead off the eighth inning. First baseman Vic Wertz lined a drive to the deepest part of the Polo Grounds in center field. Mays knew the ball was over his head. But he also knew that the Polo Grounds had nearly 450 feet before you got to the wall to the right of center. He turned and ran for the wall. At the last instant, Mays put his glove up over his shoulder and made the catch with his back to home plate. Then he suddenly stopped his sprint, whirled, and threw the ball back to the infield. The runners had to hold at first and second base; the Indians did not score. In the 10th inning, it was Mays who started the winning rally by walking with one out and stealing second base. But his biggest play didn't come at bat or on the basepaths. It came more than 425 feet from home plate. The Series between the New York Giants and Cleveland Indians was notable as the first with black players on both teams, but it was memorable for an amazing catch by the Say Hey Kid, Willie Mays.

Beginning in 1954, with the triumph of Willie Mays and the Giants and the impressive debuts of Henry Aaron and Ernie Banks, the first generation of black superstars began making their mark in baseball. Roberto Clemente would debut with the Pittsburgh Pirates in 1955, followed by Frank Robinson for the Cincinnati Reds the following year, Orlando Cepeda with the Giants in 1958, and all in 1959, Bob Gibson with the St. Louis Cardinals, Willie McCovey with the Giants, and Maury Wills with the Dodgers. In 1954, Major League Baseball teams had 7 percent black players, a percentage that would grow to 28 by 1986. Players of color would tilt the balance of power in Major League Baseball for the next couple of decades.

1955: A CHANGE HAS COME

Casey Stengel's New York Yankees had won five American League pennants and five World Series championships in his first six seasons as manager. But he knew that basic repairs would have to be made if New York was to return to the top of the AL heap. The Yankees pitching staff was the oldest in the league and in need of a makeover. An organization that once boasted about being eight to nine starting pitchers deep suddenly lacked young quality arms it could rely on. Vic Raschi was long gone and Allie Reynolds called it quits, despite a 26-11 record and 20 saves over the past two seasons. He was 37 years old and had grown weary of the game. He was unhappy with how the Yankees treated his good friend Raschi, selling out the veteran rather than paying him a little more money. Reynolds was a former AL player representative and helped negotiate a pension for the players, something badly needed, especially in the days before free agency.

Replacing Reynolds would be a challenge. He was one of his skipper's most valuable assets. He could throw a World Series shutout one day and come out of the bullpen to close it out just a couple days later. A superb big-game pitcher for the Yankees from 1947 on, he led New York to the World Series six times during his eight seasons wearing pinstripes. He had a 7-2 record with four saves and a 2.79 ERA in 15 career World Series games, and he was there for all of the record five straight World Series titles, cementing his spot in Yankees history. Reynolds had stuck around to see if the team could win one more pennant in '54, but his old Cleveland teammates snatched the title away from a New York stranglehold. As if that wasn't enough, Reynolds also hurt his back in a crash in Philadelphia when the team bus hit an overpass. Nobody was seriously hurt, but after the accident his back was never the same.

When Stengel's Yankees won an astounding five consecutive World Series from 1949 to 1953, they did it without the offensive firepower that characterized so many of their championship teams before and after. The franchise came to rely instead on three aging pitchers, an unlikely trio that won 255 games during the five-year championship run. At their best, the troika had combined for 53 victories in 1949, 55 in 1950, and 59 in '51. With Raschi toiling in St. Louis and Reynolds now in Oklahoma working in the oil business, only 36-year-old Eddie Lopat remained of the Yankees' Big Three. But with a sore left shoulder it was questionable how long he could continue. Johnny Sain, at 37, was nearing retirement age, as was 35-year-old Tommy Byrne, back for his second go-round with the club. Tom Morgan and Jim Konstanty, acquired from the Philadelphia Phillies the year before, bolstered the bullpen. Stengel had remembered Konstanty from the 1950 World Series, and when the opportunity arose to acquire him for the 1954 pennant drive, the 38-year-old relief specialist was added to the club, another of the ex–National League castoffs like Mize, Sain, and Slaughter, who could give valuable experience to a Yankees pennant run.

When Stengel's club assembled for spring training, Casey boasted that his starting eight position players would be better than anyone else's. The big question, however, was his pitching. Before the season, the Yankees and Baltimore Orioles had completed the biggest trade in baseball history—a 17-player deal that changed the face of both teams and sent shivers through baseball's hot stove league. Notables among the eight players headed to New York included pitchers Bob Turley and Don Larsen, and shortstop Billy Hunter. Among those going to Baltimore were outfielder Gene Woodling and catcher Gus Triandos. Larsen had had an awful season for a Baltimore team that lost 100 games, though he did have one surprisingly good day, which happened when he faced off against Reynolds at the end of July. Coming into the game, Reynolds had a 10-game winning streak, while Larsen had won just two of 14 decisions. On paper, the game looked like a mismatch and it was, but the Orioles were the team on the good side of a 10–0 score as Larsen pitched his only shutout of the year. It was his third and last win of the season, as he dropped nine straight decisions to finish with a 3-21 record. That was the fewest wins with at least 20 losses in a season since Jack Nabors went 1-20 for the 1916 Philadelphia Athletics. Perhaps a change of scenery would do him good.

Turley and Larsen arrived at Yankees spring training camp like cavalry reinforcements in support of Whitey Ford, the team's 26-year-old

In 1955, the Yankees and Orioles completed a massive trade that included Billy Hunter (left) and Bob Turley (center). Here they are horsing around with Mickey Mantle in the clubhouse at Fenway Park. COURTESY OF THE LESLIE JONES COLLECTION, BOSTON PUBLIC LIBRARY

ace. At a stocky 5-feet-10 and 180 pounds, Ford was never an over-powering pitcher, but he did have a sneaky fastball to go with one of the best curveballs in the game and an assortment of trick pitches, not all of which conformed to the rules. Ford got more pleasure out of deceiving hitters than blowing the ball by them, and his deceptions involved use not only of the conventional spitter but of a pitch pretty much of his invention, the mud ball, which was one part saliva and one part dirt from the mound. He did not, however, throw these disreputable pitches as often as the hitters expected. Even though Stengel favored veterans, he retained 22-year-old righty Johnny Kucks, who had pitched his way onto the team with a splendid spring. Big things also were expected of Bob Grim. The previous season Grim had won 20 games pitching as a starter and reliever, becoming the Yankees' first Rookie of the Year since Gil McDougald in 1951. Tom Morgan, a 24-year-old right-hander in his fourth season, rounded out the bullpen. Known as the Plowboy for the way he ambled to the mound, Morgan had a heavy sinker that would enable him to become a top reliever. Stengel was a firm believer in his retooled pitching staff, and confident his batting lineup would provide the necessary run support to overcome any stumble. Gene Woodling, traded to Baltimore, would be missed, and Billy Martin still had several months left on his military hitch. But Stengel still had Bill Skowron, Joe Collins, and Eddie Robinson at first, Gil McDougald and Jerry Coleman at second, Phil Rizzuto and Billy Hunter at shortstop, and Andy Carey at third. Yogi Berra and rookie Elston Howard were the catchers, and Mickey Mantle, Hank Bauer, Irv Noren, and Enos Slaughter were in the outfield with Howard also available to play there.

In their sixth home game of the season, on April 23, the recently relocated Kansas City A's got pounded by the Chicago White Sox, 29–6. The visiting White Sox, who blasted seven home runs, equaled the modern major-league record (since broken) for most runs in a single game, and Chicago's catcher Sherm Lollar established a major-league first when he notched two hits in an inning twice. By season's end, the

A's would lose 91 games and finish sixth in the AL, but bring in nearly 1.4 million fans—far more than they ever pulled in at Philadelphia.

The Yankees kicked off the 1955 season by trouncing the Washington Senators, 19–1, in the Bronx on April 13. Mickey Mantle had three hits, including a home run; Yogi Berra also homered; and Whitey Ford threw a complete game while allowing fewer hits (two) than he had himself (three, plus four RBIs). But New York's most significant player that day never got off the bench. Two days shy of eight years exactly after Jackie Robinson broke Major League Baseball's color barrier, Elston Howard became the first African-American player to don Yankees pinstripes.

The civil rights movement was in its infancy, but there was mounting pressure on the Yankees to add a black player. Prior to the season, four big-league teams—most notably, the powerful Yankees—still were

Yogi Berra poses with his eventual successor behind the plate, Elston Howard, in 1955. COURTESY OF THE LESLIE JONES COLLECTION, BOSTON PUBLIC LIBRARY

not integrated. The Brooklyn Dodgers and New York Giants had been integrated for years. Yankees general manager George Weiss repeatedly denied any racism on the team's part. In his book, *Baseball's Great Experiment*, author Jules Tygiel quotes Weiss as saying, "The Yankees are not going to promote a Negro player to the Stadium simply in order to be able to say that they have such a player. We are not going to bow to pressure groups on this issue." To be fair, the Yankees roster didn't have many holes in those years, not when the team was winning six World Series titles from 1947 to 1954. But there certainly were weak links that could have been fortified had the club not been so slow to embrace integration. The delay by America's most popular and successful team to integrate had led activists to appear in front of the Stadium carrying picket signs with messages to disparage the perceived discriminatory practices of the Yankees organization. Black men returning from the Korean War were beginning to scrutinize their status in American society, which sent them off to fight for their country, but which prevented them from voting or eating a hot meal at a segregated, whites-only lunch counter. All of this had been ignored by the organization's top brass, in particular Weiss, who had previously passed on opportunities to sign Ernie Banks and Willie Mays, among others. When it came to racial attitude, comments from Weiss suggested prejudice had indeed factored into keeping the team's lineup all-white. In his book *The Boys of Summer*, author Roger Kahn quotes Weiss as saying in 1952 that having a black ballplayer would draw undesirables to the Stadium. "We don't want that sort of crowd," he said. "It would offend boxholders from Westchester to have to sit with niggers."

The Yankees finally called up their first black player to the parent club. The 26-year-old Howard, a converted catcher who would bide his time in the outfield while Yogi Berra still was in the prime of his career, finally made his major-league debut on April 14 in Boston, taking over in left field in the bottom of the sixth. He got into his first game when Irv Noren was ejected over a call at home plate. He made his first and only plate appearance of the day in the eighth inning, lining a solid single to center field to score Mantle, though New York lost, 8–4. According to the Black Associated Press, Elston made his Yankees debut at 4:32 p.m. "Howard's appearance at-bat signaled the fall of a dynasty that had been assailed on all sides as being anti-Negro. The fans gave Howard a well-deserved round of applause, making his debut on the heretofore lily-white Bronx Bombers." Howard didn't make his first start until April 28, whereupon he went 3-for-5 with two runs scored and two RBIs in an 11–4 win at Kansas City.

Howard treaded lightly his rookie season, for the prejudice he faced didn't cease with his callup to the major leagues. When his manager first saw the burly Howard play, Stengel said, "When I finally get a Negro, I get the only one who can't run." Casey is also quoted in Robert Creamer's biography *Stengel* as calling Howard by the hurtful nickname "Eight Ball," a not-so-subtle reference to the jet-black color of that billiards ball. Several of Howard's teammates, however, welcomed the rookie. The most notable sign of his acceptance came a month after his debut. On May 14, he came to bat in the bottom of the ninth inning with two outs, two runners on, and the Yankees trailing the Tigers, 6–5. Howard laced a triple to left that scored Joe Collins and Mantle, giving New York a 7–6 win. When Howard reached the clubhouse, he found that Collins and Mantle had laid out an honorary carpet of white towels from the clubhouse door to his locker. He was officially one of them. "It was like a red carpet, laid out for me," said Howard. "I was surprised. And when they did that, I figured I was accepted just like everyone else."

Puerto Rican native Roberto Clemente broke into the major leagues with the Pittsburgh Pirates on April 17, and made inroads for Latin-American players and others from around the world. Although Clemente hit a modest .255 for the season, it quickly became apparent that he possessed remarkable defensive skills and an uncanny ability to hit. He won four NL batting titles in an 18-year career, and he won 12 consecutive Gold Glove Awards. Clemente was not only the first Latino Hall of Famer, but he also helped to open doors for scores of international players to follow. Today, Major League Baseball rosters are dotted with players from all over the world.

In February, Mickey Mantle received a $4,000 raise, which made his salary $25,000. For the first time since he joined the Yankees, Mickey was entering a season completely healthy. The knee that he injured stepping into a drain during the 1951 World Series was finally sound, and the cyst that developed on the back of the knee from playing basketball too soon after the operation was gone. Casey, who wanted Mickey to be the crown jewel player of his managerial career, thought a healthy Mantle could win the batting title. "Mantle has more ability than any player I have on the club," he said. Entering the season, Mantle was once again under pressure to reach the heights predicted for him ever since he had been a rookie in 1951. When the New York baseball writers first saw Mickey play, they placed upon him the burden of having even greater potential than the acclaimed Joe DiMaggio, primarily because Mickey ran faster than Joe and he could hit the ball farther—batting from either side of the plate. Despite having three solid seasons following a rookie year of ups and downs, Mickey was still considered only the third-best New York center fielder, ranked by pundits below the Giants' Willie Mays and Brooklyn's Duke Snider. The Mick was criticized because he possessed the physical requisites for greatness, but except for occasional flashes, he was not yet a truly great player. Mickey's bad legs hindered his development, and he struck out too much. In his first four seasons, Mickey's strikeout totals were 74, 111, 90, and 107, which is about one strikeout for every five official at-bats. One time, when the slugger kicked a water cooler after striking out, Stengel observed, "It ain't the water cooler which is gettin' you out."

Mantle was finally beginning to lay off the high inside fastballs, and as his strikeouts decreased, his home run totals increased. He clocked three titanic homers—two from the left side and one batting righty—against Detroit at the Stadium on May 13, the first Yankees switch-hitter to hit a home run from each side of the plate in a game. The Yankees won, 5–2, over the Tigers in New York, with Mantle getting four hits and driving in the Yankees' five runs. Witnesses estimated the three home runs traveled a total distance of about 1,300 feet. The Mick was ready for takeoff. He hit a home run against Chicago's Billy Pierce that traveled an estimated 550 feet beyond the left field upper deck at Comiskey Park on June 5. The next day in Detroit he sent a Bob Miller pitch skyrocketing into orbit, the first ball to clear the center field screen at Briggs Stadium. In yet another first, in the first inning of a June 21 game in New York against the Kansas City Athletics, Mantle hammered a changeup thrown by left-hander Alex Kellner that smashed into a seat in the ninth row of the center field bleachers, 486 feet from home plate. It was the first home run ball ever to reach the black seats at Yankee Stadium, until then considered to be the ballpark's Holy Grail. Mantle hit homers in bunches—and when it counted. In an August 7 game against the Tigers, with the score tied in the bottom of the 10th inning, he sent the fans home happy with a game-ending blast off Detroit's Babe Birrer, his 26th homer of the season and second of the game, into the upper stands in right for the win. Opposing pitchers struggled to find ways to retire him. During one particularly hot stretch in June, Mantle reached base 15 times in a row, hitting a home run, a triple, two doubles, a bunt single, and walking nine times (plus reaching on an error). There was lightning in his bat, but little flash in his game. "After I hit a home run I had a habit of running the bases with my head down," said Mantle. "I figured the pitcher already felt bad enough without me showing him up rounding the bases."

With Enos Slaughter and Johnny Sain traded to Kansas City in early May, and with Woodling gone to Baltimore, outfielder Hank Bauer was given the opportunity to play every day, and he shined as the team's leadoff hitter. At a time when base stealing had gone out of favor, predominantly in the power-packed AL, Stengel used a player with extra-base rather than stolen-base potential at the top of the order. Bauer wasn't particularly fast and didn't walk all that much—he just hit. Stengel liked that Bauer might lead off the game with a home run, and while he wasn't a base stealer, he could make it around the bases well enough for Casey. While Mantle and Berra were the brightest Yankees stars, Bauer became a Stengel favorite not only for his hard-nosed play but also for the results. "Too many people judge ballplayers solely by 100 RBIs or a .300 batting average. I like to judge my players in other ways," the manager said, pointing to Bauer. "Like the guy who happens to do everything right in a tough situation." He also emerged as a team leader. Mantle, a rookie in 1951, said Bauer "taught me how to dress, how to talk, and how to drink." But Bauer could be unforgiving if he felt his teammates' off-the-field activities were hurting the Yankees on-the-field performance, which might cost Bauer a World Series check. During the 1950s, a World Series share, especially a winning share, made a significant difference, sometimes equaling a player's yearly salary. Whitey Ford remembered how Bauer reacted when he thought Ford and Mantle had been overindulging themselves after hours. "He pinned me to the wall of the dugout and said, 'Don't mess with my money.'"

The pitching staff gave Stengel and GM George Weiss reason to gloat. Ford began the season marvelously with three shutouts and six wins in his first seven games, and newly acquired Bob Turley was a sensation early in the year as he won eight of his first nine games. Known as Bullet Bob for his blazing fastball, Turley pitched a one-hit shutout against the White Sox and a two-hit shutout against the Red Sox to go with five games of 10 or more strikeouts. (He also had five games of eight or more walks.) In addition, Johnny Kucks won four of his first five decisions, and veteran Tommy Byrne, tabbed by Stengel as the number three starter, chipped in with a couple of complete game victories. Don Larsen, however, was a huge disappointment. He reported to spring training with a sore shoulder and a lackadaisical attitude, and was soon banished to the Yankees farm club in Denver, where he'd remain in exile for the next four months.

In the NBA, fans who had become restless at the stalling tactics that plagued games of seasons past were now treated to more thrilling games thanks to a revolutionary rule change. The new 24-second shot clock that required teams to shoot within that specified time (or lose possession of the ball) received rave reviews. George Mikan, who had been the standard-bearer as the league gained a foothold in the public consciousness, announced his retirement.

After winning 111 games the previous year, the Cleveland Indians added Herb Score to an already strong starting rotation. Score was one of the most exciting young pitchers to arrive in the majors in years. The flame-throwing lefty, anointed as the second coming of Bob Feller, recorded a 16-10 record with a 2.85 ERA. On paper, it didn't look so good for the rest of the league, but despite an excellent season from Score, who set a rookie record with 245 strikeouts, it was clear that the Indians would not run away with the league again. As a result, the AL pennant chase was a fierce four-team contest for much of the summer, with New York, Cleveland, Chicago, and Boston battling it out.

Though Turley sputtered a bit in June, losing five games in a row, Ford was consistently excellent, and a rejuvenated Tommy Byrne sported a 9-2 record in late July after a brilliant 1–0 victory over the White Sox, with a Yogi Berra home run accounting for the game's only tally. Byrne was a daffy pitcher. He was in perpetual motion on the mound, always fidgeting with his uniform, his hair, his cap, or the ball. While warming up for an inning, he would often use a double windup, or he'd clown around by throwing the ball from behind his back. He called that pitch his kimono (wrap-around) pitch. Byrne drove everyone nuts with his wildness. While he won some important ballgames, it seemed he was always just one batter from disaster. He walked almost as many as he fanned; it was exciting to watch Byrne walk the bases loaded and then strike out the side. Tommy liked to talk to batters, sometimes telling them what pitch he was going to throw (he was known to fib), and would say anything to distract them for an advantage. One player whom he used to infuriate was Ted Williams. Right before he stepped to the plate, Tommy would bring up the delicate subject of Ted's estranged wife. The strategy worked. In 12 career at-bats against Byrne, Williams went 0-for-7 with five walks and a strikeout. Another pitcher who didn't fare well against the competition got the "fare thee well" from the Yankees. On the last day of July, shortly after he turned 37, Eddie Lopat, with a 4-8 record, was dropped from the team and claimed by the Baltimore Orioles. During the Yankees' five-year championship run, Lopat won 80 games, plus four more in seven World Series starts. He pitched 10 times for the Orioles, posting a 3-4 record, then retired.

The Hall of Fame finally came calling for Joe DiMaggio, who was inducted into the hallowed Cooperstown museum, in his fourth year of eligibility. In those days there was just a one-year waiting period before a player went on the Hall of Fame ballot, so DiMaggio first appeared on the ballot in 1953. The dominant view held that he would get elected with near-unanimous consent. "It is the countrywide belief," Grantland Rice wrote, "that Joe DiMaggio will be the next star to enter baseball's Hall of Fame." But DiMaggio was not elected in 1953; in the end he was not even close. Dizzy Dean and Al Simmons were elected, Bill Terry just missed, and DiMaggio got only 44.3 percent of the vote, eighth among players on the ballot. It seems many of the voters—more than half of them—believed that there was an unwritten rule that a player should have to wait five years after retirement to be elected to the Hall of Fame. They felt it was an affront to list a player on the ballot so quickly, and were not so eager to vote for any player before the unwritten five-year waiting period. As it turned out, the Hall of Fame agreed with the make-them-wait crowd. Later that year, they created the rule that a player could not appear on the ballot until five years after retirement. The Yankee Clipper was grandfathered onto the ballot in '54, but again he finished shy of election. In 1955—after a four-year waiting period—he was elected, but with only 88.8 percent of the vote. DiMaggio would likely have received closer to 100 percent of the vote under normal circumstances, but in 1955, some voters were still bitter that DiMaggio was cutting in line.

Everyone agreed that when Bill Haley & The Comets' "Rock Around the Clock" blared over the opening and closing credits of the

MGM film *Blackboard Jungle* starring Sidney Poitier, it caused a sensation. It was the first rock 'n' roll song used in a Hollywood film and had teens dancing in the aisles. In March alone, the record sold one million copies. The song hit number one on the *Billboard* charts and held that spot for eight weeks, remaining on the charts for nearly six months. Bill Haley and his band, meanwhile, continued to receive national attention. They became the first rock 'n' roll act to appear on *The Ed Sullivan Show*.

At the All-Star break, Whitey Ford's record stood at 10-4 with a 2.69 earned run average to help the Yankees to a five-game lead over the Indians. He pitched in his second All-Star Game, relieving Cleveland's Early Wynn in the seventh inning with the AL sporting a 5–0 lead that Mantle had sparked with a gargantuan first-inning three-run home run off Robin Roberts. Uncharacteristically, Ford couldn't hold the lead, and the NL eventually tied the game, 5–5. The contest remained knotted into the 12th inning, when Milwaukee pitcher Gene Conley—who also played as a forward in the NBA—struck out all three AL batters he faced. With the score still knotted in the bottom of the 12th inning, St. Louis Cardinals outfielder Stan Musial came to the plate and was greeted by a very tired Yogi Berra, who had been catching all game. "My feet are killing me," Yogi said to Musial. "Relax," Musial said, "I'll have you home in a minute." On the first pitch, Stan "The Man" Musial homered into the seats, winning the game. In fact, the homer off Frank Sullivan became one of a record six he hit for the NL in All-Star Games.

A new television quiz show, *The $64,000 Question*, made its summer debut on the CBS-TV network and became, almost at once, the entertainment equivalent of the California Gold Rush. In the space of 10 dizzying weeks, 47 million Americans were watching. No entertainment program in mass media history—not *Amos 'n Andy* in radio days or Milton Berle in the first years of television—had ever acquired so huge an audience so quickly or inspired so many stories in the press, such as those when a psychologist, Dr. Joyce Brothers, professional boxing expert, became the first woman to win the top prize. *The $64,000*

Question would "set back by at least a season, if not by years, TV's already enfeebled yearning to leaven commercialism with culture," *Time* magazine predicted with scornful accuracy that August.

The Yankees' top prize Whitey Ford, like a fine wine, was improving with age. He had uncommon poise and confidence. "I have never seen pressure bother him," said pitching coach Jim Turner, "and the Yankees during those days were always under pressure." On September 7, the 26-year-old lefty went to the mound at Yankee Stadium and pitched a one-hitter against the Kansas City Athletics, matching what he had done five days earlier against the Washington Senators. It was a rare feat, as only four big leaguers had ever before thrown consecutive one-hitters, but Ford's achievement came with a twist. In between his two one-hitters, he relieved the struggling starter Bob Turley in the eighth inning of a game on September 4 and retired four Senators in a row as the Yankees won, 8–3. The Yankees were a half-game behind the first-place Indians on the day Stengel summoned Ford from the bullpen, with just 20 games left in the regular season. Using a starter in relief was not uncommon in the 1950s, and Stengel particularly liked that strategy with Allie Reynolds, who turned out to be equally effective in both roles at a time when there was still the common belief that there was something inferior about relief pitching. "Casey figured that if every once in a while you loosened up between starts, you might as well pitch for two batters," said New York outfielder Irv Noren.

In the first of his back-to-back one-hitters, on September 2, Ford had a no-hitter into the seventh inning. He ended up walking four, striking out four, and surrendering two unearned runs, made possible by a single by Cuban-born Carlos Paula—who had integrated the Washington Senators in '54—that went through Noren's legs. With a day's rest, Ford returned to work, coming into the game with two Senators on base and two outs in the eighth and efficiently nailing down the victory. Three days later, Ford went back to the mound and pitched another one-hitter. Once again, he had a no-hitter into the seventh, thanks in part to an excellent backhanded play by shortstop

Phil Rizzuto on a fourth-inning line drive by Harry Simpson, one of the earliest black players in the American League. With two outs in the seventh, a short flyball to right eluded Hank Bauer of the Yankees for a ground-rule double. A wild pitch by Ford then tied the score at one, but the Yankees won in the bottom of the ninth on a bases-loaded walk to Noren. Ford also had two two-hitters during the season. But none of his 236 career wins was a no-hitter.

The biggest horse race of 1955 wasn't the Kentucky Derby. Nor was it one of the other legs of thoroughbred racing's Triple Crown. Instead, it was a match race on August 31 at Washington Park in Chicago: Nashua versus Swaps in a $100,000, winner-take-all race over one and a quarter miles. A national television audience eagerly tuned in to see once and for all which was the better horse. The match race turned out to be a mismatch. Swaps, ridden by jockey Bill Shoemaker, was the heavy favorite, but Nashua, with jockey Eddie Arcaro aboard, never trailed. Nashua pulled away with every stride in the homestretch and won easily, by 6 1/2 lengths.

However, the 1955 AL pennant race seemed destined to be decided at the wire. The Yankees, White Sox, Indians, and Red Sox were galloping neck-and-neck into the home stretch. On August 10, all four teams were bunched tightly together—Cleveland in first, a half-game ahead of New York and Chicago, with a streaking Boston squad just two games off the pace. Stengel was in a fretful state. His infield was a sore spot. Third baseman Andy Carey had fallen into a dreadful slump, and Rizzuto seemed to have lost a step or two in the field. Furthermore, he wasn't hitting, and neither was the smooth-fielding second baseman Jerry Coleman, back from Korea. When Coleman returned to the Yankees he hit only .217. He was sent to an eye doctor, who told him he'd lost his depth perception. "If you're trying to hit a baseball and you don't have depth perception, you have a problem," said Coleman. He got that corrected but then broke his collarbone. The night he came back from that injury, he got beaned. The infield seemed to lack leadership and direction. To make matters worse, Casey was without the valuable services of his infield swingman Gil McDougald, sidelined for two weeks when a batted ball hit him in the head.

New York outfielder Bob Cerv, who was said to possess almost as much power as Mickey Mantle, roped a line drive during batting practice that struck McDougald squarely on the left ear. He was standing near second base talking to coach Frank Crosetti behind a protective screen, but bent over just beyond the netting to retrieve a loose ball when he got skulled. With McDougald knocked out of the lineup, the Yankees plucked from their minor-league system 19-year-old infielder Bobby Richardson, who made his major-league debut on August 5. In the fourth inning, he walked and stole second, followed by a walk to Mantle. They both scored on Yogi Berra's 200th career home run. That was all the Bronx Bombers needed as they defeated the Detroit Tigers, 3–0. It looked like Bobby had all the tools, but when McDougald returned to reclaim his position, Richardson was sent back down to Triple-A Richmond on August 19, his 20th birthday. Eventually, the injury did cost McDougald the hearing in his left ear. He kept his deafness a secret until 1994 when he revealed it to Ira Berkow of the *New York Times*. A group of physicians read the article and told McDougald that a cochlear implant might restore his hearing. It did.

The Yankees, Indians, and White Sox took turns in first place through August. The Red Sox wilted away by Labor Day. The White Sox soon caved, too. That cleared the way for New York and Cleveland to fight it out to the finish. The Yankees trailed the Indians by a half-game on September 16, with just 11 games remaining in the season. The Indians controlled their own destiny. There were no more head-to-head matchups between the two contenders, so the Yankees were going to have to focus on winning their own games and hope that the Indians would stumble in their few remaining games. The odds favored the Indians because the Yankees had to play a three-game series against the tough Red Sox at home while Cleveland played the lowly Detroit Tigers three games. But the Tigers sent the Tribe reeling with a three-game sweep at Cleveland, while the Yankees started an eight-game winning streak that simmered the Indians nicely.

The first game of the Yankees–Red Sox series drew 50,000 fans to Yankee Stadium, a surprisingly good turnout considering that the Yankees were now televising all their games. The Yankees raced to a 3–0 lead on a Yogi Berra homer, but in the eighth inning Boston scored four runs against Ford and reliever Jim Konstanty. The day promised to be a complete disaster because in the second inning Mickey Mantle bunted down the third base line, and after he safely crossed the bag, he pulled up lame with a pulled right thigh muscle, and limped to the locker room. It seemed doubtful that Mantle, who had 37 home runs and 99 RBIs, would play during the rest of the season. Trailing 4–3 in the bottom of the ninth, the Yankees were facing right-hander Ellis Kinder, once the ace of the Boston staff, but now its top reliever. With one out, Hank Bauer drove a fastball down the left field line for a home run to tie the score at 4. Bauer had hit over .400 during the month of August, and his home run against Kinder was one of 20 he hit on the season. Two batters later, Yogi Berra hit the first pitch he saw from Kinder into the right field seats as the Yankees magically snatched a 5–4 victory from the Red Sox.

While the Yankees were winning eight in a row—two against Detroit, a three-game sweep of Boston in New York, and a three-game sweep of the Senators in Washington—the Indians had lost five of six to be suddenly on the brink of elimination. The Mantle-less Yankees, with Stengel platooning and substituting brilliantly, clinched the pennant on September 23 in the second game of a doubleheader against the Red Sox at Boston's Fenway Park. After the Bosox won the opening game, 8–4, the Yanks scored twice in the first inning of the second game to take a lead they would not relinquish on their way to a 3–2 win. Stengel called on Ford in relief when starter Don Larsen gave up a run in the seventh, and Jackie Jensen took Ford deep in the eighth, but the Yankees southpaw retired the Red Sox in order in the ninth to put an end to the 1955 American League pennant race. Writing in the *New York Post*, Jimmy Cannon described the feeling of rooting for the Yankees. "I never have been on a yacht in my whole life. But I imagine rooting for the Yankees is like owning a yacht."

The usual three-man wrecking crew led the Yanks: Mantle, Berra, and Ford. For the first time in AL history, no pitcher won 20 games. Ford led the league with 18 victories and finished second in earned run average (2.63). Bob Turley won 17 games with a 3.06 ERA. Don Larsen, back in the team's good graces, won nine of his 13 starts. The team also got unexpected help from Tommy Byrne. At the age of 35, Byrne set his career high for victories, finishing 16-5, with a 3.15 earned run average. His .762 winning percentage was the best in the league. His manager gushed. "He beat the other first-division clubs, Cleveland, the White Sox, the Red Sox, when it was them or us," Stengel said. "Without him, we don't win." Jim Konstanty (7-2, 12 saves) and Tom Morgan (7-3, 11 saves) were excellent in the bullpen. Even with Bob Grim slipping to 7-5, the Yankees had enough pitching, and more than enough hitting.

Homers off the bats of Mantle, Berra, and Bauer settled scores in a hurry. Mantle led the AL in homers (37), triples (11), walks (113), on-base percentage (.431) and slugging percentage (.611). He also batted .306 and knocked in 99 runs. Berra had less impressive stats, a .272 average with 27 homers and 108 RBIs, but those numbers combined with his clutch hitting and continued leadership behind the plate earned him his third Most Valuable Player Award in five years. Moose Skowron, Joe Collins, and Eddie Robinson shared first base and combined for 41 homers and 148 RBIs. Promising newcomer Elston Howard played 97 games in all his rookie season, finishing with a .290 average, 10 home runs, and 43 RBIs. Down the stretch, the Yankees were boosted by the return of Billy Martin from military service. Stengel immediately inserted him into the lineup; he benched Carey, moved McDougald to third, and started Billy at second. Martin was an inspiration, batting .300 and providing a missing spark. He solidified the infield defense and provided much-needed fiery leadership. With him the Yankees finished strong, winning 17 of their last 23 games, and secured their sixth pennant in seven years under Stengel's masterful leadership.

Rocky Marciano defended his heavyweight crown one last time, knocking out challenger Archie Moore in front of more than 61,000 fans at Yankee Stadium on September 21. Moore went down for the count in the ninth round. Those fans did not know it then, but the fight would be Marciano's last. He retired the following April. With the victory, Marciano improved his career record to 49-0 and remains the only heavyweight champion to retire undefeated.

The indomitable Yankees won their 21st American League pennant and arrived back at the World Series to face off with the Brooklyn Dodgers again for the third time in four years. The Dodgers had been waiting patiently to see who would win out in the AL since clinching the National League way back on the 8th of September. The ever-popular catcher Roy Campanella had one of his best seasons yet. Campy led an unstoppable Dodger attack with a .318 batting average while bashing 32 home runs with 107 runs batted in, second on the team to center fielder Duke Snider's 42 homers and 136 RBIs. Like Berra, his AL catching counterpart, the 33-year-old Campanella won the NL Most Valuable Player Award for the third time in five years. Snider, 28, led the league in RBIs and was second in the MVP voting. The Duke of Flatbush also hit his 200th career home run on May 10. Gil Hodges, 31, hit 27 home runs with 102 RBIs, and Carl Furillo, 33, hit 26 homers with a .314 batting average. Pee Wee Reese, the 36-year-old shortstop, could still play, too.

The 29-year-old veteran Don Newcombe anchored the pitching staff. He won his first 10 decisions, and by the end of July, he had an 18-1 record. Newk finished the year at 20-5, the first time a black pitcher had won 20 games in a season. Yet his season could have been even better. The Brooklyn ace won only two of his last nine starts as soreness in both his arm and back quieted his final mark. A 19-year-old lefty named Sandy Koufax won two of four decisions, but was still too raw to make an impact. A lesser-touted southpaw named Tom Lasorda made his first big-league start for the Brooklynites on May 5, and proceeded to equal a dubious major-league record by throwing three wild pitches in an inning. Both Koufax and Lasorda would make a greater impact as Dodgers in years to come: Koufax as the first pitcher to throw four no-hitters, one of them a perfect game; and Lasorda as the manager to take over for Walter Alston in 1976.

When Brooklyn owner Walter O'Malley decided he would not meet Dodgers manager Charlie Dressen's request for a multi-year contract, the owner promoted his top minor-league manager to skipper of the big-league club. "Who's he?" *New York Times* sportswriters wondered in mock concern as spring training began in 1954. Walter Alston's big-league playing career consisted of exactly one at-bat—one that ended in a strikeout in the final game of the season for the St. Louis Cardinals, on September 27, 1936. (He was batting as a substitute for Johnny Mize, who had earlier been ejected from the game.) For the last 15 years he had been managing in the bush leagues with over-the-top success. A quiet Ohioan, Alston was taking over a team coming off two straight NL pennants—and two straight World Series losses to the Yankees. It was a roster filled with talented players like Robinson, Campanella, and Snider. The team had been riding a wave of success, and expectations were high. If Alston felt a modicum of pressure, he never showed it. "He might be taken for a farmer who came to manage the town team on a Saturday," wrote a columnist of the *Atlanta-Journal*. O'Malley gave Alston a one-year contract, the first of 23 the manager would eventually sign.

The 1955 Alston-led Dodgers won a major-league best 98 games and clinched the NL pennant with three weeks to spare. It was Brooklyn's sixth NL pennant in 15 years. Alston's team never wavered. These Dodgers were the first team since the famed 1927 Yankees to hold first place from the season's first day to its last. The defending champion New York Giants finished in third place, and would have dropped even further in the standings were it not for Willie Mays's spectacular efforts.

Mays was coming off a season in which he won the batting title with a .345 average, hit 41 home runs, had 110 RBIs, and was voted the NL's Most Valuable Player. The 1955 season, however, was his breakout season. The Giants superstar led baseball with 51 home runs, 13 triples, 382 total bases, and a .659 slugging percentage, to go along with 127 RBIs and 24 stolen bases (second best), and a .319 batting average (third best). Other notable performances were staged by Milwaukee outfielder Henry Aaron (.314, 27 HRs, 106 RBIs) and Chicago Cubs shortstop Ernie Banks (.295, 44, 117).

In December 1955, Rosa Parks, a black woman in Montgomery, Alabama, refused to give up her seat to a white man on a city bus, sparking a civil rights movement that led to sweeping changes. While Major League Baseball had been integrated for nearly 10 years, African-American players still often took a back seat to their white counterparts. By the middle of the decade, three big-league teams—the Philadelphia Phillies, Detroit Tigers, and Boston Red Sox—still were not integrated. In fact, Jackie Robinson would complete his major-league career and be retired by the time those teams broke the color line. When Robinson announced his retirement, he took a parting shot at the Phillies, Tigers, and Red Sox. "If 13 major league teams can come up with colored players, why can't the other three?"

"Wait Till Next Year" had been the cry of long-suffering Brooklyn fans for years, as their beloved Dodgers often came close to a World Series title, only to fall short. In fact, the Dodgers were in embarrassing company with the historically inept St. Louis Browns (now Baltimore Orioles) and Philadelphia Phillies as the three teams yet to win a World Series. Unlike those other two October duds, the Dodgers had seven previous chances to win the elusive championship, and lost them all. What's more, each near miss had seemed worse than the last. The Dodgers had lost three heartbreaking tiebreakers in the past nine years just trying to get to the Series. When they did reach the Fall Classic they often found spectacular ways to blow it. Hitting into an unassisted triple play in 1920, allowing a passed ball in 1941, losing Game 7s

Before the start of Game 1 of the 1955 World Series at Yankee Stadium, players observe a moment of silence in honor of President Dwight Eisenhower. Ike had suffered a heart attack four days prior, on September 24th. WIKIMEDIA COMMONS

to the Yankees in 1947 and 1952, and Bobby Thomson's Shot Heard 'Round the World in '51.

It didn't appear that 1955 would be any different. The Yankees jumped to a quick two-games-to-none lead with victories in Games 1 and 2 at Yankee Stadium. Newcombe and his slump continued in the first game of the World Series, a 6–5 loss to the Yankees and Whitey Ford, with some relief help from Bob Grim. Joe Collins slapped around Newk for two homers and rookie Elston Howard also homered for the Yanks. The round-tripper to deep left field at Yankee Stadium marked the first time a black batter hit a home run off a black pitcher in the history of the Fall Classic. Newcombe would not pitch again in the series, suffering from the flu, a sore arm, and a sore back. For the first time, NBC-TV offered a World Series broadcast entirely in color, with Mel Allen and Vin Scully sharing the play-by-play duties. The first consumer color television receivers hit the market, with 5,000 units rolling off the RCA assembly line in Bloomington, Indiana. Nicknamed "the Merrill," the RCA Model CT-100 had a 12-inch diagonal screen and cost a whopping $1,000 (well over $6,000 by today's standards).

Tommy Byrne put the Dodgers in a two-games-to-none hole with a sparkling five-hit victory in Game 2 of the Series. It was the first complete-game victory by a left-hander against Brooklyn all season. Now the Dodgers were in trouble. No team had ever won the World Series after losing the first two games at the opponent's park. And the Yankees two wins had been done without Mickey Mantle—who was coming back for Game 3. The Dodgers knew they were finished if they fell behind three games to none. So the Brooklyn team had its work cut out back at Ebbets Field, a place where they had won only five of 16 previous World Series contests against the Yankees.

Inside Ebbets Field the Sym-Phony Band was in full swing. The five musicians played and danced on top of the dugout and marched through the stands playing ragtime music. When the umpires came out before the game, they played "Three Blind Mice" even though a six-man umpiring crew worked the game. In Ebbets Field there might be 30,000 fans in the park, but it would sound like 10 times as many. Up in the bleachers, you could still hear Hilda Chester, now making lots of noise with her cowbell. Warned by her doctors about the fragility of her heart and advised against too much yelling, she returned to Ebbets Field banging a frying pan and iron ladle, and made so much noise that the Dodger players soon replaced her noisemaking implements with a brass cowbell as a gift.

After taking a two-games-to-none lead on their home field, the Yankees lost all three games at Ebbets Field behind poor pitching efforts from starters Bob Turley, Don Larsen, and Bob Grim. Game 3 was the contest that turned the Series. Just as the Brooklyn faithful was on the verge of giving up hope, an unlikely hero named Johnny Podres took the mound. Podres had a mediocre 9-10 season, only his third in the big leagues, and he wasn't expecting to pitch at all in the Series. He only made the Brooklyn postseason roster after a strong outing the final week of the season following his recovery from an injury. A better script could not have been written for the occasion as Podres—on his 23rd birthday—lit up Ebbets Field with a clutch, complete-game 8–3 triumph that gave his teammates reason to celebrate. Duke Snider then took over the series. His three-run blast helped propel the Dodgers to an 8–5 Game 4 victory, and he hit two solo homers in Game 5 to set the pace for a 5–3 triumph. Suddenly, the Dodgers had the series lead at three games to two, giving them two shots to win the Series at Yankee Stadium.

The Bombers were on the brink of defeat as play shifted back across the East River to the Bronx for Game 6 at the Stadium. The Subway Series, as it was christened, was always a fan favorite, even though subway fare had gone up to 15 cents. With Newcombe unavailable, manager Alston went with Karl Spooner for Game 6. But the former phenom was no longer a blue-chip prospect. The young lefty had sensationally teased Dodger fans the prior year with two shutouts and 27 total strikeouts in two late-season starts. "We shoulda had Spooner sooner," went the cry in Brooklyn for losing the 1954 pennant. However, in 1955 he won only eight games before his arm went south. In his World Series outing, Spooner never made it out of the first inning, as the Yankees collected five runs in the first for Ford, which is all he needed in the 5–1 win. Ford had pitched the second complete-game victory by a lefty over Brooklyn in less than a week. Spooner would never appear in another big-league game.

The Yankees proved once again in the Stengel era that they were at their best in games they had to win, and it appeared they were once again poised to polish off Brooklyn. For the first time in World Series history, the home team had won the first six games. The Dodgers had yet to win a game at the Stadium in this Series and they'd yet to beat the Yankees in five previous Series tries. In fact, Brooklyn was at this point 0-for-7 in the World Series, dating back to 1916. So their prospects did not look promising. The left-handed Podres didn't quite see it that way. "Don't worry, Pee Wee," he said by way of consoling Reese after the Ford loss. "I'll shut 'em out tomorrow."

The winner-take-all Game 7 featured Podres versus Tommy Byrne, the 16-game winner who had already pitched a complete-game victory in Game 2. Podres had matched the feat in Game 3, and he would be even better in Game 7. Podres, cocky and confident at 23, boarded the team bus in Brooklyn for the 15-minute ride over to Yankee Stadium. "How many runs do you need?" asked Snider. "Just get me one," responded Podres. The Dodgers actually got him two. Gil Hodges had driven in both Dodger runs, on a single in the fourth inning following Campanella's double, and then extended the lead with a bases-loaded sacrifice fly in the top of the sixth. After the Dodgers scored their second run in the sixth, manager Alston went for the knockout blow. The Dodgers had loaded the bases with two out against Grim, pitching in relief of Byrne. Alston sent left-handed hitter George "Shotgun" Shuba up to bat for second baseman Don Zimmer in hopes of opening up a big lead. Shuba grounded out to end the inning, and now some rearranging was necessary. Alston moved left fielder Jim Gilliam back to his natural position at second base in the bottom of the sixth and sent Sandy Amoros out to left field as a defensive replacement for Gilliam. Amoros was the Dodgers' substitute outfielder, a small, smiling Cuban who spoke virtually no English. He had come up through the Dodgers' organization and was playing only his second big-league season. He proved to be the right man in the right place.

Meanwhile, Podres was shutting down the Yankees. In the third game he had tantalized them with his effective changeup, but this time he was firing fastballs, keeping the Yankees batters off-balance and upsetting their timing as they looked for the soft stuff. Podres had not been in any serious trouble through the first five innings, but the Yankees appeared to be mounting a rally in the home half of the sixth when Billy Martin walked leading off and Gil McDougald beat out a bunt, bringing the dangerous Yogi Berra to the plate with nobody out and the tying runs on base. Berra already had 10 hits, more than any other player in the Series. The outfield shifted toward right, expecting the hard-hitting catcher to pull the ball. Instead, Berra swung at an outside pitch and sliced a long fly down the left field line. As Amoros raced to his right and into the shadows enveloping the left field corner, he seemed to disappear from the view of half the people in Yankee Stadium. "I looked around and saw the ball slicing toward the line, and I saw Amoros running his tail off," Podres told *Sports Illustrated*. "Jeez, I said to myself, he's got a hell of a run."

Without breaking stride, Amoros stretched his 5-foot-7-inch frame to the fullest, stuck out his gloved right hand as far as he could reach, and made a spectacular one-handed running catch. When Amoros reappeared from out of the shadows he was holding the ball, but only for a split second. He quickly relayed the ball back to the infield to complete a double play. If Amoros had been right-handed, wearing the mitt on his left hand, the ball would probably have dropped for a double that could have tied the score and put Berra on second base with no outs. It was the play of the Series, and Podres took care of the rest to complete the shutout victory. The Dodgers finally had a World Series win against the Yankees. "Hey, Pee Wee," Podres shouted across the jubilant locker room to shortstop Reese. "What did I tell you? I said they wouldn't get a thing off me, didn't I?"

At last, there would be no cry of "Wait Till Next Year" in Flatbush. The borough of Brooklyn became a mob scene once the final out was made. People danced in the streets and the players threw a big victory party with gallons of champagne at the Hotel Bossert that lasted long into the night. A huge burden had been lifted from Brooklyn's broad shoulders after their first (and only) World Series triumph. It took some hefty hitting from Duke Snider, who belted four homers and drove in seven runs, but this Series belonged to Johnny Podres and to little Sandy Amoros, who would, in a career that lasted four more years, have just this one moment in the sun. In the Dodgers' epic victory, Jackie Robinson played at third base for six of the seven contests and though he hit poorly, he scored five times, including his shocking Game 1 steal of home.

The Yankees' bats were not exactly subdued: Bauer hit .429 and Berra .417. The Army extended Martin's furlough, which allowed him to play in the World Series, and he performed well, finishing with a

.320 batting average. Billy the Kid, as he was now being called in the media, got into a shoving match with Dodgers catcher Roy Campanella after he was thrown out trying to steal home to end the sixth inning in Game 1. Martin told the Associated Press, "I wasn't sore. I just don't like being pushed around. I might have punched him in the nose if it hadn't been the World Series." Although he missed most of the season, the Yankees voted Martin a full $5,598 share of the losers' World Series bonus. Mantle, nursing an injured leg, appeared in only three Series games and batted just .200 with only one run knocked in. Sometimes there are valid reasons to explain a sporting result. Not having to contend with a healthy Mantle batting in the middle of the lineup was the Dodgers' good fortune. Or perhaps for the Yankees it simply was not meant to be. They had come within one base hit of taking the lead in the sixth inning when Amoros made his miracle catch. Years later, lifelong baseball man Don Zimmer would kid that he deserved the most credit for Brooklyn's only World Series win. "If they hadn't taken me out of the game," Zimmer said, "Sandy Amoros couldn't have made that catch and Brooklyn never would have won." The next day, Johnny Podres drove off in the first car presented by *Sport* magazine to the World Series Most Valuable Player.

Baseball lost two legends barely a month apart. Cy Young, the all-time winning pitcher with 511 victories, died on November 4 at the age of 88. Later on December 6, Honus Wagner, the most dominant hitter of the century's first decade, passed away at 81. Beginning in 1956, baseball would honor Young with an award named after him for the year's most outstanding pitcher. Three days before the New Year, Otto Graham led the Cleveland Browns to the NFL title. Afterwards, the Browns quarterback could have gone to Disneyland, because Walt Disney's vast amusement park had opened earlier in the year in Anaheim, California. Graham then retired, leaving a record of success unmatched in pro football history. In his 10 seasons with the Browns, he took his teams to 10 league championship games. And he won seven of them. Graham, like the Yankees, couldn't win 'em all.

1956: MICKEY TOPS
THE CHARTS

ELVIS PRESLEY'S FIRST APPEARANCE ON *THE ED SULLIVAN SHOW* DREW 60 million viewers, nearly 83 percent of the national television audience, making it the most-watched broadcast of the decade. Contrary to popular belief, Presley was not photographed from the waist up; the CBS-TV audience was granted a full-body view of his pelvic thrusts and gyrating hips. The episode horrified parents, delighted America's youth, and made him a star. Presley shattered viewership records, went on to challenge the social mores of the conservative Eisenhower era, and helped bring the rock 'n' roll revolution into family's living rooms. Even on the small screen, Elvis Presley was larger than life.

While a 21-year-old crooner from Tupelo, Mississippi, was becoming one of the most celebrated and influential musicians of the 20th century, a 24-year-old hit maker on the diamond from Commerce, Oklahoma, finally started to fulfill his promise of superstardom. Few players in the history of baseball had as much talent as Mickey Mantle. The blond, broad-shouldered switch-hitter could blast the ball for tremendous distances from either side of the plate. He also had a fine throwing arm and blazing speed—he could run from home to first base faster from the right-handed batter's box than anybody in the majors got there from the left side. Headline writers referred to him as The Commerce Comet. Mantle's immense natural talent displayed on the diamond—that combination of power and speed—once prompted his manager, Casey Stengel, to say of his slugging center fielder: "He should lead the league in everything." In 1956, he nearly did.

Stengel's Yankees rallied to Florida for spring training camp having not won a World Series in two years. Unlike seasons past, the pitching was no longer a question mark. Whitey Ford was the best left-hander in the AL, and at 27, he was now the oldest regular starter on the Yankees pitching staff. Bob Turley, 25, and Don Larsen, 26, who had been key factors in the '55 pennant victory, joined two youngsters, Johnny Kucks, 23, and Tom Sturdivant, 26, to give the Yankees five solid starters. Bob Grim, Tom Morgan, and Tommy Byrne—who moved to the bullpen and was still pitching well despite his 37 years—formed an excellent relief corps. The outfield with Mantle, now in his sixth year, in center, Hank Bauer in right, and Elston Howard in left, was strong. Bill Skowron was growing nicely into the first base job, and Andy Carey started at third. Billy Martin shared the second base duties with Jerry Coleman, and Gil McDougald was now the full-time shortstop, with Rizzuto on the bench. At catcher Yogi Berra was starting his 10th full season.

Lawrence Peter Berra grew up in an Italian section of St. Louis called The Hill. He got his nickname as a kid after his friends saw an Indian actor in a movie that reminded them of Berra and from that point on, Larry was Yogi (a Hindu word for teacher). Berra began his career in the Yankees' farm system in 1943. He served in the Navy during World War II from 1944 to 1946, and then joined the Yankees' top minor-league team in Newark, New Jersey, where Mel Ott, the New York Giants manager, saw him play. "He seemed to be doing everything wrong, yet everything came out right," said Ott. "He stopped everything behind the plate and hit everything in front of it." When Berra joined the Yankees in 1946 he was a backup player, sharing the catching duties and occasionally playing left field. In Yankee Stadium, left field is notorious for its late afternoon shadows. "It gets late early out there," he said.

Berra was squat and clumsy when he joined the Yankees. One writer said he looked like "the bottom man on an unemployed acrobatic team." Some teammates mocked him as an ape by hanging from the dugout roof by one arm. But manager Casey Stengel believed in Berra from the start. Berra knew how to call a game, and Stengel dubbed him "my assistant manager." Yankees catcher Bill Dickey had just finished his Hall of Fame career, and he took on the young Berra as a student. Dickey was a great teacher, showing Berra the basics of catching, and Berra proved to be an excellent pupil. "Bill is teaching me all his experience," said Yogi. In 1949, Berra became the Yankees' everyday starting catcher, a job he would hold for a decade. Behind the plate Berra was one of the top defensive catchers in the game and a great handler of pitchers. (He called two no-hitters thrown by Allie Reynolds in 1951.) The jug-eared catcher who was built like a fireplug had surprising cat-like quickness. "He springs on a bunt like it was another dollar," said Stengel.

Berra's great catching played a big part in the team's success, and so did his solid bat. He was one of the great clutch hitters of his day, "the toughest man in baseball in the last three innings," said Baltimore manager Paul Richards. An amazing bad-ball hitter, Berra was skilled at reaching for balls out of the strike zone and hitting them out of the park. Yet for all his aggressiveness at the plate, he rarely struck out—only 12 times in 597 at-bats in 1950. Berra was the constant of the great Yankees teams of the era, bridging the team's transition from Joe DiMaggio to Mantle. So integral was Berra to the Yankees' fortunes that he was voted the AL's Most Valuable Player three times (1951, 1954 and 1955) over a five-year span—in a league that boasted such future Hall of Fame stars as Mantle, Ted Williams, Al Kaline, Nellie Fox, and Larry Doby. Even more impressive, since 1950, Berra had never finished lower than fourth in the balloting.

He was feared as a hitter, but Berra the man was easy to embrace. He had a way of rearranging the English language and warping logic.

"You should always go to other people's funerals; otherwise, they won't come to yours," is an example of the unique and witty observations he was famous for—his so-called Yogi-isms. "Slump? I ain't in no slump; I just ain't hitting," he once claimed. It's ironic that Berra was managed for most of his Yankees career by baseball's other great scrambler of the English language, Casey Stengel, the originator of Stengel-ese. A favorite of sportswriters, Berra had countless expressions and turns of phrase that are memorable because many of them don't make much sense, while at the same time, every one has some truth to it. "You can observe a lot by watching," he once said, along with "If you can't imitate him, don't copy him." Many Yogi-isms are attributed to Berra, even if he never actually said them. As he so aptly put it: "I really didn't say everything I said."

Bruised and ego-battered following their shutout loss to the Dodgers in Game 7 of the World Series, the Yankees were plagued by an alarming number of injuries right from the start of spring training. Stengel was distressed because the Yankees team off the field was almost as strong as the one on the field. Larsen barely escaped an extended stay in the infirmary. At 6-foot-4 and 215 pounds, the pitcher was nicknamed Gooney Bird by his teammates for his wild and crazy off-field antics. He had earned a reputation as an enthusiastic partygoer. Jimmy Dykes, his manager in Baltimore, once said of Larsen: "The only thing he fears is sleep." Larsen had gotten himself into Stengel's dog-house in St. Petersburg, when he wrapped his car around a telephone pole at five o'clock in the morning. "He was either out pretty late or up pretty early," said Stengel of his big pitcher, who escaped unmarked, except for a chipped tooth. When Larsen was fined by the city, his manager defended him in jest by stating, "He oughta get an award, finding something to do in this town after midnight." By season's end, Larsen would get his reward.

For Elston Howard, spring training in St. Petersburg, Florida, meant separate but equal. In his first few camps, Howard had to live with a black family in the segregated part of town. He was the only player not staying at the Yankees hotel. He spent a lot of time with another black player, Bill White, of the St. Louis Cardinals, who also trained in St. Pete. Howard was a quiet and dignified man. He worked hard and kept his head down. His locker was right next to Bauer, who gave him tips on playing the outfield, when to take batting practice, what to look for in certain situations against certain pitchers, and, of course, how to act like a Yankee. Bauer believed in Howard's ability. Whenever somebody in the stands would yell racial slurs at Howard, it was Bauer who was the first to stick his head out of the dugout. When a reporter asked why he would do such a thing, Bauer replied, "Because he is my friend."

The Yankees began the season at Griffith Stadium, in Washington, DC, on April 18. Gil McDougald, who was often overshadowed by his home-run-hitting teammates and rarely received the public recognition he deserved, had the honor of catching the ceremonial first pitch from President Dwight D. Eisenhower on Opening Day. After Eisenhower threw the first pitch, McDougald got the president to sign the ball. But there was just one problem. Ike wrote, "To *Joe* McDougald, Best Wishes. President Eisenhower." The game was noteworthy from the start, because third base umpire Ed Rommel became the first major-league umpire to wear eyeglasses during a game. It turned out to be a mere footnote, however, because Mantle started the season with a double-bang, clobbering two home runs off Camilo Pascual that were each measured as traveling nearly 500 feet. Both homers were screaming line drives that cleared the 31-foot center field wall. The first homer landed on a rooftop across from the stadium, which thrilled President Eisenhower, cheering Mantle from his seat behind the Senators dugout. The second homer ricocheted off a tree outside the park on Fifth Street. Ballpark old-timers remembered only Babe Ruth ever hitting a ball there. "One of these days," said Rizzuto, "he's going to take this league apart."

Mantle exploded out of the gate, hitting homers on successive days during the first Yankees homestand of the season. Then he cranked two home runs into the third deck of the right field stands at Yankee Stadium on May 5, and to prove those eye-opening blasts were not flukes, he went 4-for-4 and homered from both sides of the plate on May 18 at Chicago's Comiskey Park. The May 24 game at Detroit brought a 5-for-5 effort including another tape-measure homer. Nothing was going to slow him down, not even a pulled ligament in his right knee suffered on April 25. The trainer wanted him to rest the injury, but Mantle refused, and insisted on continuing to play. By the end of May the Oklahoma kid had hit 20 homers. One of Mantle's blasts, his 19th of the season on May 30, carried special significance. In the first game of a Memorial Day doubleheader against the Senators at Yankee Stadium, batting left-handed, Mickey ripped a ball off Pedro Ramos so high and hard that it appeared to the awestruck crowd that it was going to be the first fair ball ever hit out of the hallowed stadium. The ball struck 18 inches below the cornice high above the famous third-deck façade.

Ever since Yankee Stadium was built in 1923, nobody had ever come close to hitting that copper filigree. Mantle hit it with a drive many insisted was still rising when it struck. The drive was estimated at 370 feet from home plate and 117 feet above the ground. There is no telling how far the ball might have traveled had it managed those 18 inches to clear the façade, but some believe the ball would likely have wound up nearly 600 feet away from its starting point. Sitting in the stands behind third base, the comedian Billy Crystal, then an eight-year-old boy attending his first big-league game, recalled: "A priest sitting in front of me shook his head and said, 'That almost hit heaven.'" Mantle's home run won the game for the Bombers, and to add insult to injury, Mickey, again batting from the left side, would hit a slightly less impressive 450-foot blast to the top of the right field bleachers off Camilo Pascual in the second game, also providing the difference in the Yankees win.

Mantle's impressive start also elevated the hitting of Yogi Berra. With Mantle batting behind him in the cleanup spot, pitchers began worrying about walking Berra and then having to face the league's most powerful hitter with a runner on base. Getting better pitches to hit, Berra got off to a career-best start, hitting 12 home runs and batting .357 on May 18. Consequently, the teammates were touted as the most explosive batting duo since Babe Ruth and Lou Gehrig. Along with Bauer, Skowron, Howard, and McDougald joining the hit parade, the Bronx Bombers boasted a lineup of sluggers not seen in the AL since the great New York teams of the 1930s with Gehrig, DiMaggio, Lazzeri, and Dickey. Home runs were on the rise throughout the game. In one of the more sustained shows of power in Major League Baseball history, Pittsburgh Pirates slugger Dale Long connected against Dodgers pitcher Carl Erskine on May 28, giving Long home runs in a big-league record eight consecutive games. (The record was duplicated by New York Yankees first baseman Don Mattingly in 1987 and by Seattle's Ken Griffey Jr. in 1993.)

Asserting power reached a crescendo in November 1956 as Soviet premier Nikita Khrushchev's infamous statement—"We will bury you"—ushered in one of the Cold War's most dangerous phases, one rife with paranoia and conviction that both sides were out to destroy the other. Earlier that year, the Bronx Bombers also set out to bury their opponents by late spring. The surging Yankees built up a big lead over the Cleveland Indians and took quick control of the AL pennant race. After beating the Indians on May 16, they never were out of first place again. The Yankees were in a class by themselves, though sportswriters and fans were focusing on Mantle's remarkable individual feats more than those of the club. The May 30 moonshot catapulted him to national fame, prompting cover stories on him in numerous major magazines, including *Time*, *Life*, *Newsweek*, and *Sports Illustrated*, hailing his talent for long home runs and his sprinter's speed. The attention, however, came with a price. In Detroit, some two-dozen Tigers fans hopped the center field fence, mobbed Mickey, and salaamed. In Chicago, waves of spectators—one report estimated the number of fans to be about 200—took turns dashing onto the field to shake Mickey's hand and pat him on the back. Mantle never did feel comfortable in the outfield, playing in an era when fans were allowed to storm the field after the game, and he frequently had to battle his way back to the safety of the dugout. Eventually, the Yankees hired a group of men self-described as the "suicide squad," to work as quasi-bodyguards to help protect Mantle by escorting him from center field after each home game because adoring fans would jump over the rails and mob him. "We'd say, 'Here we go, Mickey, let's move,'" said one such hire, Tony Morante, still working for the club as director of stadium tours. "Here I am, with one of my idols, helping to get him to the dugout safely."

Mantle was only 20 years old in 1952 when he had the good fortune and the bad luck to follow DiMaggio as the Yankees full-time center fielder—the good fortune because New York was in the midst of a record five-year run as world champions, and the bad luck because some fans felt Mantle could do nothing that would measure up to the great DiMaggio. Now 24, Mantle awed baseball fans with his tape-measure home runs, including another legendary blast off Paul Foytack on June 18. When the Tigers left-hander wound up and delivered his pitch, Mantle uncoiled a mighty swing and, as he had many times before and after, sent the ball on a deep arc toward the left field fence. Only this time, it seemed as if the ball was not going to come down. The crowd at Briggs Stadium in Detroit gasped as Mantle's gargantuan home run easily cleared the stands beyond the fence, and disappeared outside the stadium. Mantle became just the second player after Ted Williams to knock a ball over the roof of Briggs Stadium. Mantle's victim Foytack coined it a "bazooka blast." Two days later, Mantle tattooed a ball into the top deck of the center field bleachers, something no other player had done since the bleachers were built there in the late 1930s. By June, he was leading the majors in batting with a .414 average. A slight adjustment to his left-handed batting stance contributed to his success. By moving away from the plate just a little, he was now better able to handle the high, inside fastballs, thereby turning a previous weakness into a new strength.

Teammates marveled at Mantle's prodigious power while opponents searched for ways to slow him down. Kansas City manager Lou Boudreau unveiled the Mantle Shift in June, a variation of the defensive alignment he employed a decade earlier to combat Ted Williams. It was a simple case of playing the percentages: Boudreau knew Mantle was an extreme left-handed pull hitter, and therefore more likely to make an out if more defenders were shifted to the right side of the field. So when Mantle batted left-handed with nobody on base, Boudreau moved all of his fielders out of position. The second baseman moved to deep right field near the foul line, the right fielder manned deep right-center, the center fielder played in deep left-center, the left fielder played a very deep third base, the third baseman played a shallow center field, and the shortstop took the normal second base position. Some observers were opposed to such a shift. An editorial in the *Sporting News* advocated for a rule that would outlaw such gimmicky defenses. Marty Marion, the manager of the Chicago White Sox, said he had no plans to shift against Mantle. "I am thinking about putting a fielder in the stands," he quipped. Paul Richards of the Orioles suggested his pitchers not give Mantle anything good to hit, and cautious pitchers preferring to walk Mantle heeded that advice, issuing him 30 free passes in 25 July games alone.

Both Mantle and the Yankees kept up their furious pace well into the summer, making a shambles of the league. After the July 10 All-Star break the Yankees swept a three-game series from Cleveland, and Chicago, the only other AL team with a winning record, collapsed by losing three straight at Boston. Now with a 9 1/2-game lead, the Yankees were running away with the pennant. John Drebinger wrote in the *New York Times*, "If the National League could make up its mind as to the winner of the pennant in that circuit, the World Series could start this week." Mantle, wearing a knee brace, hit only a handful of home runs in July, but then hit 12 in August to give him 47 with the coming of September. Going into the Labor Day weekend, he needed 14 homers to break Ruth's single-season record of 60 home runs set in 1927.

While he was pursuing Ruth's record, Mantle became perhaps the most famous ballplayer since Joe DiMaggio had burst onto the national scene during his remarkable 56-game hitting streak in 1941. Inspired by watching Mantle in action at Yankee Stadium, Teresa Brewer, one of the most popular female singers of the decade, released a novelty song called "I Love Mickey" in tribute to the Yankees slugger. The number was a swing and a miss. The song peaked at number 87 on the *Billboard* charts, despite Brewer and Mantle appearing on *The Ed Sullivan Show* to promote it. (While the song never truly caught on with music lovers or baseball aficionados, Brewer's songwriting partners, Ruth Roberts and Bill Katz, went on to pen the original New York Mets theme song, "Meet the Mets.")

While some people believed a Yankees pennant would be a foregone conclusion, another televised contest certainly proved to be. A cheating scandal hit the popular television quiz show *The $64,000 Question* when it was revealed that producers had been rigging the outcome of some shows by giving favored contestants the answers in advance. A winning contestant in the boxing category, Dr. Joyce Brothers, denied any knowledge of cheating, and was later called before Congress. During testimony, she stated that she was not assisted in any manner during her run for the money, and no taint of the scandal attached to her.

It was August 25, the Old-Timers' Game at the Stadium, a day when the Yankees celebrated their rich history as the great players of the past donned the pinstriped uniform for old times' sake. Earlier that morning, desperate for a left-handed-hitting outfielder, the Yankees purchased the contract of 40-year-old Enos Slaughter and decided to release the popular Phil Rizzuto, 38, who could no longer make the long throws from shortstop or get the hits that had made him so valuable earlier in his career. Scooter was called into the executive suite by general manager George Weiss and manager Casey Stengel and asked to consult with the brain trust concerning a roster move necessitated by the team having re-acquired Slaughter off waivers from the Athletics. After making several suggestions about which player should be cut from the squad, the veteran infielder was told by Weiss that he was the player about to be let go. Slaughter was inserted into the starting lineup and quickly vindicated the decision to release Rizzuto. In Slaughter's first four starts, he got six hits, including a triple, and scored five runs and knocked in two to help his new team win all four games. In that final month of September, Slaughter hit close to .300 and finished the season extremely pleased with his contribution to helping the Yankees win the pennant. An extremely dejected Rizzuto, however, would still remain with the team. The following season, he was hired as the team's third broadcaster in the booth with Mel Allen and Red Barber, manning the microphone as the voice of the Yankees for another 40 years. Rizzuto was a shameless homer, and his distinctive cry of "Holy cow!" was the rallying call of Yankees fans for two generations.

Fittingly, Mantle's 50th home run of the season on September 18 helped to clinch the AL pennant for the Yankees. Mantle connected in the top of the 11th inning off the White Sox's Billy Pierce, and Whitey Ford and Bob Grim combined to shut down Chicago in the bottom of the frame—setting off a celebration for the Yankees at Comiskey Park. Mantle's accomplishment was a big deal at the time. The Mick became just the eighth player in MLB history to slug 50 home runs in one season. His name was being dropped in the same breath as Babe Ruth (who reached the 50-homer plateau four times), Jimmie Foxx (two times), Ralph Kiner (two times), Hack Wilson, Hank Greenberg, Johnny Mize, and Willie Mays as the only players to hit at least 50 homers in one season. Adding to the excitement, Mantle also had a good chance at the Triple Crown, as he was leading both the AL and NL in batting average, RBIs, and home runs—something that nobody had done since Ted Williams in 1942. Though a pulled groin muscle in the first week of September would keep The Mick from reaching the Bambino's mark, he was comfortably ahead of Brooklyn Dodgers center fielder Duke Snider for the major-league home-run lead, 51 to 41, with three games remaining in the season. But Mantle would need to finish strong in order to fend off Boston Red Sox left fielder Ted Williams

A four-time AL batting champion in the 1940s, Ted Williams gave Mickey Mantle a run for his money right up to the last weekend of the regular season in 1956. Williams would reclaim the batting crown in each of the following two seasons.
NATIONAL BASEBALL HALL OF FAME AND MUSEUM, INC.

for the batting crown and Detroit Tigers right fielder Al Kaline for the RBI title.

The batting title race between Mantle and Williams would be decided during the final weekend of the season when the Red Sox came to town to play a three-game series against the Yankees at Yankee Stadium. Mantle led Williams by four percentage points, .354 to .350. Mantle hit his 52nd home run in the first game, which was his only hit in four at-bats, dropping his batting average one point. But Williams went 0-for-3 and his average dropped to .348. To rest his injured groin muscle with the pennant already sewn up, Mantle did not start the second game, which Boston won in 13 innings, but he entered the game as a pinch-hitter in the eighth inning and walked with the bases loaded. Williams failed to capitalize on the opportunity; the 38-year-old tallied just one hit in six at-bats and he saw his batting average fall to .345. In the third and final game, Williams walked in his first at-bat and was then removed from the game for a pinch-runner, conceding the batting title to Mantle, who did not start the season finale, but drove in a run on a pinch-hit grounder, ending the season at .353, eight points ahead of Williams. The run Mantle drove in with his groundball gave him 130 RBIs for the season. Detroit's Al Kaline, going into his final game, had 126 RBIs and a chance to tie or overtake Mantle. Mickey had to wait out nervously the news from Detroit to learn that Kaline had driven in only two runs, two fewer than Mantle.

Mantle had won the Triple Crown of both leagues, hitting .353 with 52 homers and 130 RBIs, joining Williams, Gehrig, and Rogers Hornsby as the only players to ever do so. Additionally, he led both leagues in total bases with 376, runs scored with 132, and slugging with a .705 percentage. His performance made him a unanimous selection for the league's MVP award, as well as recipient of the prestigious Hickok Belt as the Professional Athlete of the Year. More importantly, Mantle's production drove the Yankees to another pennant, Casey Stengel's seventh in eight years, tying the mark set by Joe McCarthy with the Yankees from 1936 to 1943.

The Yankees ran away with the AL pennant with a record of 97-57, nine games ahead of the Indians, who had a trio of 20-game winners in Herb Score, Early Wynn, and Bob Lemon, yet once again, played second fiddle. In fact, it was the second time in five years that Cleveland had a trio of 20-game winners without a pennant to show for it. New York's offense led the league in runs per game, total runs, home runs, runs batted in, and slugging percentage. In addition to Mantle, the Yankees were led by Yogi Berra, who would have won a fourth MVP award were it not for his teammate. Berra drove in 105 runs—the fourth straight season with 100 or more RBIs—and only struck out 29 times in over 500 at-bats. Complementing Mantle's power surge, Berra, along with Bauer and Skowron, all topped 20 home runs. The 5-foot-11, 195-pound Skowron had already become legendary for his physique. "His muscles had muscles," a familiar saying, was often applied to Moose. He was a powerful right-handed hitter who was hurt by the great distances to left field and left-center field at Yankee Stadium, but had great power to the opposite field and occasionally took advantage of the Stadium's short porch in right field. Lefty-hitting Joe Collins and righty-swinging Bob Cerv led a deep bench that enabled Stengel to take advantage of the lefty versus righty percentages and play to his players' strengths. Shortstop Gil McDougald had his best season yet, with a .311 batting average, and his .405 on-base percentage was second on the team only to Mantle's .464. McDougald played so well that he was named the All-Star shortstop in the AL, the third different position he started in an All-Star Game.

Whitey Ford, called the Chairman of the Board because of the cool, corporate-like efficiency of his pitching style, led New York with 19 wins, and he just missed winning 20 when he lost, 1–0, in his last start of the season. Ford went 19-6, with a league-leading 2.47 ERA and .760 winning percentage. Johnny Kucks compiled an outstanding 18-9 record as the number two starter behind Ford. The 24-year-old right-hander, who grew up in Jersey City, New Jersey, right across the Hudson River from New York City, made his first (and only) All-Star team. Kucks was known as a fast worker. The Yankees liked to name him the starting pitcher for the last game of a road series because he pitched quickly and games ended in plenty of time to catch a train to the next city. But the hot dog vendors and beer salesmen at Yankee Stadium weren't so pleased on August 24 when Kucks needed only 73 pitches to blank the White Sox, 2–0, in a two-hour contest. Tom Sturdivant, another unexpected contributor, won 16 games, Don Larsen finished the year with 11 wins, and Bob Turley won eight of 12 decisions. With the addition of youngsters Kucks and Sturdivant, Tommy Byrne moved to the bullpen and posted seven wins and six saves. Tom Morgan had a team-leading 11 saves, and unfortunately for Bob Grim, his slider—which was his best pitch—had wrecked his arm, though he still managed to contribute six wins.

The Brooklyn Dodgers began their home-away-from-home experiment with a 10-inning, 5–4 victory over the Philadelphia Phillies on April 19 in the first regular-season major-league game ever played at Roosevelt Stadium in Jersey City, New Jersey. Dodgers owner Walter O'Malley moved seven of his team's home games to Jersey City as a thinly veiled warning to New York City officials that he wanted a new ballpark—or else. The Dodgers won the first six games at Roosevelt Stadium before losing their last, 1–0, to the New York Giants on a Willie Mays home run on August 15. With 36 home runs and 40 stolen bases, Mays was the National League's first 30-30 player—though at the time nobody recognized it as a significant achievement—and Mays would do it again the following season.

The world champion Brooklyn Dodgers had their hands full all season before finally securing the NL pennant by just one game over the Milwaukee Braves. Don Newcombe, a 20-game winner for the third time in six big-league seasons, which were interrupted by two years of military service during the Korean War, was exceptional from July through September, when he won 17 of 18 decisions and had a scoreless streak of nearly 40 innings. He finished with a 27-7 record—the last victory coming on the season's final day to seal the last pennant the

Dodgers would ever win in Brooklyn. Newcombe won the NL Most Valuable Player Award and the very first Cy Young Award. In addition to Big Newk, the Dodgers pitching staff was reinforced by clutch performances from 39-year-old Sal "The Barber" Maglie, returning from the Mexican League and pitching the Dodgers to victories in several must-win games down the stretch, including a September no-hitter. The aging hurler finished with a 13-5 record and a 2.97 ERA. The Barber was a sharp addition to a fine Brooklyn staff that included Carl Erskine, Roger Craig, Clem Labine, and a pair of unproven youngsters, Sandy Koufax and Don Drysdale.

For the fourth time in five years, the World Series pitted two fabled rivals, the New York Yankees against the Brooklyn Dodgers—the Damn Yankees against Dem Bums. The Dodgers, anxious to prove that their 1955 World Series triumph over the Yankees was no fluke, were hoping to get off to a quick start as the teams congregated at Ebbets Field in Brooklyn for the opening game of the Fall Classic. President Eisenhower threw out the ceremonial first pitch with relish. Ike was one of the better all-around athletes to ever serve in the White House. The West Point linebacker had famously battled Jim Thorpe in the 1912 Army-Carlisle game. (The Native American sports legend—who only months before had won Olympic gold in the pentathlon and decathlon at the Stockholm games and was dubbed The World's Greatest Athlete by the king of Sweden—scored two touchdowns and kicked three field goals to help the Indians defeat Army, 27–6.) Eisenhower played several sports while at West Point, but would later call not making the baseball team "one of the greatest disappointments of my life, maybe my greatest."

The first game of the Series was won by Brooklyn behind the pitching of veteran right-hander Sal Maglie, who struck out ten Yankees and overcame a first-inning two-run homer by Mickey Mantle to go the distance for a 6–3 win. Whitey Ford started the Series for the Yankees, as he was to do a record total of eight times in his distinguished career, but Brooklyn pounced on him early, and he was gone by the fourth inning after home-run blasts by Jackie Robinson and Gil Hodges. Game 2 pitted Newcombe against Larsen. Neither starter made it out of the second inning. Newcombe fell apart and was lifted after giving up a grand slam home run to Berra, and Larsen, after being staked to a 6–0 lead, immediately unraveled and couldn't hold it. The Gooney Bird was wild, issuing four walks in less than two innings. He came out, and the Yankees went on to lose, 13–8—the most runs ever scored against them in a Series game to that point. The heart of Brooklyn's lineup—Snider, Robinson, and Hodges—combined for seven hits, five walks, seven runs, and seven RBIs.

Down two games to none, the Yankees hoped to right the ship when they returned to the Stadium for the next three games. As it turned out, Game 2 would be the last time a New York starting pitcher would need relief in the Series. The Bronx Bombers prevailed in Game 3, 5–3, on the strength of Ford's complete game and on homers by Martin and Slaughter, whose three-run shot in the sixth off Roger Craig was the fatal blow that put New York ahead to stay. It was Slaughter's first round-tripper since being picked up from Kansas City in late August. The Yankees knotted the series at two games apiece with a decisive 6–2 victory in Game 4 as Sturdivant pitched a strong nine innings. Martin's single in the fourth gave New York the go-ahead run, while homers by Mantle and Bauer in the sixth and seventh innings iced the game. Bauer's homer was hit off 20-year-old Don Drysdale pitching in relief. Sandy Koufax sat through his second World Series in a row without making an appearance.

Don Larsen arrived at the Stadium on the morning of Game 5 thinking he would spend the rest of the World Series in the bullpen. But when Larsen got to his locker, he found a baseball tucked into his left shoe. It was Stengel's way of letting him know he would be starting. "I just stood there, very surprised," said Larsen, who had lasted less than two innings as a starter in the Yankees' Game 2 loss. "I didn't want to mess it up." A near-sellout crowd jammed their way into Yankee Stadium for the pivotal Game 5 as Larsen took the mound against Maglie. Pitching without a windup, a style he had adopted late that season, Larsen set the Dodgers down in order over the first three innings. Maglie retired the first 11 Yankees he faced, but number 12, Mickey Mantle, rifled a home run into the short right field porch near the foul pole for a 1–0 New York lead. Every inning, Larsen retired three batters in a row. Few Dodgers even came close to reaching base. In the second inning, Jackie Robinson drilled a line drive off the glove of third baseman Andy Carey, but shortstop Gil McDougald grabbed the deflection and threw him out. Mantle made the best defensive play, racing back and to his right to chase down Gil Hodges's long line drive for a backhanded catch in the fifth. And in the seventh, Duke Snider flied out to Mantle in Death Valley in deep left-center field, where the distance to the fence was 457 feet.

As the game rolled on, and as the perfect frames piled up, Larsen noticed his teammates began to ignore him, strictly adhering to the time-honored superstition to avoid conversation with a pitcher throwing a no-hitter. Larsen continued to keep Brooklyn at bay, and in the sixth, the Yankees picked up their second run on Bauer's single that drove in Carey. By now the fans at Yankee Stadium began to realize that through six innings Larsen had allowed neither a hit nor a runner to reach first base. Pitching flawlessly, Larsen got the Dodgers out in order in the seventh and eighth innings, and while he realized he was working on a no-hitter, he was more concerned about winning the game. The tension reached its peak in the ninth inning. You could have heard a pin drop in the big ball yard in the Bronx after Carl Furillo opened the ninth by flying out on the warning track for the first out. Larsen dodged a bullet when Campanella lashed a liner out of play near the foul pole before hitting an easy grounder for the second out. Now only pinch-hitter Dale Mitchell—an extra outfielder recently acquired by the Dodgers from the Indians—stood between Larsen and perfection. With the count one ball and two strikes, he threw a fastball that some observers thought was wide of the plate. Umpire Babe Pinelli signaled strike three, setting off a deafening roar in the Stadium with

64,519 fans making more noise than the nearby River Avenue express train rumbling past the station. Catcher Yogi Berra rushed to the mound and jumped into Larsen's arms to celebrate the only no-hitter and perfect game in World Series history. "It never happened before, and it still hasn't happened since," said Berra. It was Pinelli's last call, for he retired immediately after the Series, ending a career that spanned 22 major-league seasons and six World Series. Mitchell, a lifetime .312 hitter, would make one more pinch-hitting appearance in the Series, grounding out in Game 7, before he also retired. It's ironic that the most famous at-bat of his career ended in a strikeout, since he had a great eye and rarely struck out.

Larsen needed only 97 pitches to record his perfect game in a 2–0 victory—the first game in which no runner reached first base in the major leagues since April 30, 1922, when Charley Robertson of the White Sox stopped the Tigers, 2–0. It was also the first World Series no-hitter after 307 games, beginning in 1903. In retiring 27 batters in a row, Larsen's control was so sharp that he went to three balls on only one batter—Reese, in the first inning. He also struck out seven, including five on called strikes.

Almost forgotten in the postgame frenzy was the fine game Brooklyn's Maglie pitched that day—in eight innings he allowed the Yankees only two runs on five hits, one of them a homer by Mantle. Maglie pitched well enough to win most ballgames, but his performance didn't match Larsen's. Larsen's gem gave the Yankees a three-games-to-two Series lead. A journeyman pitcher had triumphed at a time when the Yankees needed it most with one of the most spectacular achievements in baseball history. "Sometimes, I wonder why it happened to me," said Larsen, adding, "I think about it every day."

Thanks to Larsen's perfect performance, the Yankees regained the Series lead as play shifted back to Brooklyn with the Yankees needing only a single win to wrap up the championship. The Dodgers, with their backs to the wall, eked out a 1–0 win in 10 innings at Ebbets Field on a game-winning single by Jackie Robinson. Bob Turley allowed just four

After a mediocre season, Don Larsen delivered a historic pitching performance in the 1956 World Series. TOPPS ® TRADING CARDS USED COURTESY OF THE TOPPS COMPANY, INC.

hits and struck out 11 but was bested by Clem Labine, who pitched a masterful seven-hit shutout. The winning run was set up when Jim Gilliam walked and was bunted to second by Pee Wee Reese. The Yankees chose to walk the left-handed slugger Duke Snider, who led the NL with 43 homers, and face the right-handed-hitting Robinson, playing on weary 37-year-old legs. Robinson lined Turley's second pitch to left field. Slaughter, who had spiked Jackie at first base as a member of the 1947 St. Louis Cardinals, was playing left. Jackie's drive took off as Slaughter charged in. He had misjudged the flight of the ball, and as it sailed over his head, Gilliam raced home from second with the winning run. It would turn out to be the last hit in Robinson's glorious Hall of Fame career, a game-winning blow over the head of one of his early antagonists.

There was a little more pressure than usual on the Yankees as the series came down to a winner-take-all seventh game at Ebbets Field.

New York had coasted to another pennant, but they hadn't won a World Series in two seasons with the 1954 pennant loss to Cleveland and the surprising seven-game loss to Brooklyn in the 1955 Series. Two seasons without a Series triumph was considered a severe team slump around the Bronx in the 1950s. Stengel's well-rested ace Whitey Ford seemed the logical choice to start the decisive Game 7. But the game was played in Brooklyn, and Ford had pitched poorly in his previous two starts there. Playing a hunch, Stengel went with New Jersey native Johnny Kucks. The 24-year-old right-hander had won 18 games during the regular season but had made only two relief appearances so far in the Series. Dodgers manager Walter Alston stuck with his ace Newcombe, who didn't last through the second inning in his earlier start against the Yankees and was still looking for his first career World Series victory.

As so often happened in October, Newcombe found trouble in the very first inning. Berra drove a low fastball high and hard over the right field screen for a two-run homer. The ball bounced onto Bedford Avenue and, adding insult to injury, reportedly struck Newcombe's red Cadillac that was parked in the players' lot, leaving the automobile dented, much like Newcombe's confidence. Berra nicked Newk again for another two-run homer in the third inning. Then Elston Howard took him deep to the left field seats to start the fourth, and Big Newk was gone. Bill Skowron wrapped up the scoring with a grand slam homer in the seventh, and that locked up the Yankees 9–0 rout. It was a typical win for the Bronx Bombers with all nine Yankees runs coming as the result of homers. Kucks, whose big strength was keeping his pitches low, was on his game as he shut the Dodgers down with a masterful, three-hit performance. He walked three and struck out one, ending the game by whiffing Jackie Robinson. For the Dodgers, the 1955 defending World Series champions, it was another bitter defeat. They had carried the Yankees to a seventh game again but fell short. Their best pitcher, Newcombe, couldn't get them a win—Newcombe finished his World Series career with a 0-4 record and 8.59 ERA—and all of Brooklyn's hitters were handcuffed in clutch spots by the Yankees pitchers.

The New York Yankees trounced the Brooklyn Dodgers as handily as Ike Eisenhower defeated Adlai Stevenson. The Yanks pounded 12 home runs against Dodgers pitching, with six coming off the bats of Berra and Mantle. Berra had a great series. He hit a grand slam homer in Game 2, caught the only perfect game in Series history in Game 5, and hit two more homers in Game 7—the first player in major-league history to hit two home runs in an elimination game. He batted .360 for the Series, with 10 RBIs. Mantle slammed three home runs, walked seven times, scored six runs, and drove in four. The Bronx Bombers, usually noted for their offensive firepower, this time relied on pitching to subdue the Dodgers. After using 11 pitchers in the first two games, the Yankees proceeded to get five consecutive complete-game performances from five different pitchers in Games 3 through 7. In the last three games hurled by Larsen, Turley, and Kucks, the Dodgers were held to just seven hits and one run in 27 innings.

The Yankees' triumph was a total team effort, but the Series will forever belong to Don Larsen, whose perfect game is the greatest game ever pitched and is ranked as perhaps the finest single performance by any player in World Series annals. Larsen's regular-season major-league career may be a mediocre one, but he's still remembered as the only man to throw a perfect game in the October Classic. "It can't be true," he said after the game. "Any minute now I expect the alarm clock to ring and someone to say, 'Okay, Larsen, it's time to get up.'" Dick Young, writing in the next morning's *New York Daily News*, summed it up best: "The imperfect man pitched the perfect game."

The '56 Series was the last fling for the Boys of Summer. Jackie Robinson, soon to be 38, retired in the offseason, rather than accept a trade to the New York Giants, the Dodgers' fiercest rival. His strikeout to end the Series turned out to be the Dodgers infielder's final major-league at-bat. He announced his retirement from the game in a controversial article in *Look* magazine, in which he took a few parting shots at the remaining segregated teams in the majors. The century's first African-American ballplayer finished his 10-year major-league career with a lifetime .311 batting average. Pee Wee Reese, the team leader and impeccable shortstop, and Roy Campanella, the great catcher, would play in '57, but both men were in their late 30s and looked like they had little left. Don Newcombe followed up his MVP season by winning only 11 games. Unfortunately, the '56 Series was to be the last Subway Series for 44 years, as the Dodgers (along with the New York Giants) were California dreamin'.

The super fantastical Yankees had won their sixth World Series title in eight seasons, a feat that no team would come close to over the next half-century. The win gave the franchise its 17th championship, and once again gave the Yankees bragging rights to the city. By reclaiming the world championship from Brooklyn, the Yankees had atoned for their 1955 Series loss to the Dodgers. The baseball world had returned to normal—Casey Stengel again was a winning World Series manager. Mickey Mantle was the toast of the town. He won the Triple Crown, the MVP award, and then capped off his great season with three homers in the World Series, won by the Yankees over the Brooklyn Dodgers in seven games. On October 20, Mickey celebrated his 25th birthday, assured that he was the most gifted man in all of baseball.

1957: BRAVES NEW WORLD

THOUGH MICKEY MANTLE FINISHED EIGHT HOME RUNS SHY OF BABE Ruth's single-season home run record of 60, set in 1927, his sensational Triple Crown performance catapulted him into the stratosphere of stardom. Mantle was an awesome figure with a bat in his hand, and journalists of the day crafted him as an Adonis. His tape-measure blasts became a symbol of America's post–World War II swagger, at a time during the Cold War when the country needed an icon of national exceptionalism. Thanks to his incredible feats on the baseball diamond, the hayseed from Oklahoma had become the most visible man in the nation. Mantle came into baseball when television, a sleeping giant, was just beginning to stir. His face appeared on TV sets seemingly every day—playing in a game, as a guest on a talk show, or starring in a commercial. Popular magazines published cover stories on Mantle seemingly every week, crafting the image of an American hero. He was equally awesome at the box office, and was the number one draw in baseball. Mickey's appearance in a three-game series in a place like Kansas City, Cleveland, Detroit or Chicago, where the home teams often were struggling at the gate, guaranteed a crowd. He was 24-karat at the box office. He was Elvis Presley in cleats, Marlon Brando with a cannon right arm. Just a glimpse of Mickey Mantle in the flesh raised goose bumps. Wherever Mantle went in the city that never sleeps—Toots Shor's, El Morocco, the 21 Club, the Latin Quarter, the Stork Club, Danny's Hideaway—all eyes gawked at him when he walked through the door. Mickey was an idol. One fan asked Lenox

Hill Hospital for Mantle's tonsils, which doctors there had removed in the offseason. In February, the New York Chapter of the Baseball Writers' Association of America presented Mantle with their Player of the Year honor, at an awards dinner at the Waldorf Astoria. Casey Stengel gushed, "Mickey is the greatest hitter I've seen for distance of any modern-age ballplayer. I've seen him hit balls so far in this park [Yankee Stadium] and in Washington that even the President came out to see him twice." Mantle wanted to double his salary from the $32,500 he made in '56, so he diplomatically asked general manager George Weiss for $65,000. According to Mantle, "[Weiss] told me I was too young to make that kind of money." Weiss wouldn't budge, but Yankees co-owner Del Webb agreed to meet Mantle's price—an investment that paid off handsomely.

After winning seven pennants and six world championships in his eight seasons as Yankees manager, Casey Stengel had already become one of the most successful skippers in postseason history. Many fans were beginning to wonder if the regular season was simply a formality, that for the Yankees, October action was de rigueur. The 1957 edition of the Yankees was a slugging team with a new Murderers' Row: Mantle, Yogi Berra, Elston Howard, Hank Bauer, and now Tony Kubek, a rookie who could play both infield and outfield, to join a strong nucleus of infielders Bill Skowron, Billy Martin, Jerry Coleman, Gil McDougald, and Andy Carey. To Stengel's world championship squad was added pitchers Art Ditmar and Bobby Shantz, who had won 24 games and the Most Valuable Player Award for the Philadelphia A's in 1952. Now Casey had Whitey Ford, Johnny Kucks, Tom Sturdivant, Bob Turley, Don Larsen, and Ditmar to start, with Bob Grim, Tommy Byrne, and Shantz in the bullpen. "You should clinch the pennant by Mother's Day," it was suggested to Stengel. Casey shrugged his shoulders. He had a much later date in mind: sometime around the Fourth of July.

The usually pessimistic Stengel had to admit that he presided over a dominant team, but, he predicted, "I don't think it's gonna be a runaway." Stengel liked his team's chances, but as was his nature, he worried. Mantle's Triple Crown performance of 1956 confirmed Stengel's boast of Mantle as the next best thing in baseball. But Mantle and his running mates, Ford and Martin, were mischievous devils—Stengel called the three "whiskey slick" because of their various late-night hijinks—and Stengel feared it was just a matter of time before their carefree attitude caused an incident. Indeed, in Florida, at spring training, Mantle, who seemed snake bitten, injured himself while fooling around on the golf course with Martin. The two decided to play bumper cars with their electric golf carts. When Martin rammed Mantle's cart, the center fielder fell off, and the cart toppled on his leg. The Mick sprained ligaments in his left foot and needed crutches to get around. It was explained to the press that he had hurt himself stepping in a hole during fielding practice. An embarrassed Stengel was none too pleased to explain the incident to Weiss, and though spring training went well, Stengel grew ornery, and took out his frustrations on innocent bystanders. In late March, Stengel was arrested and released on $50 bail after he allegedly cursed at and kicked a newspaper photographer during an exhibition game in St. Petersburg. It was a bad omen for a ballclub that to this point had capably coped with the pressures of always being the prohibitive favorite to win the World Series. "If we're going to win the pennant," said Stengel, "we've got to start thinking we're not as good as we think we are."

The Chicago White Sox started like a house afire, and put some distance between themselves and the Yankees in April and May. Chicago had a new manager, the former Cleveland skipper, Al Lopez, in place of the fired Marty Marion. The White Sox lineup featured three future Hall of Fame position players in Nellie Fox at second, Luis Aparicio at short, and 33-year-old Larry Doby in center. Fox, 29, and Aparicio, 23, formed the slickest double-play combination in the league. Aparicio, the 1956 AL Rookie of the Year and a sure-handed defender, led the league in stolen bases and would do so for nine seasons in a row. Fox was a .288 lifetime hitter known for choking up on the grip of his bottle bat with a wad of chewing tobacco bulging in his cheek. Though he was an unimpressive physical specimen at 5-foot-9 and 155 pounds, Fox was the heart of the team and a perennial All-Star. In 1957, he led the league in hits and was selected as the Gold Glove Award winner when only one Gold Glove was awarded per position between the National and American Leagues. Doby, acquired in a trade with Cleveland, battled a wrist injury but still managed to drive in 102 runs for Chicago the previous season. The left fielder was Minnie Minoso, a .298 hitter over his career, and one of the game's truly fine players. Sherm Lollar, who ranked below only Yogi Berra as a catcher, was behind the plate. On the mound, the lefty Billy Pierce led the league with 20 wins. Chicago was a team on the rise.

The CBS-TV television network aired the final episode of the classic comedy *I Love Lucy* starring Lucille Ball and Desi Arnaz. The show went out on top, as it was the highest-rated program in the country at the time. Unlike the front-running Ricardos, from Opening Day through the end of June, the Yankees had spent just four days on top of the AL standings, when the White Sox hiccupped, in early May. The Yankees won six games in a row, the last three in Chicago at Comiskey Park, to claim a temporary hold on first place. But after losing the next two games in Cleveland, the Yankees fell to second place and stayed there well into June. The highly rated Indians, the AL pennant winners of 1954, were off to a slow start. But they had to like their chances in the first game of a May series against the Yankees. Cleveland sent Herb Score to the mound against New York's Sturdivant. The 23-year-old Score, in only his third major-league season, was already rated as one of the best pitchers in the league. He was signed to a $60,000 bonus in 1952 by Cy Slapnicka, the scout who brought the Hall of Fame pitcher Bob Feller to the Indians. Now Score seemed a left-handed version of Feller. The Indians' brilliant southpaw was the AL Rookie of the Year in 1955, when he had a 16-10 record, 2.85 earned run average, and 245 strikeouts, tops in the major leagues and a record for a rookie that stood for 29 years, until Dwight Gooden of the New York Mets broke it in

1984. Score was even better in '56, posting a 20-9 record, 2.53 earned run average, and 263 strikeouts, again the most by any pitcher in the big leagues.

The Indians boasted a strong starting pitching staff of Bob Lemon, Early Wynn, and Mike Garcia, but it was the young phenom Score who was becoming one of the star attractions of the major leagues. In March, the Boston Red Sox had offered the Indians $1 million for Score—an extraordinary sum for the time—but were turned down by Cleveland's general manager, Hank Greenberg, who said that Score "may become the greatest pitcher in the game's history." Score was on his way to fulfilling that prediction. Coming into this game he had already fanned 39 batters in 36 innings. At that point, Score, in his five outings, had posted a 2-1 record with three complete games. In the top of the first inning, Stengel's lineup had Bauer leading off, followed by McDougald and Mantle, but as things turned out Score wouldn't be in the game long enough to face The Mick. Bauer grounded out to third baseman Al Smith to begin the game. That brought up McDougald, playing shortstop that day.

McDougald excelled as a sure-handed fielder and productive hitter at whichever infield position the Yankees needed him to play. Alternating between second base, third base, and shortstop for Casey's clubs, he led AL infielders in double plays at third base in 1952, second base in '55, and shortstop in '57. The versatile McDougald was a valuable member of the Yankees championship teams. His first season was in 1951. Mantle was baseball's most highly touted rookie that season, but it was McDougald, who hit .306 with 14 homers, who was honored as the winner of the AL Rookie of the Year Award. A timely hitter, McDougald belted the first World Series grand slam by a rookie, a bases-loaded home run off Larry Jansen of the New York Giants in Game 5 at the Polo Grounds. But what he is forever remembered for is the role he played in a frightening accident that severely injured Score, and which put a promising pitching career on hold.

The incident occurred in the first inning of a night game at Cleveland's Municipal Stadium, on May 7. The ballgame was barely three minutes old. With the count two balls and two strikes, Score, throwing his 12th pitch of the evening, went with the heater. McDougald was right on it and ripped a screaming line drive back up the middle. The ball was headed directly at the pitcher. "I can remember seeing the ball coming right into my eye," Score said. "Boy, it had got big awfully fast, and it was getting bigger. There was really nothing I could do about it." Unable to get his glove up in time, the ball struck Score squarely in the face, the force of the blow so great that the baseball rebounded to third base. Score crumpled to the ground and remained there for several minutes. A hush of tremendous concern overwhelmed the spectators. The public address announcer asked, "Is there a doctor in the stands?" Here's how *Sports Illustrated* described the gruesome scene: "The marvelous discipline of the game prevailed for another second or so. McDougald ran toward first and the Cleveland third baseman fielded the ball and threw it to first base for the curiously inconsequential out. Then players converged on the fallen pitcher. McDougald took one look and felt ill. Score, still conscious, was lying with his body in a defensive embryonic curve, bleeding frighteningly from the face. Amid an awful hush the loudspeakers called for doctors and a half dozen of them began hurrying across the grass."

Members of both teams rushed to Score's side. Ice packs were applied and a stretcher brought out. Score was carried off the field and taken to Cleveland's Lakeside Hospital, where he spent three weeks being evaluated by doctors. He had suffered severe hemorrhaging in the right eye and a swollen retina as well as a broken nose. A prominent eye specialist examined him and reported hemorrhaging in the eye so severe it might permanently endanger Score's sight. His plight brought 10,000 letters with good wishes. People in his hometown of Lake Worth, Florida, sent him a 125-foot-long get-well telegram with 4,000 names, and a California man offered to donate an eye to him.

Bob Lemon, who relieved Score that night, wound up going 8 1/3 innings in relief for a 2–1 victory. Recalled Lemon: "Herb Score was as good as you can get. He was a left-handed (Bob) Feller. He had an outstanding fastball and a hellacious curve. When he was on, it was fourteen or sixteen strikeouts." Lemon said he recalled arriving at the mound while Score was still on the ground. Blood was everywhere, Lemon said. "I can still remember watching the grounds crew use rakes to cover up the blood," he said. Afterwards, a distraught McDougald addressed reporters. "If Herb loses the sight in his eye I'm going to quit the game," he said.

McDougald, Bauer, and Berra tried to visit the hospital the next morning, but were turned away, as were all visitors. Score never blamed McDougald. When Indians general manager Hank Greenberg told Score that McDougald was trying to see him, he showed admirable compassion. "Please tell Gil that I don't blame him for what happened. It's part of the game, that's all." Score was sidelined for the rest of the season, his vision fuzzy and his depth perception impaired. Interviewed by Gay Talese of the *New York Times* the next spring, Score recalled, "When the line drive struck me I wasn't aware of the acute pain . . . I fell but I never lost consciousness. I remember saying, 'St. Jude, stay with me.' My middle name is Jude. He's the saint of impossible causes. I was bleeding from the mouth and I knew there were a lot of people around me. When they took me off the field on the stretcher, I remember saying to Mike Garcia, 'They can't say I didn't keep my eye on that one.'"

Everyone was watching Mickey Mantle and he continued to impress. He once again made big news by going 3-for-4 and belting a game-winning home run deep into the right field seats with two out in the eighth inning to lead the Yankees to a 4–3 win over the Orioles at Municipal Stadium in Baltimore on May 12, putting New York into second place, percentage points behind Chicago. Three nights later, the Yankees would be in the news again, but with some unwanted headlines. What started as a birthday celebration turned into a drunken brawl—the infamous Copacabana Incident—resulting in injuries, a lawsuit, a trade, and a more guarded tone between players and members of the media.

The evening of May 15 started out innocently enough. It was a celebration for Billy Martin's upcoming 29th birthday, a party suggested by Mantle. The two men were extremely close friends; in fact, when Mickey's third son was born at year-end he would be named Billy, after Martin. Mantle organized a celebratory gathering at the Copacabana nightclub, in Manhattan. (The Copa, then at 10 East 60th Street, is now located in Times Square at 268 West 47th Street.) Martin and Mantle were there, as were Berra, Ford, Bauer, and Kucks. Several wives went along, too. The players weren't looking for trouble, but they found it anyway. The entertainer Sammy Davis Jr. was headlining that night when a group of bowlers entered the nightclub and began heckling Davis with racial epithets. The Yankees, being big fans of Davis, took offense to the name-calling and came to his defense. While there are many versions of what happened next, it is clear that a scuffle developed in the hallway outside the men's room at the Copacabana. Bauer was involved. The cops were called. And one of the bowlers, a delicatessen owner from the Bronx, ended up with a concussion and a broken jaw. He claimed Bauer had belted him and sued for damages. Bauer, an ex-Marine, claimed he didn't lay a hand on him; if he did, he said, the guy wouldn't be around to file a lawsuit. Yankees general manager George Weiss was so upset with the players that he slapped all but one with $1,000 fines, a harsh sum in those days. Kucks's lowly status on the payroll got him off with a $500 fine. To the front office the scandal was deadly serious, though it turned into a laugh when a reporter asked Yogi what had happened. "Nuthin," said Berra. "Nobody did nuthin' to nobody."

Eventually the Copacabana incident was settled. During his grand jury testimony, Mantle was asked to explain how a man came to be unconscious on the floor near the Copa bathroom. Mantle thought about the question and then answered, "I think Roy Rogers rode through the Copa, and Trigger kicked the guy in the face." The jurors laughed and the district attorney threw out the case for insufficient evidence. The Yankees' lawyers then advised Bauer that he now could sue in turn. "Forget it," he snapped. "What would I do if I won? Take the guy's delicatessen?"

The day after the fight, Stengel was plenty steamed. He was not a manager to crack down hard on his players when they got a little spirited, but the fact that so many of his players had so very publicly broken curfew called for discipline. Stengel scratched Ford from the start he was due to make and replaced him with Turley, and Berra was benched in favor of Howard. "I won't pitch Ford because the whole world knows he was out until two [o'clock] in the morning," Casey growled. Bauer stayed in the lineup, though Stengel dropped him to eighth in the batting order. As for Mantle, Stengel left him alone, letting him bat third, as usual. "I'm not mad enough to take a chance on losing a ballgame and possibly the pennant," the manager explained. Neither Martin nor Kucks were scheduled to play in the May 16 game and were unaffected. The moves proved to be magical, like most of The Old Perfessor's. Turley threw a four-hit shutout against the Athletics with eight strikeouts. The Yanks won, 3–0. One of those three runs came from a solo shot by Mantle.

Though Bauer was considered the main combatant in the case of the dented delicatessen owner, George Weiss, the general manager, put the blame on Martin. A reputation for post-midnight alcohol-fueled donnybrooks had followed Martin around since 1952, so it came as no surprise when Weiss held Martin responsible for the incident. "Lots of people look up to Billy Martin," said Yankees pitcher Jim Bouton. "That's because he just knocked them down." One month after the Copa incident, Martin was among many pugilists participating in a bench-clearing brawl at Comiskey Park. Billy singled out Chicago's Larry Doby. That was the last straw. Weiss felt the hard-drinking, hot-tempered second baseman was a bad influence on his young superstar Mantle. So Martin had to go. Despite Stengel's affection for Martin, Weiss traded Martin along with pitching prospect Ralph Terry to the Kansas City Athletics on June 15 in exchange for Harry Simpson and relief pitcher Ryne Duren, in a deal generally acknowledged to have stemmed from the brawls.

Martin's significant contributions to the Yankees dynasty as a player were now history. He had a .333 lifetime batting average with five home runs and 19 RBIs in five World Series, and he was on the winning side four times. He made a terrific running catch in 1952 to save Game 7 for the Yankees. The following year he hit .500 to lead the Bombers to their fifth straight title. The trade also cleared the way for a young, talented, and far more clean-cut prospect, Bobby Richardson, to take Martin's spot at second base. Ironically, on June 16, Martin's first game for the A's happened to be against the Yankees. Martin had two hits, including a home run, and scored three runs in an 8–6 New York win. For a long time Billy blamed Stengel for his exile to Kansas City, claiming the old man hadn't stood up for him. Eventually they had a tearful reconciliation.

With the Copacabana incident behind them, the Yankees went on a tear during the month of June, winning 21 of 30 games to overtake the White Sox, AL leaders for much of the first two months. Many games were won in the late innings. Berra led off the bottom of the 13th inning with a game-ending home run to defeat the White Sox on June 22. A week later, Joe Collins doubled in the 10th inning for a victory over Kansas City to keep the Yankees in a first-place tie with Chicago. Young Al Cicotte, who pitched four shutout relief innings, picked up his first major-league victory. (Cicotte's great-uncle, Eddie, was a pitcher and integral member of the Chicago Black Sox team that threw the 1919 World Series.) The team's propensity to rally late in games, which were normally played in the afternoon, led to the catch-phrase "five o'clock lightning," referring to the time when the Yankees' offensive power usually struck, and delivered a crippling blow to their opponent in the late innings. The day before Memorial Day, in a game against Washington, won 7–6 by the Yankees in come-from-behind fashion, Berra's ninth-inning RBI was the "five o'clock lightning" the

Billy Martin (left) was Mickey Mantle's frequent off-field companion during his playing days with the Yankees. Ultimately, their late-night carousing led to Martin's trade to Kansas City. NATIONAL BASEBALL HALL OF FAME AND MUSEUM, INC.

Yankees needed to take the series three games to one. Lightning struck twice for the Yankees with two wins in their final at-bat against the Red Sox. Berra hit a bases-empty homer in the bottom of the 10th to give the Yankees a 3–2 win in April, and pitcher Bob Grim stroked a three-run homer for a 5–2 Yankees win in September.

Sixteen years after Pearl Harbor, Japanese prime minister Nobusuke Kishi received a warm welcome when he visited the United States to address Congress in Washington, DC, stressing Japan's intention to fight communism. He also donned a Yankees cap to throw a ceremonial pitch in the Bronx, and then was one of 63,787 fans at Yankee Stadium to see the Bronx Bombers split two with the White Sox, winning 9–2 before falling, 4–3, on June 23. Mantle went 6-for-9 with a home run, a double, and four RBIs in the twinbill, and he leaped high to grab a long flyball off the bat of Larry Doby to rob a homer. The big day put

The Mick atop the AL with a .392 batting average and 21 home runs, and one behind Washington's Roy Sievers with 51 RBIs.

Another chart topper, Jerry Lee Lewis, had a runaway hit in "Whole Lotta Shakin' Goin' On," and his invitation to perform on Steve Allen's Sunday night variety show gave Lewis enormous exposure, and his performance—marked by pounding piano rhythms and acrobatics on the piano bench—pushed sales of the song past the six million mark.

The Yankees sent eight players, the most of any team, to the All-Star Game in July: Mantle, Berra, McDougald, Skowron, Richardson, Howard, Grim, and Shantz. The event was marked by controversy that caused the commissioner to intervene prior to the game. Cincinnati fans stuffed the ballot boxes and had apparently elected an NL starting squad of all Reds: George Crowe at first base, Johnny Temple at second, Don Hoak at third, Roy McMillan at shortstop, Frank Robinson in left field, Gus Bell in center, Wally Post in right, and Ed Bailey as catcher. An investigation by the league office found that more than half the ballots had come from Cincinnati, and that the *Cincinnati Enquirer* had printed up pre-marked ballots and distributed them with the Sunday newspaper to make it easy for Reds fans to vote for their hometown favorites. Before the voting results were announced, commissioner Ford Frick declared that Crowe, Bell, and Post were disqualified as starters, naming Stan Musial, Willie Mays, and Henry Aaron in their place. The game resulted in the AL defeating the NL, 6–5. Brought in from the bullpen by Stengel to protect the one-run lead, Bob Grim got the final out of the game, getting pinch-hitter Gil Hodges on a game-ending fly out to left field. Due to arm trouble, Grim was now used exclusively in relief, and was selected for the All-Star team in that role for the AL squad. Partisan voting brought about the demise of elected All-Star teams, at least for a time. The ballot box stuffing by Cincinnati fans resulted in the major-league players, coaches, and managers making the All-Star choices from 1958 to 1969. As part of Major League Baseball's attempts to modernize its marketing of the game, the vote again returned to the fans for the selection of the eight starting position players for each team for the 1970 game, and fan balloting remains today.

The Yankees hummed along like a great, efficient machine, equaling June's success with a matching 21-9 record for July. The Yankees stood three games ahead of the second-place White Sox when the teams met for a Sunday doubleheader on July 14 in Chicago. The Yankees lost the first game to the White Sox, 3–1. A rollicking Comiskey Park was jammed with 48,244 fans, some 1,500 more than official capacity. A win in the nightcap would pull the Sox within one game. The Yankees were in peril in the second game, trailing 4–0 in the ninth inning, when pinch-hitter Bill Skowron hit a bases-loaded home run to tie the game—it was Moose's second pinch-hit grand slam of the season—and pitcher Tommy Byrne hit a home run to put the Yankees ahead. The Sox went scoreless in their half of the ninth inning and the crowd filed silently out of Comiskey, knowing a treasured opportunity had been wasted.

Opportunity was the reason Reverend Martin Luther King Jr. established the Southern Christian Leadership Conference to fight segregation and discrimination. King had rocketed into the national consciousness the previous year as the leader of the Montgomery bus boycotts, in Alabama. The local affiliate of the National Association for the Advancement of Colored People (NAACP) decided to challenge the city ordinance requiring segregated seating on public buses, and Rosa Parks became the woman to challenge the law. King led the successful black boycott of the buses, which soon brought the city transportation system to the verge of bankruptcy. King's role in the bus boycott attracted wide media attention and made him a national figure. To achieve his objectives, King employed demonstrations, sit-ins, boycotts, and protest marches. His insistence on nonviolence, as well as his constant refrain that all black people wanted was to be treated equally under the law, resonated with millions of white voters, who came to support his movement.

The Yankees marched into July with Mantle leading the way and performing more late-inning heroics. He hit a home run in the 10th inning to beat the Orioles on July 1, and hit for the cycle—a single, double, triple, and a home run—to win another game against the White Sox, July 23. Mantle's last hit was a bases-loaded triple that capped a five-run rally in the seventh inning of a 10–6 victory. His titanic clout in the third inning landed in the last row of the right-center field bleachers—465 feet away. "They ought to create a new league for that guy," Chicago lefty Jack Harshman said of Mantle. The home-run ball nearly struck the Stadium's massive electronic scoreboard, the famous 50-foot-tall black behemoth with sparkling lights that towered above the right-center field grandstand. A magnificent Longines clock sat 25 feet above the scoreboard. A banner running the length of the bottom of the scoreboard carried an advertisement for Ballantine beer, then the third-largest brewery in America. Ballantine's advertisement—"It's a Hit! Ballantine Beer & Ale"—and its distinct three-ring logo (representing purity, body, and flavor) was a familiar visual backdrop for Yankees fans and TV viewers alike. It was announcer Mel Allen who made the brew part of baseball vernacular, describing each of the Yankees' all-too-frequent home runs as a "Ballantine blast." With his 4-for-5 display, and four runs knocked across, Mantle stood atop the AL leaderboard in batting average (.367) and runs batted in (69), and his 26 home runs put him just one behind Ted Williams.

By the end of August, Mantle was hitting .376 with 34 home runs and 90 RBIs, when he landed in the hospital with what the Yankees' front office called a bad case of shin splints, which is precisely what Mickey had told them. In fact, he had injured himself playing 18 holes of golf with friend and teammate Tom Sturdivant—violating one of the few prohibitions that Stengel had for his players on off days. Angry at missing a putt, Mickey lost his temper and took a wild swing at a low-hanging tree limb with his putter. It snapped in two, flew off at the handle, and crashed at full speed into his left shin. Mantle was hobbled for 10 days, but no one—least of all Stengel—knew the real story of what had happened. Mickey covered up the truth and invented a different, more acceptable accident, a tale that involved bumping into an endtable.

American Bandstand made its national television debut on ABC-TV, beaming images of clean-cut, wholesome teenagers dancing to Buddy Holly & The Crickets singing "That'll Be The Day." The Yankees did not fade away in August, winning nine of 10 to start the month, including three more walkoff victories from three different sources: Enos Slaughter, Joe Collins, and Bill Skowron. Moose (the nickname came from his grandfather, who thought Bill looked like Mussolini and shortened Mussolini's name) carried a .300 batting average in each of his first four big-league seasons. Part of Skowron's hitting profile was his powerful opposite-field home-run swing. He used one hand to slam shots over the short right field porch when it seemed that he was fooled by outside curveballs. "I don't always swing at strikes," he said. "I swing at the ball when it looks big."

Racial tensions were at an alarming high in September, fueled in part by the furor over Arkansas governor Orval Faubus's refusal to desegregate Little Rock Central High School. The Supreme Court ruled, in the 1954 decision known as *Brown v. The Board of Education of Topeka, Kansas*, that public schools must be desegregated. But when the first nine African-American students at Little Rock Central arrived for classes, the Arkansas National Guard, which acted on Faubus's orders, turned them away. Three weeks later, the students began classes under the protection of Army troops sent by President Dwight D. Eisenhower. About the same time, Althea Gibson was striking a blow for equal opportunity on the tennis courts. On September 8, Gibson became the first African American to win the US Open singles title. The 30-year-old Gibson, who already had made history by winning at Wimbledon in June of 1956, breezed past 1947 champ Louise Brough 6–3, 6–2 in the final. She capped a run in the tournament in which she did not lose a single set. Vice President Richard Nixon presented Gibson with the championship trophy.

Despite his checkered past, Mantle led the Yankees again and threatened to win a second straight Triple Crown if not for the leg injury at the end of August that ruined the last month of his season. Mantle achieved a career high in batting average at .365 with 34 homers and 94 RBIs, and for good measure he led the team with 16 stolen bases. Those power numbers had decreased from his remarkable season of a year earlier, but pitchers now worked more carefully to the switch-hitting outfielder, as evidenced by his major-league-best 146 walks. His 121 runs scored also led the majors. Combining Mantle's hits and walks, he reached base more than half the time he came to the plate and would exceed a .500 on-base percentage (as did Ted Williams). Mantle would have earned his second-straight batting title had it not been for 39-year-old Ted Williams's stellar .388 effort. Although he lost the batting title to Williams, Mantle would win his second straight Most Valuable Player Award.

The Yankees were so good they overcame a slow start from Berra. He hit poorly in spring training and his woes continued for the first three months of the season. In early June, Yogi was struck by a foul ball that shattered the protective catcher's mask and broke his nose. After several stitches, Berra was back in the lineup but batting only .228—yet reminded reporters in a Yogi-ism that would reverberate 15 years later, "The season ain't over 'til it's over." When the season was over, Berra had amassed 24 homers, driven in 82 runs, and played in his 10th straight All-Star Game. First baseman Bill Skowron hit .304 with 17 homers and 88 RBIs en route to his first All-Star Game. Bauer hit 18 homers with 65 RBIs and led the league with nine triples. McDougald chipped in with 13 homers and 62 RBIs, and Tony Kubek, thanks to solid fielding at three positions and a .297 batting average, took AL Rookie of the Year Award honors.

On the mound, New York pitching led the major leagues with the lowest earned run average and the most strikeouts. Stengel juggled a deep staff that included six different Yankees pitchers winning 10 or more games. Ford missed much of May and all of June with a sore left shoulder, but the Yankees didn't miss a beat. With Sturdivant, Turley, Grim, and Larsen a combined 51-24, the Yankees survived Ford's two-month bout with tendinitis. Shantz started 21 games, came out of the bullpen nine times, won 11, saved five, and had the lowest ERA, 2.45, on the team. As a spot starter and reliever, Ditmar won eight games and saved six more. Following two undistinguished seasons, Grim made a comeback, winning 12 games and leading the league with 19 saves. Stengel used him to quell rallies, which meant that Grim rarely entered a game with the bases empty.

The Ford Motor Company introduced a new automobile, called the Edsel, which was a miserable flop. The Edsel, named for Edsel Ford, Henry Ford's son who died of cancer in 1943, was the subject of an intense marketing blitz while still on the drawing board. Automotive writers roundly trashed the Edsel, going so far as to compare the oval-shaped vertical grille to a vagina—racy stuff for 1957. Interestingly, it was Ford's president Robert McNamara who convinced the board to bail out of the Edsel project; a decade later, it was McNamara, then secretary of defense, who couldn't bring himself to quit the disaster of Vietnam, even though he knew a lemon when he saw one. While the Edsel became synonymous with failure, by contrast, the Yankees, with their unparalleled success and accompanying gallery of legends, had become a proud and distinct part of Americana. The popular stand-up comic Joe E. Lewis commented on the coldly efficient, perpetually victorious Yankees: "Rooting for the Yankees is like rooting for U.S. Steel." It was business as usual for the red-hot Yankees; like a corporate juggernaut, they swept a three-game series from the White Sox at Comiskey Park in late August upping their AL lead to 6 1/2 games. Berra hit a three-run homer in the eighth inning off Paul LaPalme to snap a 6–6 tie in the series opener, and the Yankees all but wrapped up their record-setting eighth AL pennant in nine years. New York finished the season with a 98-55 record, eight games better than the White Sox, who once again finished in second place.

The Milwaukee Braves, forerunners of baseball expansion after their move to Wisconsin from Boston in 1953, beat out the St. Louis Cardinals for the National League flag. Henry Aaron's game-winning home run in the 11th inning against the Cards at County Stadium in late September clinched the franchise's second pennant since the 1914 Miracle Braves. Nine years earlier, the Boston Braves had reached the World Series, but in 1953 the Braves moved to the beer-brewing town of Milwaukee, Wisconsin—the first Major League Baseball franchise shift in 50 years. Now the Braves were back atop the NL standings. Manager Fred Haney's Milwaukee squad had top-flight talent in the batter's box and on the mound. Right fielder Henry Aaron, the NL's Most Valuable Player in just his fourth major-league season, led a powerful lineup. Aaron hit .322 with a league-leading 44 home runs and 132 RBIs. Eddie Mathews, a perennial All-Star at third base, chipped in with 32 homers and had already amassed 200 career longballs by age 25. On the mound, Milwaukee's rotation boasted 56 wins from Warren Spahn, Bob Buhl, and Lew Burdette. Spahn was already a Hall of Fame–caliber hurler, and now, at age 36, he was only getting better. Spahn won 21 games (his eighth 20-win season) and became the first left-handed pitcher to win the Cy Young Award. Buhl, an 18-game winner, and Burdette, winner of 17, were able complements.

The Yankees, playing in their eighth championship round in nine seasons under Stengel, made their customary October journey to the World Series, but the Braves were a well-balanced team and not intimidated by the perennial champion Yankees. The matchup seemed well scripted for Game 1 with future Hall of Fame left-handers Ford and Spahn matching up for the opener. "If you had one game to win and your life depended on it," Stengel once said of his left-hander, "I would go with Ford." Stengel's life didn't hang in the balance of Game 1, but Ford pitched like it did, allowing the Braves only five hits in nine innings. Spahn allowed the Yankees nine hits, and the Bombers won the opener at the Stadium, 3–1. Burdette, a longtime Yankees farmhand who made it to the big club for a cup of coffee in 1950 before being traded away in a deal for Johnny Sain, started the second game for the Braves against another left-hander, Bobby Shantz. Burdette frustrated the fastball-hungry Yankees bats by throwing an assortment of junkball pitches, including an alleged spitter. When accused, the 30-year-old right-hander replied: "Who me? I just throw a mean curve and a sharp drop." Burdette allowed two early runs but settled in and shut the Yankees down with only seven hits through nine innings. Hank Bauer did the only serious damage against Burdette with a home run, but a triple by the young Aaron and a homer by veteran shortstop Johnny Logan gave the Braves a 4–2 victory as they tied the Series at a game each.

A 20-year-old rookie from Milwaukee, Tony Kubek, returned home in the enemy uniform of the Yankees for the third game at County Stadium. In the first World Series game ever played in Milwaukee, Kubek, a native son who doubled as both a utility outfielder and infielder, celebrated his arrival with two home runs in a 12–3 Yankees rout that put the Bronx Bombers ahead two games to one. Bob Buhl was the victim of the New York onslaught that began with three runs in the first inning on Kubek's first homer, two walks, a sacrifice fly, and a single by Harry "Suitcase" Simpson, who earned his colorful nickname with five big-league clubs, half a dozen minor-league teams, and another seven Negro Leagues addresses. Don Larsen gained the decision with seven-plus innings of solid relief work.

The fourth game turned out to be the most dramatic of the series. A three-run blast by Aaron and a solo shot by first baseman Frank Torre in the fourth inning off Yankees starter Tom Sturdivant built an apparently safe 4–1 lead for Spahn. In the ninth inning, after retiring the first two batters, Spahn allowed back-to-back, two-out singles to Berra and McDougald, and then, on a full count to Elston Howard, the Milwaukee ace blinked and surrendered a game-tying three-run home run hit into the left field stands. Milwaukee manager Fred Haney stayed with Spahn, who retired Andy Carey for the final out of the frame. Haney sent Spahn back to the mound for the 10th inning. That certainly looked like a mistake as Kubek beat out an infield hit and Bauer tripled him home and the Yankees—who were one strike away from defeat—pulled ahead, 5–4. Spahn then retired Mantle to end the threat. A stubborn Milwaukee club wasn't done just yet. Vernal Leroy "Nippy" Jones batted for Spahn to lead off the bottom of the 10th. Left-hander Tommy Byrne let loose a wild curveball that may or may not have hit Jones on the foot. The pitch skipped past catcher Yogi Berra. The home plate umpire, Augie Donatelli, called it a ball. Jones claimed that the pitch had struck his right foot, and insisted he be sent to first as a hit batsman. While a heated discussion ensued, the 32-year-old reserve infielder picked up the ball, showed it to the umpire, and insisted the black smudge on the ball was from the shoe polish on his cleat. Donatelli agreed, reversed his call, and awarded Jones first base. Berra and manager Stengel argued the call, to no avail. Casey went to his pen and gave the ball to Bob Grim. Red Schoendienst, who had come to the Braves in a July trade with the Giants, bunted pinch-runner Felix Mantilla to second base, setting up a key at-bat for Logan, who smashed a long double, sending Mantilla home with the tying run for the Braves. Then Mathews delivered the big blow in the next at-bat, taking Grim downtown for a long two-run home run to right field to turn what could have been a heartbreaking loss into a Braves 7–5 triumph to even the Fall Classic at two games each. "It's a funny thing," Nippy Jones said in a 1991 interview. "Nobody remembers Mathews' home run to win the game. But they remember me getting hit on the foot."

Burdette was back on the bump again as the Milwaukee starter in the fifth game against Ford, and both pitchers were brilliant. Facing the Yankees gave Burdette just a little more incentive as he went after his second victory over his former team. The only run came in the bottom of the sixth, when Braves first baseman Joe Adcock singled to right field, scoring Mathews. Ford allowed only six hits in seven innings, but Burdette topped that with a seven-hit shutout. Gil McDougald almost changed the outcome with a fourth-inning leadoff drive to deep left field, but Wes Covington saved the day for Milwaukee by jumping above the wall to grab it. The 1–0 victory gave the Braves a three-games-to-two advantage and had the team's fans dancing down Wisconsin Avenue.

The sixth game was another thriller at Yankee Stadium with the Bronx Bombers taking the victory in old-fashioned Yankees style with the long ball. Turley faced Buhl in a pitchers' duel. Berra, playing in his 53rd World Series game, a new record, got the Yankees going by hitting his 10th series homer with a man on in the third, to give the Yanks an early 2–0 lead. After the Braves tied the game at 2 on home runs by Aaron and Torre, Hank Bauer connected for a homer off Milwaukee reliever Ernie Johnson in the bottom of the seventh, tying a World Series record by hitting in his 13th straight game. Turley, who allowed only four hits, shut the Braves down the rest of the way. The victory evened the series at three games each.

For the third straight year, the series had gone the limit, and for the third straight year, the decisive game would be a shutout. For the deciding seventh game at the Stadium, manager Haney bypassed Spahn (who was ill with the flu) and brought Burdette back on only two days rest. He had other pitchers available but opted to go with the hot hand, and Burdette made him look like a genius. Stengel had Sturdivant rested, but played a hunch and started Larsen, making his first Series start since his perfect game of a year earlier. Defense would determine the outcome of the game. Kubek's error on an apparent inning-ending double play opened the floodgates for four runs in the top of the third inning, and that was more than enough for the Braves. The final score was 5–0, and again Burdette shut down the Yankees on seven hits. Third baseman Eddie Mathews ended any thoughts of a Yankees comeback when he made a nifty play on Skowron's groundball headed down the line with two outs and the bases loaded in the bottom of the ninth. Mathews snared the hot shot and stepped on the bag for a Series-ending force-out to preserve Burdette's second shutout in three days, and give the city of Milwaukee its first major-league baseball championship. Ironically, Burdette had pitched only one shutout all season before his two Series shutouts, and the Yankees themselves were whitewashed just twice during the regular season. In the clubhouse following Game 7, Braves manager Haney exclaimed, "If Lew could cook, I'd marry him." The city of Milwaukee felt the same. It was only the fifth year of big-league baseball for Milwaukee after nearly half a century with only a minor-league team. The beer parties went long and loud as the Braves came home to a victory parade.

The key for the Braves in the World Series was Burdette. Including the final six innings of his first start, he shut out the powerful Yankees for 24 consecutive innings. In all, he won three games in the Series with an ERA of 0.67. He struck out 13 and allowed only 25 baserunners in 27 innings of work. Burdette was the first pitcher since Cleveland's Stan Coveleski in 1920 with three complete-game victories in a World Series, and the first to throw more than one shutout in a Series since Christy Mathewson for the Giants in 1905. Throughout his career, people said that Burdette was so good because he threw illegal spitballs—he fidgeted and touched his hat and face so much on the mound that, his manager said, he could "make coffee nervous"—but no one could ever prove it. When a reporter asked how he was able to start three games, win three games, and toss two shutouts, Burdette replied, "I exploit the greed of all hitters." Burdette was an easy choice for World Series MVP, although he received plenty of help from Mathews—who had three doubles, a homer, and walked eight times—and Aaron, who batted .393 in the series with 11 hits, including three home runs and a triple, and seven RBIs.

The Yankees offense was stifled. Removing the 12-run outburst in Game 3, the New Yorkers scored a total of just 13 runs in the other six games. They lost three of the last four games, two by shutout. Berra (.320), Kubek (.286), and Bauer (two homers, six RBIs) delivered key hits throughout the Series, and Jerry Coleman ended his playing career with a flourish, hitting .364. The Colonel, as he was known, retired as the owner of four World Series rings to go along with his numerous medals and ribbons accrued as a Marine Corps pilot. Mantle again played in pain, entering the Series troubled with a leg injury. Then in the first inning of Game 3, Mickey severely damaged his right shoulder diving back into second base on an attempted pickoff play and was out of the starting lineup for the rest of the Series.

For the Yankees, although they had continued to add AL pennants to their collection, it was their second World Series loss under Stengel in the last three attempts. Some of the glow surrounding Stengel was beginning to dim. The club was dealing with rumors of the impending retirement of their aging skipper. Stories about the 67-year-old Stengel sleeping on the bench filtered into the press. "What about it?" Casey bellowed when confronted with the player gossip about his dugout naps. "A lot of players my age are dead at the present time." It was a bitter Series for the Yankees. Especially bad was the feeling in Milwaukee when the three games were played there. Stengel grew angry and called the Milwaukee fans "bush," and the Braves fans retaliated with choice insults. But the greatest affront of all was the seizing of the championship trophy from New York where it had resided since 1949, thanks to the Yankees, Giants, and Dodgers.

The biggest baseball news, however, took place off the field as both the Brooklyn Dodgers and New York Giants announced plans to pack up and move to California. The Dodgers played their last home game at Ebbets Field on September 24. The end came quietly, with just 6,702 fans watching Danny McDevitt pitch a shutout for Brooklyn. The *New York Times* reported that among the tunes played between innings by stadium organist Gladys Gooding were "Am I Blue," "After You've Gone," "Don't Ask Me Why I'm Leaving," "Que, Sera, Sera," and "Thanks for the Memories." Five days later, the Giants were trounced by Pittsburgh by a 9–1 score before 11,606 fans in the finale at the Polo Grounds. The Dodgers and Giants moved west to play in California in 1958, leaving the Yankees alone in New York. They'd pretty much had the place to themselves anyway.

1958: A WESTERN FRONTIER

IN THE 1950S, AMERICANS WERE ON THE MOVE. AT THE START OF THE decade there were 25 million registered automobiles, and the first Holiday Inn opened in Memphis, Tennessee. Construction of the 41,000-mile interstate highway system that would span the nation was underway. The new interstate highways were at least four lanes wide and were designed for high-speed driving. They were intended to serve several purposes, chief among them: eliminate traffic congestion; make coast-to-coast transportation more efficient; and make it easy to get out of big cities in case of an atomic attack. By 1958 there were 67 million registered automobiles and 100 Holiday Inns with its iconic sign a familiar sight on US highways. Postwar American families, then growing at four million children a year, fueled the proliferation of Holiday Inns. Railroads were fading and plane travel was still expensive, but gasoline was cheap. The expansion of the vast highway system, coupled with inexpensive gasoline, encouraged the public to buy cars worthy of extended road trips. This gave auto manufacturers confidence to build a wide spectrum of large cars with powerful engines. Station wagons were big enough for everybody. Families took vacations that changed the face of the American road. One of the decade's most famous literary works, Jack Kerouac's *On the Road*, was published. Baseball franchises were on the road, too. As spring training commenced, five of the 16 original franchises had been relocated to a different city.

Soviet advances in space technology took off with the launch of the Sputnik satellite. America was on the verge of exploring the final frontier, too, having established the National Aeronautics and Space Administration (NASA). For Major League Baseball, the final frontier was the West Coast, and the big leagues finally stretched all across the country when the Dodgers moved from Brooklyn to Los Angeles and the Giants moved from New York to San Francisco. Big-league teams would now be forced to travel across the country, to the land of sunshine, palm trees, and orange groves in California.

New York fans were stunned, though not exactly blindsided. Rumors had been circulating for months. But still the official news was greeted with disbelief. How could two of baseball's most glamorous, tradition-steeped franchises run out on their faithful fans? The answer, of course, was money. The Giants played in a 52,000-seat stadium, the Polo Grounds, but they also had a parking problem and were feeling the pinch of a population shift to the suburbs. After drawing 1.15 million fans in their championship season of 1954, attendance skidded to 629,179 in 1956, last in the league. The Dodgers had a different kind of problem. They had the fan support and population, but they did not have an adequate facility. Aging Ebbets Field seated only 32,000 and that simply was not enough. The perennial pennant contenders regularly had drawn one million fans to their games, but that figure might easily have doubled in a more spacious stadium. Dodgers president Walter O'Malley had made no secret of his dissatisfaction and had even transferred seven home games to Roosevelt Stadium in Jersey City each of the last two seasons.

It seemed only fitting that the Dodgers and Giants should be opponents when West Coast fans got their first taste of major-league baseball. And it seemed only right that the home teams should prevail. The Dodgers and Giants immediately resumed their longtime rivalry when they met at San Francisco's intimate Seals Stadium on Opening Day, April 15, as 23,448 fans turned out to watch the hometown San Francisco Giants pound the Dodgers, 8–0, behind the six-hit pitching of Ruben Gomez. Hall of Famer Ty Cobb was on hand for the historic game, as was Mrs. John McGraw, widow of the late, great Giants manager. The Opening Day atmosphere was festive, especially when the Giants jumped on Dodgers starter Don Drysdale and two relievers in an eight-hit attack that included a two-run single by Willie Mays and a home run by rookie Orlando Cepeda. Three days later, the Dodgers played in the massive Los Angeles Memorial Coliseum for the first time, and a National League–record crowd of 78,672 watched the home team jump to a 5–2 lead and then hold off the Giants for a 6–5 victory. Seals Stadium and the Los Angeles Memorial Coliseum were being used temporarily until Candlestick Park and Dodger Stadium were completed.

The Dodgers would play their first year in Los Angeles without eight-time All-Star catcher Roy Campanella, whose career ended tragically on a wintry January night when his rental car spun out of control on an icy Long Island road, bounced off a telephone pole, and flipped over—resulting in a spinal injury that would confine him to a wheelchair for the rest of his life. The 36-year-old Campanella, a three-time winner of the NL's Most Valuable Player Award, was scheduled to move with the Dodgers to Los Angeles for the 1958 campaign, but that move, along with everything else in Campy's life, now was on hold. He had been driving to his Glen Cove, New York, home at three o'clock in the morning after making a television appearance in Manhattan. Campanella was pinned in the car for about 30 minutes as rescuers worked to pry open the doors. The burly 5-foot-9, 225-pounder was rushed to Community Hospital where a four-hour, 15-minute operation was performed to repair two fractured vertebrae in his neck. He had some movement in both arms after the surgery, but none in his fingers, or the lower part of his body. He would never walk again. Campanella joined the Dodgers in 1948 and compiled a .276 average with 242 home runs in 10 major-league seasons.

Four Yankees stars—Whitey Ford, Yogi Berra, Mickey Mantle, and Bill Skowron—appeared on *The Ed Sullivan Show* to strut their vocal stuff by singing "Take Me Out to the Ball Game," alongside the song's lyricist, 79-year-old Jack Norworth, on April 13. During the players' appearance on the show, Berra took a moment to deliver well wishes to Campanella. Baseball fans made a big deal of the golden 50th anniversary of the 1908 classic song written by Norworth and composer Albert Von Tilzer. The idea for the song struck Norworth while riding the New York subway. He saw a poster that said, "Baseball Today—Polo Grounds." In 15 minutes, he wrote the lyrics to a chorus that would come to define the baseball experience for generations to come. The song, including two verses that are rarely heard, tells the tale of a liberated woman named Katie, who would rather her boyfriend take her to the ballpark than to the theater. Norworth, who also wrote the words to the classic "Shine on Harvest Moon," cowrote more than 2,000 songs with Von Tilzer.

"Take Me Out to the Ball Game" was an instant number one hit in 1908, and the optimistic spirit of the song's refrain still endures. One of the most familiar of all American tunes, it is still sung every day at just about every ballpark in the land. Oddly, at the time they had written the song, neither Norworth nor Von Tilzer had ever been to a baseball game. In fact, Von Tilzer would not see his first game until 1928, and Norworth didn't attend his first game until he was honored on Jack Norworth Day at Brooklyn's Ebbets Field, in 1940. And the first time he heard his song performed at a game was in 1958, when the Dodgers, newly arrived from Brooklyn, honored him at the Los Angeles Memorial Coliseum to commemorate the tune's half-century mark. The makers of Cracker Jack presented him with a trophy. The song has been recorded more than 100 times, by musicians as diverse as the Andrews Sisters and the Goo Goo Dolls, and it inspired a 1949 movie musical starring Frank Sinatra and Gene Kelly. It is thought to be the third-most commonly played song in America after "The Star Spangled Banner" and "Happy Birthday To You."

In January, the Yankees announced an unprecedented 140 games would be televised in 1958 on WPIX-TV. The decision to telecast such a large number of games, including 63 road contests, was prompted by the departure of the Dodgers and Giants to California. The Yankees reportedly received $850,000 in the sale of TV rights, the largest TV income in baseball. The Yankees were rich in position players, too. Casey Stengel's nucleus of veterans and youngsters was the envy of the league. In center field was Mantle, the most feared hitter in baseball, coming off his second straight superstar season, who despite surgery on his right shoulder in the offseason signed a $65,000 contract (after some hard bargaining with general manager George Weiss). Hank Bauer was back in right field. There was Skowron at first base, with Andy Carey at third. Stengel wanted to get his favorite young player, Tony Kubek, into the lineup on a regular basis, so he moved Gil McDougald, the best shortstop in the league the previous year, to second base and installed Kubek at short. There was a school of thought that said McDougald was the best second baseman in the league and that Kubek might be even better at short than McDougald. That put Bobby Richardson, who had played 97 games in '57, on the bench. At age 42, Enos "Country" Slaughter hit .304 as a part-time outfielder and he contributed in any way that Stengel needed. The other major change involved left field, where Norm Siebern, the 1957 Minor League Player of the Year, replaced Elston Howard, who proved so versatile; Howard could catch and play the outfield, a quality Stengel liked. Stengel hinted during spring training that he would give starting catcher Berra, at age 33 the oldest of the Yankees regulars, more rest and Howard more playing time behind the plate.

Stengel worried about the health of his pitchers. Don Larsen had an inflamed right elbow. Bob Turley had a tender shoulder. Ford had been the victim of arm trouble the year before. Tom Sturdivant, a holdout following his excellent '57 season, finally signed for a $6,000 raise to $18,000, but showed up late to spring training and never got on track. Johnny Kucks and Art Ditmar could be counted on to put forth their best efforts. But Ditmar in 1956 had been 12-22 for the A's, leading the Philadelphia staff in most of the positive and negative pitching categories when Weiss traded for him, which was consistent with Weiss's traditional practice of acquiring pitching talent without regard to win-loss record. You have to be a very good pitcher to lose 20 games in one season. Why would a manager keep putting you out there to pitch, time after time, if you didn't have a chance to win the game? Stengel knew that even the strongest team could not win without a group of solid starting pitchers, no matter how good your relief corps.

The Yankees had acquired Ryne Duren in the Billy Martin trade. He replaced Bob Grim as the Yankees main pitcher out of the bullpen. Duren had a blazing fastball, wore thick glasses, and was occasionally wild, making batters wary of digging in against him. Besides his tremendous velocity, he had a regular habit of entering the game and throwing his first warmup pitch over the head of his catcher and off the screened backstop in Yankee Stadium. He blamed the errant throw on his bad eyes hidden behind Coke-bottle glasses. The fans always roared. Three familiar faces were gone from the team. In addition to the retirement of infielder Jerry Coleman, pitcher Tommy Byrne, 38, also retired, and first baseman Joe Collins was sold to the Philadelphia Phillies during spring training. Rather than report, he retired. The 34-year-old first baseman had spent his entire 10-year career with New York and appeared in seven World Series with the team, finished with a lifetime .256 batting average, and had won many games with his clutch hitting.

After a terrible spring training that had Stengel walking the beach of St. Petersburg in the wee hours, the Yankees turned it on when the real games began. Riding early winning streaks of six and 10 games, the Yankees ended the pennant race before Memorial Day. After sweeping a May 25 doubleheader in Cleveland, they had a 25-6 record and a huge nine-game lead. The key, as it turned out, was their pitching. Seven times they shut out their opponents in that first 31-game sprint, and eight other times they held them to one run. Of the six games they lost, three were by one run, another by two. Only once were they soundly defeated. Ford, their ace since Allie Reynolds had retired, was having his best season to date. Watching Ford, said fellow Yankees pitcher Ralph Terry, "was like watching a pitching textbook in the flesh." A complete game, 6–1 victory in the first game of that May 25 matchup put his ERA at 1.64. He would keep it under or near two all season. Rivaling him was Turley. He won his first seven starts, all complete games, including four shutouts and a one-hitter. He ran his record to 13-3 in July and started the All-Star Game in Baltimore. Kucks, however, was never able to come close to duplicating his splendid 1956 form. The highlight of his season came on June 3 when he shut out Chicago, 13–0, allowing only two hits, to put his record at 4-1. Larsen won seven of his first eight starts, and though Ditmar and Sturdivant scuffled, behind Ford and Turley, the Yankees continued to cruise.

Arnold Palmer won his first Masters golf tournament. Stan Musial got hit number 3,000. Charles de Gaulle became premier of France. Mantle scored on his third inside-the-park home run in a month as the Yankees beat Early Wynn and the White Sox, 12–5, in a doubleheader split in the Bronx, on June 5. (After a 14-17 season in 1957—Wynn's first losing season in nine years—the Indians sent Wynn to the White Sox for the popular Minnie Minoso. The trade proved a good one for both teams.) Then Chicago took the nightcap, 3–2. Mantle's most home runs against a pitcher are the 13 he hit against Wynn, a future Hall of Famer. Major League Baseball passed a new rule for the season requiring all players to wear protective batting helmets when hitting. Earlier in the season, Mantle drilled a liner through the box for a single. Wynn then fired several pickoff attempts at Mantle's legs. "Now that Mantle wears a protective helmet, pitchers [are] throwing at his legs and feet," said Stengel. Wynn had a willingness to back hitters off the plate, or even to send them spinning to the dirt. To those who suggested that he would throw at his own mother, Wynn famously replied, "I would if she were crowding the plate." Wynn was one of the most intimidating pitchers of the 1950s. Mantle once said of him, "That SOB's so mean he would (expletive) knock you down in the dugout."

Mantle continued to play hurt and in pain. He missed a week of games in early May when his surgically repaired shoulder acted up on him. There was not a day when he took his glove to center field or his bat to the plate that Mantle was not favoring one damaged knee or the other. "Hitting the ball was easy," Mantle once said. "Running around the bases was the tough part." His proneness to leg injuries was a concern. When Mantle was forced to miss a few games nursing a pulled tendon in his right leg, fans wondered why he couldn't keep from getting hurt and stay in the lineup. Writer Dan Daniel called Mantle a "brittle hero."

Later, after a June letdown, when first the Red Sox and then the Tigers and then the Indians made faintly threatening noises, the Yankees again roused themselves. In a five-week drive, they won 24 and lost eight, sent their rivals spinning, and increased their already substantial first-place lead to double digits by the Fourth of July. Giving Berra a rest behind the plate, Howard filled in admirably on July 15 and went 4-for-4 with a double, a triple, and a walk; though the Yankees lost, 12–5, to Detroit, they still held a 12-game lead over Boston. Howard's batting average reached a robust .354, but he would not have enough plate appearances to qualify for the batting title should his average hold up. Stengel was adamant about platooning his players; Howard ended the year hitting .314 with 11 homers and 66 RBIs in 103 games, 67 behind the plate.

Gil McDougald's pinch-hit single drove in the deciding run as the AL edged the NL, 4–3, in the All-Star Game at Baltimore's Memorial Stadium. On July 25, the Yanks beat the Indians, 6–0, behind Ford, whose ERA dropped to 1.68, to give Casey's team a 14 1/2-game lead, the largest he had ever enjoyed with the franchise. A week later, when Berra was 3-for-4 with a double, a home run, and six RBIs to lead the Yanks over the White Sox, 6–1, the lead over the Indians had swelled to 17 games. Berra continued to come through in the clutch, with two more walkoff home runs. In late July, he swatted Ned Garver's third pitch into the lower right field stands in the 10th inning with a man aboard to break a 1–1 tie with Kansas City. Two days after the Labor Day holiday, his three-run homer in the bottom of the ninth off Leo Kiely won the game for New York, 8–5.

Baseball and Yogi Berra were both in prime time, and Berra parlayed his sports celebrity into multiple business ventures, the most successful being as a spokesman for Yoo-Hoo chocolate drink. A series of Yogi Berra Yoo-Hoo ads followed throughout the 1950s that featured Yogi promoting the "Drink of Champions." He became, in effect, the face of the franchise. A typical Yogi story, as told by the man himself: "One time I was in the office and the phone rang when no one else was around. I always answer a ringing phone, so I did. The woman who was calling asked if Yoo-Hoo was hyphenated. I said, 'No ma'am, it's not even carbonated.'" The impact of Berra's involvement with the company was almost instant. Within a few years, Yoo-Hoo became one of the fastest growing soft-drink brands in America, and Berra became one of a new breed of baseball players who were making good money off the field. In addition to his involvement with Yoo-Hoo, Berra also did a number of other print and TV ads during the 1950s for an assortment of sponsors, among them Kraft Italian salad dressing, Camel cigarettes, Spencer chemicals, Ballantine beer, Shelby bicycles, and Prest-O-Lite batteries. His advertising work put him in a new spotlight, with his name sometimes appearing in the *New York Times* business section. It wasn't just baseball fans who recognized Berra—Madison Avenue now knew the name, too.

Berra was one of the great catchers in the game—he went the entire season without an error behind the plate—and now he was becoming almost as famous for his pitches. The lovable Berra was a fixture as a pitchman in commercials, lending his name to everything from cat food to cigarettes to beer to athlete's foot spray. He also, for better or worse, is forever linked in the public imagination to a cartoon bear whose name is uncannily similar to his own: Yogi Bear. The cartoon character Yogi Bear first hit TV screens in 1958 as a supporting character on *The Huckleberry Hound Show*. By the time Yogi Bear made his debut, Berra the ballplayer was a household name. Soon after, Berra tried to sue Hanna-Barbera Productions, Yogi Bear's creators, for defamation of character. (Apparently, Berra didn't love that he was occasionally addressed as

Yogi Bear.) Luckily for the Jellystone Park native, Berra dropped the suit. Hanna-Barbera insisted there was no connection between their smarter-than-the-average bear and the baseball player, but despite his creators' contention to the contrary, all signs indicate that Yogi Bear was indeed named after Yogi Berra. In any case, Yogi's name was a source of yet another famous Yogi-ism. After appearing on a pregame radio show in St. Louis with announcer Jack Buck, the Yankees catcher was paid with a check made out as "Pay to Bearer," which prompted Yogi to say, "You've known me long enough to know how to spell my name."

In July, Stengel and several star players, including Mantle, Musial, Ted Williams, Bob Feller, and Robin Roberts were called as witnesses before the Senate Anti-Trust and Monopoly Subcommittee of the Judiciary. The committee was seeking information on proposed legislation to exempt baseball and other team sports from the antitrust laws. When the inquiring senators attempted a squeeze play to get a direct answer to a direct question, Casey's clever verbal gymnastics left them confused but laughing. When Stengel was asked why baseball should be exempt from antitrust regulation, he replied in classic Stengel-ese: "I would say I would not know, but I would say the reason they want it passed is to keep baseball going as the highest-paid ball sport that has gone into baseball, and from the baseball angle—I am not going to speak of any other sport. I am not here to argue about these other sports. I am in the baseball business. It has been run cleaner than any other business that was ever put out in the 100 years at the present time." When Stengel's hour-long rambling and his characteristically spirited but nonsensical responses were completed, the baffled politicians let Stengel go and called on Mantle to answer the same question. He brought down the house by deadpanning, "My views are just about the same as Casey's."

The spirit of the times reflected an age of innocence. *Leave It to Beaver*, one of the most beloved situation comedies in American television history, received an Emmy nomination for best new program. The show revolved around the Cleavers, a quintessential middle-class, stable family, who live in Mayfield, USA. The Cleavers were a perfect American family—kind, prosperous, and white—perfect at least for America in the 1950s. *TV Guide* dubbed the show "the sleeper of the season."

No American League team was sleeping on the Yankees. The team's record stood at 71-36 and New York had an insurmountable 16 1/2-game lead on August 8 after Ford twirled a three-hit shutout over Boston. Two days later, Casey had Whitey warm up in the bullpen in case he needed him to save a game. But the move backfired when his trusty lefty hurt his elbow and pitched the rest of the season in pain. Ford never won another game in the regular season. Feeling pressure because he had won the World Series just once the previous four years, Stengel may have panicked when the Yankees started coasting down the stretch and damaged his top starting pitcher. The Yankees imploded after August 8, going 21-26 after that date, the next-to-worst record in the AL down the stretch. They had a losing 15-16 record in August, and could only break even at 12-12 in September. This was the worst stretch they had ever had under Stengel. It mattered little, as the Yankees lead was as big as the recently completed Seagram Building in New York City, designed by Ludwig Mies van der Rohe.

The Yankees sailed to their ninth pennant in 10 years with a September 14 clinching date. But they had limped to the finish line. In the train car to New York after they clinched the AL pennant in Kansas City, Duren got into a scuffle with first base coach Ralph Houk and shoved Houk's cigar in his face. More embarrassingly, news reports revealed that general manager George Weiss, determined to prevent a repeat of Copa-like publicity, hired private detectives to follow the Yankees players and find out what they were up to at night. Mantle and Ford, suspecting they were being tailed, slipped their pursuers, but not the choirboys Kubek, Richardson, and Kucks. The detective reported that they spent the night playing Ping Pong at a local YMCA.

Three days after the Yankees clinched the AL pennant, Mantle put on a show at one of his favorite venues. Despite a stiff wind blowing in at Briggs Stadium in Detroit, Mantle poled a Jim Bunning pitch down the right field line over the roof and across Trumbull Avenue, some 500 feet away. Mantle's two-run homer, his 41st of the season, was all that Bunning allowed the Yankees hitters as the Tigers won the game, 5–2. There was joy in the Motor City as Chrysler celebrated assembly of its 25 millionth vehicle, a Windsor model sedan, in Detroit. The home team Tigers, however, finished flat at 77-77, 15 games back.

With seven games left to play in the regular season, New York was simply playing out the string. Before a crowd of 10,941 on the last day of summer, Baltimore's Hoyt Wilhelm entered the record books by pitching a no-hitter for the Orioles against the Yankees at Memorial Stadium, on September 20. The Orioles won, 1–0, thanks to catcher Gus Triandos's eighth-inning home run. It was the first-ever win for the 36-year-old knuckleballer as a starter following eight previous starts and 361 relief appearances over seven major-league seasons. Besides the few spectators who had to brave a steady rain, many more Americans witnessed history, as this was the nationally televised *Game of the Week*. With the Yankees down to their last out and Wilhelm on the verge of a no-hitter, Hank Bauer tried to bunt. Not everyone subscribed to baseball's unwritten rulebook. "If he's going to get a no-hitter, let him earn it," Bauer said to the *Chicago Tribune*. "I was trying to get a hit. That's baseball. I'm sorry it rolled foul." Bauer eventually popped out to second base, ending the game and giving Wilhelm his unlikely no-hitter.

The Yankees and Milwaukee Braves met for the second consecutive year in the World Series. The Yankees won the AL by 10 games, and the Braves won the NL by eight games. It was a clash of what were clearly the game's most powerful clubs. Both teams had identical 92-62 records. Both had two pitching aces. Turley won 21 games to pace the AL, and Ford, who was 14-7, led the league in ERA (2.01). Warren Spahn led the NL with 22 wins, and Lew Burdette was right behind with 20. The Braves had no relievers who reached double digits in saves, but New York's Duren led the AL with 20. The Yankees offense had Mantle, who led the AL with 42 home runs, and Berra (22 homers), along with the usual supporting cast that included a bevy of capable hitters such as Skowron, Howard, Bauer, and McDougald. Henry

Aaron and Eddie Mathews, who combined for 61 home runs, and Wes Covington, who added 24 in just 90 games, led Milwaukee's offense. Surprisingly, neither team had a 100-RBI man, though Mantle, Berra, and Aaron all drove in 90 or more runs.

On paper, these were two extremely well matched teams. The Yankees had a .268 team batting average to .266 for the Braves. Milwaukee hit 167 homers, just three more than New York. And the Braves pitching staff had a 3.21 composite ERA to 3.22 for the Yankees. The defending world champion Braves were confident of becoming the first NL team to win consecutive world championships since the New York Giants had done it in 1921 and '22 with a young outfielder named Casey Stengel. Stengel, who had first played in a Series as a member of the 1916 Brooklyn Dodgers against Babe Ruth's Boston Red Sox, was edgy coming into this World Series. The Dodgers had defeated Casey's Yankees in 1955 and the Yankees had come back to beat them in 1956. The Braves had won the seventh game of the 1957 Series to take the title. The 68-year-old Stengel knew only a Series victory could soften that blow.

The World Series was a rematch of the '57 Fall Classic, and the Yankees were looking for revenge. They didn't get it in the opener before 46,367 fans at County Stadium, however. Two of baseball's greatest left-handers—Ford and Spahn—were expected to make the opener of the Series a sizzling pitching duel, and they did not disappoint. The result was a tense struggle that wasn't decided until extra innings when Spahn, in typical fashion, was still around trying to finish what he started. Ford had been relieved in the eighth by Duren, and the game remained tied at 3 after regulation play. Milwaukee outfielder Bill Bruton, playing in his first World Series game, hit a two-out game-ending single in the 10th inning to drive in the winning run against the Yankees. In Game 2, Bruton hit a home run to lead off the game in another Braves victory. The Yankees ace Turley sure didn't look like the game's best pitcher in Game 2. He gave up a leadoff homer, and after just five batters, Stengel yanked him. Turley didn't get out of the first inning, recording only one out as the Braves demolished the Yanks, 13–5. Burdette pitched another complete-game victory over his former team and contributed a three-run homer to the onslaught. After the Braves won the first two games at home, Stengel still had faith in his team. "I'll pay you when we return," he told the visiting clubhouse man in Milwaukee, meaning that he expected to be back for a Game 6.

The Series moved to Yankee Stadium for Game 3, which was played before a crowd of 71,599 fans. The Yankees sent Larsen, who won nine games and had been slowed by an elbow injury, to face the Braves' 32-year-old right-hander Bob Rush, who had won 10 games in his first year with Milwaukee. Just as Game 2 was all Braves, Game 3 was all Yankees. Larsen scattered six singles to shut out Milwaukee for seven innings before giving way to relief ace Duren, who completed the whitewash for a 4–0 New York victory. Right fielder Hank Bauer accounted for all four Yankees runs with a two-run single in the fourth and a two-run homer in the seventh. It was Bauer's third home run of the Series, and with his 3-for-4 performance, he established a major-league record by collecting at least one hit in 17 consecutive World Series games. Bauer was Stengel's ideal Yankee, a hard-nosed tough guy who played every game as if it was his last. After the Japanese attack on Pearl Harbor, Bauer joined the US Marine Corps. He spent 32 months of World War II in the South Pacific as a combat platoon leader, sustained at least 20 attacks of malaria, received shrapnel wounds to his back on Guam and to his thigh on Okinawa, but recovered to win 11 campaign ribbons, two Bronze Stars, and two Purple Hearts. During one harrowing mission on Guadalcanal, Lieutenant Bauer was one of only five Americans who survived. His war experience hardened him for life, prompting *Sports Illustrated* columnist Jim Murray to write that Bauer's face "looked like a clenched fist." Bauer kept his Marine Corps crew cut throughout his baseball career, which the war delayed the start of until he was 26 years old, but he made the most of his playing time. And he was at his best under the nerve-rattling pressure of World Series competition.

Game 4 featured a rematch of the Game 1 starters, Ford and Spahn, and again Spahn came out ahead. He put on a pitching clinic that made the Yankees look like amateurs, twirling a two-hit shutout in which only one batter made it past first base. Ford pitched effectively but was undone by the sun in left field. Norm Siebern, starting in place of the injured Howard, lost two flyballs in the glaring sun, and the Braves scored a couple of easy runs due to his shaky outfield play. The next day, newspapers roasted the 24-year-old rookie. One headline blared: "Siebern Sunburn Singes Yanks" but Stengel came to the defense of his left fielder. "I'm not asking waivers on him, and you can print that!" he said. Siebern had taken over as the Yankees' regular left fielder and batted .300 with 14 home runs during the season. He also won a Gold Glove Award for his fielding, and solidified left field, a Yankees sore spot. But Stengel did not use him again in the Series.

The Braves had won three of the first four games and were on the brink of a second straight championship. The Yankees had dug themselves a big hole, and looked bad doing it. Turley took the mound again in a must-win game. In the 54-year history of the World Series, only one team had ever come back from a three-games-to-one deficit to win the whole thing, the 1925 Pirates. It was a crisp, sunny afternoon in New York. Turley, who couldn't get out of the first inning in Game 2, faced the Yankees killer Burdette, going for his fifth consecutive World Series win over the Yankees, in Game 5. Facing elimination, Turley tossed a five-hit shutout and fanned 10 Braves for a 7–0 win. Howard, back starting in left field, made a key play in the sixth inning, catching a sinking line drive and then turning it into a double play to choke off a Milwaukee rally and hold New York's 1–0 lead. Energized by Howard's defense, the Yankees exploded for six runs in their half of the sixth to knock Burdette out of the game and give Turley his first Series win.

The sixth game was a beauty. Back at County Stadium, Ford and Spahn matched up for the third time in the Series, each on two days rest. The score was tied at 2 after nine innings, with Spahn still pitching.

McDougald led off the 10th inning with a home run. Spahn retired the next two batters before singles by Howard and Berra chased Spahn from the game. Skowron greeted reliever Don McMahon with another hit, driving home Howard to put the Yankees up, 4–2. Duren took the mound in the bottom of the inning, entering his fifth inning of relief work. Shortstop Johnny Logan walked with one out, but Duren struck out Mathews. After Logan took second on defensive indifference, the Braves' most dangerous hitter, Henry Aaron, came through with a single to score Logan and bring the Braves to within one run. The Milwaukee crowd was delirious, and roared even louder after Joe Adcock singled Aaron to third. Stengel had seen enough. He pulled Duren and called on Turley on very short rest to face Frank Torre. With the tying run on third and the winning run on first, Bullet Bob overpowered Torre with a fastball. Torre could only hit a soft liner to second baseman McDougald for the final out of the game. Major League Baseball had its fourth consecutive seven-game World Series.

The Yankees were looking to complete an unlikely comeback in the deciding Game 7. Having learned their lesson the previous October, rather than sleep at a downtown hotel, and be forced to interact with the hometown populace, this year the team stayed a half-hour drive from County Stadium at Brown's Lake Resort to avoid boisterous Braves fans distracting the visitors and possibly disturbing their sleep. A few minutes into the ride, the Yankees' biggest star thought the bus was much too quiet on its way to County Stadium. So Mantle broke the silence. "For God's sake!" he bellowed. "We're here. We might as well win the damn thing. Quit (peeing) in your pants!" Mickey's pep talk broke the tension. According to reports, in the dugout before game time the Yankees seemed a happy, carefree, almost cocky bunch. The Braves, on the other hand, as a group appeared to be tense, worried, and visibly sobered by the task at hand.

With everything on the line, Larsen and Burdette squared off in Game 7 as they had in 1957. Just like the previous year, Larsen was finished after two and a third innings, mainly due to wildness. Stengel usually had his starters on a short leash in big games, and the deciding contest of this series was no exception. With a one-run lead in the bottom of the third inning, the Yankees manager pulled Larsen with one out and men on first and second and again waved to the bullpen for Turley, pitching in his third straight game. The move worked; Turley worked out of a major jam without a run scoring. The game was tied at 2 apiece in the sixth. Burdette, attempting to reprise his role as Series hero, had pitched five shutout innings, but his magic evaporated in the eighth as the Yankees erupted for four runs. The decisive rally started with two outs when Berra doubled and was singled home by Howard. Andy Carey followed with another single and then Skowron swung at a high outside fastball from Burdette and slugged it over the wall in right field as he had done so many times during the previous four seasons. The three-run blast deflated the Braves and gave the Yankees a 6–2 lead. Turley polished off Milwaukee by retiring the last six outs to complete a two-hit relief job over 6 2/3 innings that preserved the four-run lead and wrapped up the victory. The Yankees had captured their eighteenth World Series championship.

The Braves and their fans were shell-shocked. They had been within a single win of winning a second straight world title, and had Spahn and Burdette on the mound, with three tries between them, to nail it down. Columnist Red Smith felt the Braves should have won the Series, and was unsparing in his assessment. "New York won because Milwaukee wouldn't," he wrote in the *New York Herald-Tribune*. Bruton led the Braves with a .412 batting average. Aaron hit .333, but did not manage a home run and drove in just two runs. Mathews fanned 11 times while batting .160. Spahn batted .333 with three RBIs—one more than Aaron. Berra would often talk to the opposing batters in order to distract them. According to Aaron, Berra kept telling him to "hit with the label up on the bat." Finally, Aaron turned and said, "Yogi, I came up here to hit, not to read."

New York had plenty of outstanding hitters in the Series and out-homered Milwaukee, 10 to three. Bauer had 10 hits, four of them homers, and drove in eight runs. A veteran playing in his ninth Series, he topped the Yankees sluggers with a .323 average. McDougald batted .321 and crashed a pair of homers. Skowron played a key role with seven RBIs, driving in the winning run in the sixth game and hitting the decisive three-run homer in the clincher. Howard was an unsung hero for the Yankees. His impact didn't become notable until Game 5, when his diving catch in left field preserved a Yankees lead and turned the momentum of the Series in New York's direction. In Game 6, he threw a runner out at the plate, singled and then later scored the deciding run to give the Yankees a win. With the Series on the line in Game 7, he hit a two-out, RBI single to drive home the go-ahead run. Howard was later given the Babe Ruth Award, presented by the Baseball Writers' Association of America, as the top player in the Series, although the *Sport* magazine World Series MVP Award was won by teammate Bob Turley.

This was certainly the Series of Bullet Bob Turley. He picked up two wins and a save in the Series—all in a span of just four days. Manager Casey Stengel had a lot of confidence in Turley, and for good reason. He pitched 16 1/3 innings in four games, and shut the Braves down with a single run in almost seven innings of relief in the deciding seventh game. Turley drove home the Corvette as the *Sport* magazine World Series MVP, and he finished second behind Red Sox slugger Jackie Jensen for the AL MVP. He also won the Cy Young Award as the game's best pitcher, the first Yankees pitcher to win the award, edging out runner-up Spahn by one vote. He was named both the *Sporting News* AL Pitcher of the Year and Major League Player of the Year. During the winter a panel of writers and broadcasters awarded him the diamond-studded Hickok Belt as the Professional Athlete of the Year. At 28, Turley was on top of the sports world.

The Yankees had their sweet revenge victory over the Braves, and Stengel, who had once managed the Braves when the team was based in Boston, had evened the score over the 1957 winners. The Series victory was the Yankees sixth of the decade and seventh in the last 10 years.

Stengel tied Joe McCarthy with seven World Series championships, a high-water mark for a major-league manager. Stengel toasted his team once more as the best in baseball, the best in New York. But he could hardly know that he was celebrating what would be his final World Series triumph.

1959: THE BEGINNING
OF THE END

WITH THE DODGERS AND GIANTS GONE FROM THE CITY AND TRANS-planted to California, the Yankees were the only baseball team in New York. The Yankees front office expected a big increase in attendance in 1958. That never materialized. The team ran away from the pack and sprinted to the pennant. A late-season slump and general fan disinterest combined to curb attendance. During the winter, the Yankees officials were bemoaning a drop in season attendance of 70,000 fannies in the seats. As the decade was winding to a close, the euphoria of Big Apple baseball was beginning to deteriorate.

Football now was the sport on everyone's mind. The New York football Giants also now called Yankee Stadium home, and on December 28, the Baltimore Colts beat the Giants, 23–17, in overtime at Yankee Stadium to win the National Football League championship. The thrilling climax to the pro football season has commonly come to be called "The Greatest Game Ever Played." The truth is, there have been far better played games in the history of the NFL. But for sheer drama and lasting impact, the 1958 title game stands alone. "It may have been the best thing to ever happen to the NFL," said Colts defensive tackle Art Donovan, one of the many future Pro Football Hall of Famers on the field that day. That's because nationally televised sports broadcasts still were relatively new. And because some 50 million Americans were glued to their television sets and transfixed by the spectacle of the tightly contested championship game, it generally is credited with putting the NFL into the national consciousness. Add to that the drama of a fourth-quarter comeback and the first overtime game in league history, and there's a reason the game earned its lofty title as the greatest ever. With the NFL championship at stake, a Yankee Stadium crowd of 64,185 watched the Colts tie the game, 17–17, on a Steve Myrha field goal with seven seconds left. Regulation play ended that way, and many of the players did not know what came next. After all, no NFL title game had ever been tied after four quarters. Sudden-death overtime is what they learned came next: The first team to score would win the game and the title. Eight minutes into professional football's first-ever sudden-death overtime period, Baltimore's Alan Ameche crashed through from the 1 yard line and barreled into the end zone for the winning touchdown, ending a contest that would help establish pro football as a major national sport. By the end of the next decade, the NFL would grow from 14 to 26 members because of a merger with the 10-year-old American Football League that was made in television heaven. After a whirlwind courtship in the 1950s, television executives made a solid commitment to sports programming—and particularly to pro football—as the new decade dawned. It was a sensible, mutually profitable marriage, a business arrangement that made plenty of dollars and sense.

Vince Lombardi was hired as the head coach of the Green Bay Packers on January 28. Although Lombardi had no previous NFL head coaching experience, he was the respected offensive coordinator for the Eastern Conference champion New York Giants. "Gentlemen, I've never been associated with a losing team," Lombardi told the Packers players in his first team meeting. "I do not intend to start now." Those were bold words, considering that Green Bay was just 1-10-1 in 1958. But Lombardi remained true to his intentions, and hiring him turned out to be a shrewd move by the Packers. In another fast-growing—and just plain fast—sport, NASCAR founder Bill France took stock cars off the beach, where they had been racing for years, and onto the newly built Daytona International Speedway for the inaugural Daytona 500 race. The finish was literally too close to call, as it took NASCAR three days to declare Lee Petty the winner. Fidel Castro marched into Havana to mark the success of the Cuban Revolution. The Barbie doll was introduced. Alaska became the 49th state, with Hawaii to follow as the 50th. *Bonanza*, the first television western series broadcast in color, began its 14-year run on NBC-TV. Along with the *Wonderful World of Disney*, *Bonanza* was responsible for boosting color TV sales from virtually nonexistent to more than 50 percent by 1971. Buddy Holly, Ritchie Valens, and the Big Bopper were killed in a plane crash.

The four-time defending American League champion New York Yankees still had an abundance of talent. Whitey Ford, Bob Turley, the reigning Cy Young Award winner, and Don Larsen fronted the pitching staff, followed by Duke Maas, Art Ditmar, and Bobby Shantz, with Ryne Duren in the bullpen waiting for the call. Mickey Mantle in center field disappointed a lot of folks by not batting .400 or breaking Babe Ruth's home run record, but the 27-year-old was capable of doing it this season, if he could just stay healthy. In right field, Hank Bauer at 36 was a tick slow getting around on a fastball, but was still one of the toughest hitters in the game with the winning run on base. Twenty-five-year-old Norm Siebern, despite his World Series setbacks, was slated to be the regular starting left fielder. Coming off his exquisite World Series exploits, a season of superiority was projected for 26-year-old first baseman Bill "Moose" Skowron. The double-play combination was comprised of two sure-handed 23-year-olds, with Tony Kubek the shortstop and Bobby Richardson taking over at second base. Gil McDougald, now 31, was a dandy utility infielder. The third base position was to be shared between the platoon of the righty-swinging Andy Carey and the lefty-swinging Jerry Lumpe, with Lumpe getting most of the playing time due to the predominance of right-handed pitching. Carey, still just 27, had once been the Yankees' primary third baseman, but he was no longer an everyday player. He started only 70 games in 1957 and 90 in '58. Carey had regressed as a hitter, a circumstance that caused manager Casey Stengel no end of frustration.

Yogi Berra was now 33 and had been a big-league catcher for 14 years and had caught more than 1,400 big-league games. He did not react quite so quickly behind the plate as he once did, and he did not throw so well anymore. In 1958, when Berra had slowed down, Elston Howard had stepped up and hit solidly. With the emergence of Howard at catcher, in 1959 Berra on occasion could be moved to left field to save his legs. But Berra, in a bad year for him, still hit 22 homers and drove in 90 runs. He wouldn't sit on the bench very often. The roster was turning over with newcomers Kubek, Richardson, Lumpe, and Siebern in the starting lineup, and yet the team's depth and versatility remained unmatched. Stengel could take Berra, Howard, McDougald, Kubek, Lumpe, Siebern, and Richardson, and mix them around to suit his fancy.

The 1959 Yankees squad, like all of the Yankees teams during the decade, was comprised of a roster perfectly constructed for a manager like Stengel who liked to tinker with his lineups. None of his teams during the decade had been loaded with superstars, nor had they crushed the opposition in the fashion of Joe McCarthy's squads of the 1930s. What the Stengel Yankees had was a balance of hitting, fielding, and pitching. In some cases, Stengel's Yankees would have five or six hitters with more than 10 home runs as well as five or six pitchers with 10 or more wins. Just once during the five pennant-winning seasons between 1949 and 1953 did the famed Bronx Bombers lead the league in home runs. In fact, Yankees teams of the decade were almost as likely to boast the league's best earned run average as they were to lead the league in homers. The team's hitters led the league in home runs four times while its pitchers recorded the lowest ERA five times during the decade. The Yankees under Stengel stressed fundamentals. The Old Perfessor believed that most games are lost, not won. Stengel had lineups with such typically sound all-around and versatile players as Bauer, Howard, Kubek, Martin, McDougald, Richardson, Rizzuto, and Woodling. The pitchers were in the same mold, capable of starting one game and relieving in another. One intangible all Stengel-led Yankees teams possessed was complete confidence in their ability to perform as a collective unit. Casey instilled confidence into his players. He was a great leader of men, and his Yankees teams were never inclined to play scared. Nor did they ever foolishly underestimate an opponent. The Yankees merely expected to win.

So it came as an awful surprise when the Yankees started the season miserably, falling below .500 at the end of April. The lone bright spot was Skowron, who rocketed out of the gate with 11 RBIs in his first seven games. He also showed a flair for the dramatic. On April 22, his solo home run to deep left field off Chuck Stobbs in the top of the 14th inning accounted for the lone run in the Yankees victory over the Washington Senators at Griffith Stadium. Ford went the distance for the win and fanned 15 batters, equaling the club mark established by Bob Shawkey in 1919. (Ron Guidry set a new record by striking out 18 California Angels batters in 1978.) The hard-fought victory was just what the Yankees needed to jump-start their season. But uncharacteristically, the team proceeded to lose nine of their next 10 games. The Yankees traveled to Los Angeles in early May to play an exhibition game to benefit the crippled Dodgers great Roy Campanella before a Memorial Coliseum crowd of 93,103—at the time, the largest crowd in baseball history. Another 15,000 fans were turned away at the gate. "Everybody loves Campy. He was like a little Santa Claus," said his former teammate Don Zimmer. The game, won by the Yankees, was a mere postscript to the main event of saluting Campanella. The emotional ceremony began with Pee Wee Reese pushing the wheelchair-bound catcher into the darkened stadium that was illuminated by fans holding lit candles flickering in the air.

Back to business, the Yankees hoped to get back on track after sweeping a doubleheader from the Washington Senators, winning 6–3 and 3–2, at Yankee Stadium on May 10. In the first game, Mantle smacked a 410-foot home run into the left field bullpen and scored two runs. In the second game, he singled and scored the winning run when Siebern doubled with one out in the bottom of the 10th inning. New

York teams of old would have put the pedal to the metal and taken off. Inexplicably, they stalled again, losing seven of eight games, and Berra's 148-game errorless streak came to an end when he made a throwing error on his 34th birthday. So badly were things going early in the season that on May 20 the Yankees sank into the AL cellar. It was the first time since May 1940 that the Bronx Bombers were in last place. Yankees haters were gleeful, and called the team the Basement Bombers. To make matters worse, Hoyt Wilhelm continued his dominance over them, pitching a one-hitter in the Orioles 5–0 victory at Memorial Stadium in Baltimore. Lumpe's single to left in the eighth spoiled the knuckleballer's bid for another no-hitter. New York now had lost 20 of its first 32 games. The team was still stationed in last place on May 30, the latest date in a season the Yankees were in last place since 1914 when they called the Polo Grounds home. The day the Yankees plunged into the basement, they truly hit rock bottom. Shantz and four relievers were ripped for 19 hits, including three homers, during a 13–6 drubbing by the Tigers at Yankee Stadium. The Yankee Killer, Frank Lary, tossed a complete game and improved to an 18-5 career mark against them. Frustration mounted for the few fans who remained. Mantle hit a meaningless two-run home run off Lary in the ninth inning. While rounding the bases on his home run, Mantle was lustily booed as the fans showed their disgust for the sinking fortunes of their team's woeful season. "I don't care who you are," said Mantle, "you hear those boos."

The Bronx Bombers, winners of nine AL pennant flags in 10 years, were the cellar-dwellers of the league. New York's pitching woes weighed down a team never able to join the race. The pitching staff was plagued by an unusually high number of sore arms. Ford's elbow was balky, Sturdivant had arm trouble again, and there were whispers Kucks, a good pitcher a few years back, but whose sinker failed him, might be all through. Many of the team's key position players were bedeviled by injuries. Howard, McDougald, and Bauer missed games with minor injuries, Mantle was out for more than a week with a broken finger, and Skowron, who was playing with a corset wrapped around his aching back, pulled a leg muscle running out an infield single that put him on the shelf for a while. With so many regulars missing from the lineup, the team was losing on a consistent basis. A flu bug struck down Mantle, Duren, Carey, and Sturdivant for varying lengths of time. Then a case of mononucleosis sidelined Carey for more than two months. The Yankees sick list read like an All-Star Game lineup. Perhaps the toughest break was the absence of Skowron, who was leading the team in home runs, batting average, and runs batted in. On July 25 in Detroit, he entered the game in the ninth inning as a pinch-hitter. He remained in the game at first base but while reaching for an errant throw collided with baserunner Coot Veal of the Tigers. The result was a fractured wrist and an end to Skowron's season. He appeared in only 74 games. Mantle was plagued by injuries throughout his career, but so was Skowron, never playing a full season through his first five campaigns. In 1955, he was out for more than 40 games with a torn thigh muscle; in '57, he missed 30 games after damaging his back lifting an air conditioner. At other various times, Moose had a separated shoulder, a torn knee, and strained ligaments. "He seems to like the clang of the ambulance," quipped Stengel.

Needing a starting third baseman and a pitching upgrade, the Yankees traded Sturdivant, Kucks, and Lumpe to Kansas City for Panamanian third baseman Hector Lopez and right-handed pitcher Ralph Terry. The Cleveland Indians slugger Rocky Colavito hit home runs in four consecutive at-bats in a game in Baltimore. Lou Gehrig had been the last player to homer in four straight trips to the plate, in 1932. The most bittersweet accomplishment of the season belonged to Harvey Haddix. For 12 innings, the Pittsburgh Pirates left-hander got out the host Milwaukee Braves in order. No one in Major League Baseball history ever had taken a perfect game to extra innings. The trouble was, Haddix's Pirates couldn't score off Braves starter Lew Burdette either. Finally, in the bottom of the 13th inning, Haddix lost it all on one swing of the bat by Joe Adcock. Golfer Mickey Wright won the US Women's Open at the Churchill Valley Country Club in Pittsburgh.

She was the first golfer to win consecutive Women's Open titles. Ohio State University junior Jack Nicklaus won the prestigious US Amateur golf championship.

The Yankees, accustomed to being the big man on campus, would eventually make a run at the top spot and, after beating the top-ranked White Sox in the opener of a big four-game weekend series on June 26, were only two games out of first place. The Yankees seemed poised to finally make their move. But it was not to be. They lost the next day when Turley was unable to protect a three-run lead, surrendering a two-out grand slam home run to Harry Simpson hit to deep right field in the bottom of the eighth inning. The next day they were swept in a Sunday doubleheader that featured Early Wynn's 9–2 win over Ford in the opener to fall back to fifth place. The season was in danger of wasting away when New York came to Boston on July 9 for a five-game series. The Yankees stood 4 1/2 games out of first place, and needed to make a statement. Everyone expected them to turn their season around; doing so at the expense of the Red Sox would be better still. It would not happen. The Yankees lost five straight at Fenway Park. Boston beat Turley, Ford, Terry, and Larsen by scores of 14–3, 8–5, 7–3, and 13–3. In the third game of the series, the New York bullpen imploded in the bottom of the 10th inning and Boston shortstop Don Buddin hit a game-ending grand slam home run off Turley in relief to slap the Yankees with a heartbreaking defeat. New York came to Beantown down 4 1/2 games and left town down 7 1/2 games, never to get much closer to the first place White Sox. The Yankees record dropped to a disappointing 41-43 mark as the massacre in Boston cast a pall over the season.

The best pitching duel of the year took place on the night of July 17 in the Bronx. Ralph Terry of the Yankees and White Sox veteran Early Wynn matched zeros for eight innings at Yankee Stadium. The two pitchers combined had allowed only one hit through eight innings, an infield single by Terry in the sixth. In the top of the ninth, Chicago rookie Jim McAnany singled to center to spoil Terry's no-hit bid. Jim Landis added a second hit to drive home two runs and give the Sox a 2–0 win. Wynn completed a dazzling two-hit shutout on his way to capturing the Cy Young Award. The game was a microcosm of the season for the Yankees. When they pitched well, they didn't hit; and when they hit well, their pitching collapsed. Mel Allen sparked a monumental television innovation as he worked the game for WPIX-TV. Videotape was just beginning to be used to show game highlights on Red Barber's postgame show. After McAnany's single to spoil the no-hit bid, Allen called to the director in the control room to see if he had videotaped McAnany's hit using the station's cutting-edge recording technology. He had, and WPIX showed the first instant replay (though it wasn't exactly instant). After a while, viewers finally saw McAnany's ground-ball single up the middle for a second time, in what may be the first baseball instant replay using videotape. Slow motion replay made its debut on television sports, but it was full speed ahead for professional football, which would overtake baseball as America's favorite sport in the coming decade. The rapidly growing popularity of pro football led to the formation of a new league to compete against the NFL. The American Football League made plans to start play in 1960.

Massachusetts senator John F. Kennedy, who was just beginning his campaign for the presidency, and his brother Bobby were sitting in the stands at Fenway Park on July 20. The Indians had built up a three-run lead over the Red Sox by the late innings, and there had been little for Boston fans to cheer about until the Red Sox had loaded the bases with two outs in the bottom of the ninth inning, bringing third baseman Frank Malzone to the plate. He drilled a double off the Green Monster to clear the bases and beat Cleveland. Perhaps the Kennedys had brought the luck of the Irish. The next day at Comiskey Park, Vic Wertz of the Red Sox singled to center in the eighth inning of a 2–1 loss to the Chicago White Sox. Boston manager Billy Jurges then sent Elijah Jerry "Pumpsie" Green into the game to run for Wertz. Green became the first African American to play for the Red Sox. Boston was the last of the 16 teams in the major leagues to field a black player, 12 years after Jackie Robinson. Green finished the season as a .233 hitter with one home run in 50 games, beginning an unspectacular five-year career. This was the first year that Major League Baseball broke with tradition and played two All-Star Games, in an effort to boost the players' pension fund. In the inaugural All-Star "doubleheader" each league scored a win, with the NL triumphing, 5–4, at Forbes Field in Pittsburgh on July 7, and the AL winning, 5–3, at the Los Angeles Memorial Coliseum, the first All-Star Game played on the West Coast, on August 3. Willie Mays's triple in the bottom of the eighth inning off Whitey Ford plated Henry Aaron and was the difference in the NL victory in the first game. The triple made Mays 4-for-4 in four All-Star Games against Ford. Don Drysdale of the Dodgers started both games for the NL. In the first game, he pitched three perfect innings. But he took the loss in the second game, allowing a Yogi Berra third-inning home run that put the AL ahead for good.

The All-Star Games of the decade served to remind fans in case anyone had forgotten: Many of the very best players in the sport were African-American. This was the heyday of Mays and Aaron, Ernie Banks and Don Newcombe, and Frank Robinson and Jim Gilliam. The American League integrated more slowly, and it's inarguable that this allowed the National League to develop a near-monopoly on black superstars in the 1950s. The AL had previously dominated All-Star Games from 1933 to 1949, winning 12 of the first 16 Midsummer Classics. But beginning in 1950, the NL became the dominant league, winning 33 of the next 42 All-Star Games (with one tie). Not only was the NL dominant over the AL in All-Star Game play, for that matter, African-American players dominated the NL awards in the 1950s. Black players who won the NL Rookie of the Year Award in the decade were Sam Jethroe in 1950, Mays in 1951, Joe Black in '52, Gilliam in '53, Robinson in '56, and Willie McCovey in '59. Campanella's MVP award in 1951 was the first of three for him in the 1950s. Mays won in '54, and Newcombe, Aaron, and Banks also won MVPs. Banks was the first black player to win the award twice in a row when he earned it in 1958 and '59. When Newcombe won his MVP in '56, he also won a brand new award as well: the Cy Young Award to honor the league's best pitcher. Baseball hadn't even been integrated for a decade, and there was Newcombe, a black man, standing alone as the first player to have Rookie of the Year, MVP, and Cy Young awards in his trophy case. From 1949 (when Jackie Robinson was the first black player named MVP) to 1959, black players claimed nine of 11 NL MVP awards. The AL simply had no comparable black players. It should be granted that the MVP award, like the league championship, was being passed around the Yankees clubhouse during this period. With nine pennants in 11 years, it's to be expected that New York was going to be disproportionately represented in the AL MVP voting—and they were, taking six awards from 1949 to 1959.

The Little League World Series was played for the first time at its present site in Williamsport, Pennsylvania. Hamtramck, Michigan won the championship by beating Auburn, California, in the final. Hamtramck became the first team from the United States to win the tournament since foreign teams had begun to participate. NASA announced the selection of America's first seven astronauts, who possessed the right stuff for the first orbital flight to take place in 1962. Americans bought 100 million Hula Hoops. Pantyhose were rolled out. Paul Anka had a hit with "Put Your Head on My Shoulder" and Chubby Checker performed "The Twist" on *American Bandstand*, launching a dance craze.

The Yankees continued to trip over themselves, playing only well enough to bounce around the .500 mark. Hope sprung when they swept a doubleheader from the visiting White Sox before 57,000 fans at Yankee Stadium on July 19, winning the second game, 6–4, on Mantle's 20th home run of the season. In the first game, 43-year-old outfielder Enos Slaughter belted a pair of two-run home runs in a 6–2 win. Once again, it was all just a tease to tantalize the fan base. Unlike years past, when the Yankees would take off on one of their inevitable summer hot streaks, New York continued to stumble in July, posting a losing record for the month that dropped them down to fifth place and out of contention, 10 1/2 games back. In August, the team won as many games as they lost, and plummeted in the standings to 16 1/2 games behind the pennant-bound White Sox. They were under .500 as late as Labor Day, and were mathematically eliminated from the race on September 9. "You kind of took it for granted around the Yankees that there was always going to be baseball in October," lamented Ford.

The Yankees were brought down by a combination of subpar performances from Mantle and Turley, and from aging players Berra and Bauer whose best years were well behind them. Mantle still hit for power, with 31 home runs, but his batting average dipped to .285 and his RBIs, 75, had fallen off badly. Berra, Siebern, and Bauer all experienced dropoffs in their production, too. Richardson and Kubek both hit well for average, but they combined for only eight homers. Lopez, obtained from the A's early in the season, was a pleasant surprise with 16 homers, 69 RBIs, and a .283 batting average, while Howard hit for power, with 18 homers and 73 RBIs. Stengel's annual prediction that Berra would catch less was again wrong. In fact, Yogi caught 116 games, more than the previous year. Though Howard reached his career high in games played, the platoon system made him feel like a part-time player, with 50 games at first base, 44 behind the plate, and 28 in the outfield. Ford was again the big mound winner, with 16 victories, followed by Maas with 14, and Ditmar with 13, but the rest of the pitching staff, with the exception of Duren, had poor showings. Duren hit his stride and was extraordinary out of the bullpen. He made 17 consecutive relief appearances, from May 10 through July 14, without giving up a run, a stretch of 31 1/3 scoreless innings, but his season ended abruptly in September when he fell at Yankee Stadium and broke his wrist. He ended his second superb season with 14 saves, 96 strikeouts in 76 innings, and a career-low 1.88 ERA.

It was a dismal year for the Yankees. After four consecutive pennants, the Bronx Bombers bombed out, finishing in third place, 15 games behind the AL champion White Sox, who were managed by Al Lopez, the same man who managed the Cleveland Indians when they finished ahead of the Yankees in 1954. "Injuries ruined the team," general manager George Weiss explained, but he also thought that his players maybe weren't hungry enough. The Yankees won only four games more than they lost. Their final record of 79-75 was their worst showing in 34 years. Despite his long record of success in New York, there were rumblings for 68-year-old Yankees manager Casey Stengel to be canned. After the season, Weiss's primary focus was on getting the players needed to rebuild the Yankees and restock the farm teams. As the fall of 1959 progressed, it became clear that to be back on top in 1960, Weiss was willing to consider trading almost any of his veterans (except Mantle) to obtain reliable hitting, preferably a left-handed-hitting corner outfielder. Weiss turned to the Kansas City Athletics, his one reliable trading partner, and by giving Kansas City four Yankees players—veteran Hank Bauer, former outstanding pitcher Don Larsen, talented young outfielder Norm Siebern, and the ever-promising first

After dominating major league baseball for most of the 1950s, the Yankees ended the decade in disappointing fashion, finishing third in the American League with a 79-75 record. Here, a young fan watches batting practice before a late-season game against the Red Sox and looks forward to "next year" and a new decade.
PHOTO BY LYNN HARRINGTON. REPRINTED BY PERMISSION OF SHERWOOD HARRINGTON

baseman "Marvelous" Marv Throneberry—he finally acquired Roger Maris, a player whose development he had been watching all season, as well as Kent Hadley and Joe DeMaestri. Bauer, who won nine AL pennants and seven World Series during his 11 seasons with the team, heard of the trade on the radio and, though he thought he deserved better, he understood the business of the game. "When you're walking to the bank with that World Series check every November, you don't want to leave," he said. "There were no Yankees saying, 'Play me or trade me.'"

Yet another trade between the Yankees and Athletics raised eyebrows. The A's had relocated to Kansas City from Philadelphia following the 1954 season. Owner Arnold Johnson had owned Yankee Stadium, as well as being a friend and business associate of Yankees owners Dan Topping and Del Webb. This association prompted much speculation, and at times open outcry, about deals between the two clubs. Between 1955 and 1959, the two teams engineered 16 trades, involving 61 players, making it appear that Kansas City was no more than a minor-league outpost for New York. The Chicago White Sox general manager, the former major-league slugger Hank Greenberg, was widely quoted as saying to Weiss, "It sure must be great to have your own farm team right there in your own league." To all experienced baseball observers it was clear that the smooth-swinging, left-handed-hitting Maris was the centerpiece of the trade. Slotted to replace Bauer in right field, Weiss fully expected that the 25-year-old Maris, a pull-hitting outfielder with power, would take full advantage of Yankee Stadium's short right field porch. Maris was projected to team with Mantle to anchor a lineup that was determined to return the Bronx Bombers to their accustomed spot atop the baseball world. The deal for Maris would turn out to be Weiss's last major trade for the Yankees and his last great coup as general manager.

The team rebounded in 1960 to capture the pennant before losing a heartbreaking seven-game World Series to the Pittsburgh Pirates. In the aftermath of the 1960 Series, Topping eased both Stengel and Weiss out of their positions. At Topping's request both the 70-year-old manager and the 66-year-old general manager announced at their press conferences that they had decided to retire. Stengel managed to convey that he was not quitting voluntarily, implying that the Yankees had labeled him too old to manage. "I'll never make the mistake of being 70 again," he said. While the Yankees appeared in the World Series each year over the next five years, they won just twice, and then fell into a drought of 12 years without another postseason appearance.

Today, people look back on the 1950s with misty-eyed nostalgia. It was the time of the hip-swiveling, groundbreaking music of Elvis Presley, the wacky comedy of *I Love Lucy*, the screaming teens of *American Bandstand*, the fads of 3-D movies, and college kids stuffing themselves into phone booths. It all seemed so simple and innocent then. Of course, there was that hydrogen bomb thing, too, with the world for the first time facing the possibility that humans could destroy themselves completely. The Cold War, a war of competing ideologies, bred constant tension between the Soviet Union and the West. Indeed, as was the case in any other decade, the 1950s were a mishmash of the good and bad, the wonderful and the tragic, the thrilling and the ordinary. And, as in any other decade, sports in America provided a similar mix of highlights and lowlights. Mississippi State's basketball team in 1959, winners of 24 out of 25 games and ranked number three in the country, declined an invitation to play in the National Collegiate Athletic Association championship because that NCAA tournament was integrated. The 1960s would bring sweeping changes to sports and society, but that decade would have to wait.

EPILOGUE

THE YANKEES PLAYED IN EIGHT WORLD SERIES IN THE 1950S, WIN-
ning six of them. Even when the Yankees didn't win the World Series,
it was still a New York story. From the National League, the New York
Giants won in 1954 and the Brooklyn Dodgers in 1955. Baseball fans
living in the Big Apple had only to board a subway to see every game
in the World Series in five different seasons of the 1950s. After the
1957 season, the Dodgers moved to Los Angeles and the Giants moved
to San Francisco. The West Coast edition of the Dodgers and Giants
faced the Yankees five more times in the World Series, the Yankees
winning in 1962, 1977, and 1978, and losing in 1963 and 1981.

Major League Baseball named Joe DiMaggio as "The Greatest
Living Player" in 1969. That year, Paul Simon remembered DiMaggio in song, wondering where the former baseball star had gone. The
song "Mrs. Robinson," written by Simon and performed by Simon
and Garfunkel, won the Grammy Award for Record of the Year. The
reference to DiMaggio is "one of the most well-known lines that I've
ever written," said Simon, who grew up a fan of Mickey Mantle. When
asked why Mantle wasn't mentioned in the song instead of DiMaggio,
Simon explained that the number of syllables in DiMaggio's name fit
the beat. For his part, DiMaggio, sensitive to any derogatory public
comment that could affect his legacy, was puzzled by Simon's lyric,
saying he hadn't gone anywhere, and sought an answer to the meaning
of the song when he and Simon were dining at the same New York
restaurant. Only when Simon explained his motives to express a feeling
that true heroes are a thing of the past, and that the line was meant as a

sincere tribute to DiMaggio's grace and dignity, was DiMaggio molli-fied. When DiMaggio died in 1999 at the age of 84, Simon performed "Mrs. Robinson" at Yankee Stadium in DiMaggio's honor.

Despite an injury-riddled career, Mickey Mantle put up impressive numbers. He played in 20 All-Star Games, led the league in home runs four times, and hit .300 or better 10 times. He was a three-time American League Most Valuable Player and finished in the top five another six times. He played on 12 pennant winners and seven world championship teams. He holds World Series records for home runs (18), runs scored (42), RBIs (40), walks (43), extra-base hits (26), and total bases (123). "He is the best one-legged player I ever saw play the game," said his manager Casey Stengel. In his final World Series, in 1964 against the St. Louis Cardinals, Mantle hit three round-trippers, drove in eight runs, and batted .333. That season marked the end of the lengthy Yankees dynasty that had started in the 1920s with Babe Ruth, and peaked in the years from 1949 to 1964. Mantle's fortunes sank along with those of his team. By 1968 he could no longer take the pain of playing every day and his numbers reflected it. At 37, he had undergone seven surgeries in his career. On the eve of the 1969 season, Mantle decided that he did not want to sign a contract, and he retired. The team and fans paid tribute to the last great superstar of the Yankees dynasty by retiring his uniform jersey number 7 at a Mickey Mantle Day ceremony at Yankee Stadium, on June 8, 1969. In his speech, Man-tle spoke of the Yankees tradition. "To retire my number with numbers 3, 4, and 5 tops off everything," he said. "I often wondered how a man who knew he was dying could get up here and say he's the luckiest man in the world. Now I think I know how Lou Gehrig felt." Mantle was elected to the Hall of Fame in 1974. As the first baseball star Yankees fans could watch on television, he remains a fan favorite and is still one of baseball's most popular superstars even 50 years after playing his last game. Early in 1995 he was diagnosed with liver cancer, brought on by his years of hard drinking. He had a liver transplant but died in August of that year at age 63.

Roger Maris and Mantle formed one of the best one-two punches in the sport; they were known as The M & M Boys. Maris won the 1960 AL Most Valuable Player Award in his first year with the Yankees, batting .283 with 39 home runs and 112 RBIs. In 1961, he broke Babe Ruth's single-season record for home runs in a season with 61, a record he held until 1998. Maris again won the AL MVP Award in 1961 with his 61 homers and 141 RBIs. With the Yankees, Maris won the World Series in 1961 and '62. He also won the World Series again in 1967 with the St. Louis Cardinals.

Whitey Ford was the only Yankees pitcher of the era to make it into the Hall of Fame. He is the club's all-time leader in games won, games started, innings pitched, shutouts, and strikeouts. Ford's lifetime record of 236-106 gives him a career winning percentage of .690, the highest of any major-league pitcher since 1900 with 200 or more wins. He also posted a consistently low earned run average that stayed below three in 11 of his 16 major-league seasons, never rising higher than 3.24 throughout his career. Ford led the American League in victories three times and in earned run average and shutouts twice. He won the Cy Young Award in 1961, when pitchers in both leagues competed for only one award. Ford saved his most impressive performances for when it counted most—in the World Series. The Yankees won 11 pennants during Ford's years with the club, and he helped the Yankees win eight World Series titles. Had it not been for Army duty during the Korean War, he would have won two more, in 1951 and '52. The left-hander still holds several important World Series pitching records, including most Series (11), most games (22), most opening-game starts (eight), most innings pitched (146), most strikeouts (94), and most wins (10). He allowed only 44 earned runs in his 22 World Series starts. "If the World Series was on the line and I could pick one pitcher to pitch the game, I'd choose Whitey Ford every time," said teammate and lifelong pal Mickey Mantle. In 1960 and '61, Ford started four World Series games, won them all, and allowed no runs. On his way to his fourth straight World Series shutout in Game 4 of the 1961 Series, Ford injured his ankle and had to leave the game. He departed that game with a streak of 32 consecutive scoreless innings, having broken Babe Ruth's World Series record. As a Boston Red Sox pitcher, the Babe pitched 29 consecutive scoreless innings in the 1916 and 1918 World Series. Ruth would often say this was his proudest accomplishment in baseball, greater than any of his batting feats. In the 1962 Series, Ford continued his streak, ending up with 33 consecutive scoreless innings— still the World Series record for a starting pitcher. The Yankees manager, Casey Stengel, limited Ford's starts, resting him four or five days between appearances, and saving him for use against the better teams in the league. Stengel would hold out Ford against cellar-dwelling teams like the Washington Senators and Philadelphia Athletics, so he could start against division rivals such as the Cleveland Indians and Detroit Tigers. Only once during the decade under Stengel did Ford start more than 30 games in a season. But in 1961, when Ralph Houk took over as the Yankees manager, he moved Ford into a regular four-man rotation and the durable lefty thrived on the bigger workload. In 1961, Ford led the league with 39 games started—10 more than the year before—and innings pitched (283). He posted a spectacular 25-4 record to lead the major leagues in wins and winning percentage (.862). That season, he won his only Cy Young Award and then earned the World Series Most Valuable Player Award. Two years later, at the age of 35, he started 37 times and went 24-7. It's possible that Stengel's conservative use of Ford might have robbed the pitcher of at least 40 more career wins. In 1963, Ford again led the league in wins with 24, winning percentage at .774, games started, and innings pitched. After 13 straight seasons of at least 11 victories, Ford suffered his first losing seasons in 1966 and '67, his final major-league campaigns. Still, he sported impressive earned run averages of 2.47 and 1.64, respectively. After retiring following the 1967 season, Whitey and his good buddy Mickey were enshrined in the Hall of Fame together in 1974.

The Yankees retired Phil Rizzuto's jersey number 10 and dedicated a plaque in Monument Park at Yankee Stadium, on August 4, 1985, the day when Tom Seaver won his 300th career game, becoming the first to ever achieve the feat at Yankee Stadium. Among many of the gifts given to Rizzuto as part of the pregame festivities, the Yankees brought on to the field a cow wearing a halo—a real, live holy cow, named Huckleberry. For some reason, Rizzuto's Hall of Fame induction vote total always seemed to come up short, even though he was an integral member of seven World Series winning teams. Throughout the years of being passed over for the Hall, he had said he would accept entrance any way into Cooperstown—"If they want a batboy, I'll go in as a batboy." In 1994, after a 38-year wait, Scooter finally did get the call telling him that he was voted into the Hall of Fame.

By the late 1950s, with the emergence of Elston Howard at catcher, Yogi Berra had moved to left field to save his legs. From there, he helped the Yankees win two more World Series in 1961 and '62—bringing Yogi's record total to 10 World Series rings won as a player. He holds World Series records for at-bats, games, hits, and doubles. He played 19 years in the majors and played in 18 All-Star Games. When he retired, his 313 career home runs as a catcher (358 overall) stood as the record for catchers until Johnny Bench, Carlton Fisk, and then Mike Piazza broke it. He was elected to the Hall of Fame in 1972 and was chosen to baseball's All-Century Team for the 1900s. When he retired as a player in 1963, he immediately took over as manager of the Yankees, leading the team to the 1964 World Series against the Cardinals. He lasted one season in that role, but moved across town to become a coach with the Mets in 1965. Berra became manager of the Mets in 1972 and managed the team to the 1973 World Series. He returned to manage the Yankees to a third-place finish in 1984, but was unceremoniously fired just 16 games into the '85 season, vowing never to enter Yankee Stadium while George Steinbrenner owned the team. After 14 years of self-imposed exile, Berra had settled his differences with The Boss, and returned to Yankee Stadium for Yogi Berra Day, on July 18, 1999. Don Larsen threw out the ceremonial first pitch to Berra, who had been Larsen's battery mate in the only World Series perfect game at Yankee

Stadium in 1956. Pitching for the Yankees that day was David Cone, who pitched a perfect game of his own.

Elston Howard bided his time in the outfield while catcher Berra still was in the prime of his career. In time, Howard would become a star himself. He topped a .300 batting average three times, with a career-best .348 average in 1961. By then, he was the catcher and Berra had been moved to left field. Howard proved to be an excellent receiver. A two-time Gold Glove Award catcher, his career fielding average of .993 ranks among the highest ever for a catcher. A baseball pioneer, Howard was one of the first catchers to use a hinged catcher's mitt, which eventually led to the modern one-handed catching technique popularized by Cincinnati's Johnny Bench in the early 1970s. Howard also popularized the use of the batting donut, a donut-shaped weight that slips over the bat and allows the on-deck batter to swing a heavier bat, so it will feel lighter when he's at the plate. In the past, waiting batters had swung several bats at the same time. Howard batted .274 and slugged 167 home runs during his 14-year career. His best season was in 1963, when he won the American League's Most Valuable Player Award—the first African American to win the award in the AL. (Black players had won it in the National League 12 times.) That season, Howard hit .287 with 28 home runs and 85 runs batted in to lead New York to a first-place finish for a fourth consecutive season. "The Most Valuable Player isn't me," Howard told reporters after winning the award. "He wasn't playing. If Mickey Mantle had been in there, he'd have won it." Howard was selling himself short, for he may have been the only person in 1963 who did not believe he was deserving of the award. Thanks to Howard's leadership, the Yankees, incredibly, overcame injuries that would have decimated most other teams. Mantle hit 15 home runs in 65 games before being sidelined with a broken foot and torn knee cartilage. Maris played in only 90 games that season, but the Yanks persevered and even prospered. With Howard behind the plate, flawlessly handling the pitching staff and driving in a bushel of clutch runs, New York won the AL pennant by 10 1/2 games. The only sour note in the season was their staggering loss to the Los Angeles Dodgers in the World Series in four straight games. Howard played over 1,400 games with the Yankees and was an AL All-Star nine consecutive years from 1956 to 1965. He was also a member of AL pennant-winning Yankees teams in nine of his first 10 seasons. Ironically, Howard finished his career with the Red Sox in 1968. Only nine years earlier, Boston had become the last major-league team to integrate. The Yankees traded Howard to the Red Sox in August 1967 and he helped spark their amazing run to the World Series, only to lose to the St. Louis Cardinals in seven games. It was the sixth time Howard had played on a World Series–losing team, a record he shares with Pee Wee Reese of the Brooklyn Dodgers. Howard was a member of four World Series–winning teams with the Yankees. Always a respected clubhouse leader, after Howard retired he became a Yankees coach until his death in 1980. His uniform number 32 was retired in 1984 and a plaque unveiled in Monument Park that reads: "A man of great gentleness and dignity . . . one of the truly great Yankees."

Following his World Series perfect game, Don Larsen pitched well for two more years for the Yankees, but never again had a brush with greatness. By the summer of '59 there was talk of moving him, because of his strong bat, to the outfield (which never happened), and after that season he was traded to Kansas City, where he lost 10 of 11 decisions. He was mainly a relief pitcher in his declining years, and for a variety of teams. Coincidentally he did beat the Yankees in a Series game at Yankee Stadium six years to the day after his perfect game, despite pitching only a third of an inning. He was pitching for the San Francisco Giants then, and he entered Game 4 of the 1962 World Series in the sixth inning in relief of Bobby Bolin. Larsen pitched to two batters and got the side out in a tie game. He was lifted for a pinch-hitter, Bob Nieman, in the next inning. Nieman walked to load the bases, and Giants second baseman Chuck Hiller then hit a grand slam to win the game for San Francisco. Larsen was the winning pitcher. He never pitched in another World Series, and he won only 12 games in the next four years before calling it a career in 1967 at the age of 38. He finished with a lifetime record of 81-91. "People said I didn't do enough in my career," Larsen said, "and maybe they're right. But I had one great day."

Bill Skowron played in seven World Series with the Yankees, winning four rings. He hit .375 in the 1960 Series against Pittsburgh with two home runs and six RBIs. The Yankees bested the Cincinnati Reds in the 1961 World Series in five games, with Skowron adding a homer and five RBIs. The Yankees made it two straight world championships in 1962 with a hard-fought Series triumph over the San Francisco Giants. Skowron scored the only run in the deciding Game 7 on a double-play grounder by Tony Kubek. Following the 1962 season, the Yankees, in need of pitching help and with young first baseman Joe Pepitone waiting in the wings, traded Skowron to the Los Angeles Dodgers for right-handed pitcher Stan Williams. Skowron batted .294 as a member of the Yankees, with a .346 on-base percentage and a .496 slugging percentage. When he was traded he seriously considered retiring. His alma mater, Purdue University, offered him the head baseball coaching position. He turned it down and reported to Los Angeles. Skowron hit only .203 with a meager four home runs, but when the Dodgers met the Yankees in the 1963 World Series, the Moose went loose. He batted .385, hit a home run, and drove in three runs as the Dodgers beat the Yankees in four straight games.

As a ballplayer, Jerry Coleman played on Yankees teams that won four World Series titles and he was the Most Valuable Player of the 1950 World Series. But he earned a spot in the Baseball Hall of Fame as a broadcaster. Coleman began his broadcasting career in 1960 with CBS-TV conducting pregame interviews on the network's *Game of the Week* broadcasts. Three years later, he began a seven-year stint calling Yankees games on WCBS radio and WPIX-TV. It was Coleman who called Mickey Mantle's 500th career home run in 1967. Coleman became the lead radio announcer for the San Diego Padres in 1972, a position he held until his death in 2014 at age 89—except for 1980, when the Padres convinced him to manage the team. He was known in San Diego for his signature catch phrases: "Oh Doctor!" and "You can hang a star on that one, baby!", which he would deliver after a spectacular play. Coleman received the Ford C. Frick Award in 2005 for his broadcasting contributions.

Despite pitching only eight seasons for the Yankees, Allie Reynolds ranks among the team's all-time Top 10 in wins (131), win-loss percentage (.686), and shutouts (27)—and his 41 saves rank in the Top 20. In his eight years in New York he started 209 regular-season games and relieved in 86. In 1989, he was honored with a plaque in Monument Park at Yankee Stadium.

The 1958 World Series was Hank Bauer's ninth and last as a member of the Yankees, but he appeared in one more eight years later, when he managed the Baltimore Orioles to a four-game sweep of the Los Angeles Dodgers.

Johnny Mize collected four World Series rings with New York, hitting .286 with three homers and nine RBIs in 18 Fall Classic games. By the time he retired, he had played in 10 All-Star Games and homered in every major-league stadium. Though he missed three prime seasons to serve in the US Navy during World War II, Mize had a career batting average of .312 with 359 home runs, 1,337 runs batted in, 2,011 hits, and his .562 career slugging percentage ranks 13th all time. He was inducted into the Baseball Hall of Fame in 1981, after waiting nearly 30 years.

Billy Martin's passion for drinking and fighting overshadowed a brilliant career as a clutch performer. The trade following the Copacabana incident to Kansas City in 1957 was the start of Martin's travels—from the A's to the Tigers to the Indians to the Reds to the Braves to the Twins, before embarking on a stormy managing career. As a manager, his burning desire to win helped propel the Yankees to the American League pennant in 1976 and a World Series championship in 1977. Whenever he put on the Yankees uniform as a player or as a manager, Martin instilled a fiery emotion in his teams. Unfortunately, he is best remembered as a hard-drinking brawler whose battles during the 1970s with Reggie Jackson and George Steinbrenner turned Yankee Stadium into the Bronx Zoo. During his five separate stints as New York's skipper, Martin became involved in several highly publicized drunken fights that each time would lead to his undoing. "Billy the Kid" got bounced from a Texas strip club; threw punches at pitcher Ed Whitson in the parking lot of a Baltimore drinking establishment; and flattened a marshmallow salesman at a hotel bar in Minnesota, to name but a few incidents. Alcohol also played a part in Martin's death on a snowy Christmas Day in 1989. The 61-year-old was a passenger in a car driven by his friend when the vehicle slid off the road and crashed in upstate New York, less than a mile from Martin's home. Both men were drunk at the time of the accident. The driver survived, but Billy did not.

After slipping to a third-place finish in 1959, George Weiss retooled the Yankees and the team returned to the World Series the next year. For this accomplishment, Weiss was named the *Sporting News* Executive of the Year for a fourth time, more than anyone else in the history of the award. But Weiss and Stengel were "retired" by the Yankees after the disappointing 1960 Series loss. Weiss still had one last act. National League baseball returned to New York with the expansion Mets in 1962. Weiss was named the team's president, and immediately hired his old friend Casey Stengel to manage the club. The on-field results were historically poor. The '62 Mets posted the worst record (40-120) in MLB history, and the next three seasons the team lost 111, 109, and 112 games. After the 1966 season, the 72-year-old Weiss finally retired. He was inducted into the Baseball Hall of Fame in 1971, and died one year later. Stengel lamented his friend's passing, saying, "George's death is a tough thing on baseball. He was successful and great and capable in every way, shape, and form. He wasn't a terrific mixer but George sure knew how to pick men. Why, you can't stay in baseball that long by pulling players out of an icebox."

With the Mets Stengel served as front man for a team of lovable losers he dubbed "the Amazin' Metsies" for four seasons before retiring in 1965. Warren Spahn was on Stengel's horrible 1942 Boston Braves and also pitched again for Stengel on the terrible 1965 Mets, at the age of 44. Spahn famously said: "I played for Casey before and after he was a genius." The next year, Stengel was elected to the Hall of Fame, and his number 37 jersey is retired by both the Yankees and the Mets. Stengel died in 1975.

Ted Williams's career statistics—including 521 home runs and 1,839 runs batted in—are doubly impressive when you consider that he missed nearly five full seasons to the wars. Since he averaged 32 home runs a year through 1951, it's reasonable to speculate that he lost 150 homers while in the service. And he still came within 300-odd hits of attaining the magical 3,000 hits mark. Coincidentally, Casey Stengel and Williams were enshrined together at the Baseball Hall of Fame in 1966. Stengel did not have to wait long after his managing days to be enshrined into the Hall of Fame. The Veterans Committee voted him in just seven months after he managed his final game for the New York Mets. Williams was also voted into the Hall of Fame in atypical fashion. Despite his sometimes-stormy relationship with the media, Williams received 282 votes by the writers, which was the most in Hall of Fame history at that time. He received 93.4 percent of the vote and became just the eighth player elected by the Baseball Writers' Association of America on his first appearance on the ballot. In his storied career, Williams was never afraid to be himself. He refused to tip his cap to fans for most of his 19 seasons in Boston, and maintained a contentious relationship with reporters. Yet Williams's fearlessness showed in other, more noble ways. He served in two wars, even though it cost him some of the prime years of his career. And in his Hall of Fame induction speech on July 25, 1966, he advocated for the inclusion of African-American players. "I hope that some day the names of Satchel Paige and Josh Gibson in some way could be added as a symbol of the great Negro players that are not here only because they were not given the chance," Williams told the crowd. African-American players who had played in the Negro Leagues prior to Major League Baseball's integration had no representation in the Hall of Fame to that point. "That was a groundbreaking statement, and it opened people's eyes to the other half of baseball history," said James A. Reilly, author of *The Biographical Encyclopedia of the Negro Leagues.* "It definitely had a positive effect on getting Negro Leaguers into the Hall." In 1971, baseball commissioner Bowie Kuhn established a commission to induct Negro Leagues legends. Both Paige and Gibson led the list of inductees.

Herb Score was on his way to superstardom when a batted ball hit by Gil McDougald felled him. Although his vision returned after being hit by the line drive, Score's career was effectively ruined. Clearly lacking his pre-injury dominance, he never recovered his brilliant form, thanks in part to elbow problems, winning just 17 more games over five years with the Indians and White Sox. Score retired after 1962, and then broadcast Indians baseball games for more than 30 years. Bob Feller, who was near the end of his career when Score arrived, likened him to Sandy Koufax of the Dodgers, a future Hall of Famer. "Herb Score had just as good a curveball as Koufax and a better fastball," he said. "He would have been probably one of the greatest, if not the greatest, left-handed pitchers who ever lived."

Gil McDougald never had another good year with the bat after the incident involving Herb Score and retired after the 1960 season, at age 33, when it appeared that either the Los Angeles Angels or the Washington Senators would pick him up in the first expansion draft in baseball history. Even though he had a few seasons left, McDougald decided to retire rather than leave the Yankees.

Bobby Richardson was selected to the American League All-Star team eight times as a sure-handed second baseman for the Yankees from 1955 to 1966, winning the Gold Glove Award five times. He was also a pesky batter who was nearly impossible to strike out. He fanned only 22 times in 630 plate appearances during the 1963 regular season. Richardson was at his best in World Series play. In 1960 against Pittsburgh, he drove in 12 runs, including six in one game, and made history as the only World Series Most Valuable Player to be chosen from the losing team. In the 1964 Series he collected a record 13 hits against the St. Louis Cardinals.

Ralph Terry's name is synonymous with one of the most famous moments in baseball history. He surrendered a home run to Pittsburgh second baseman Bill Mazeroski in the bottom of the ninth in Game 7 of the 1960 World Series, to win the championship for the Pirates. The home run was the most dramatic conclusion to a Game 7 in World Series history. Afterward in the Yankees clubhouse, the press hounded Terry, the losing pitcher. When asked if he had thrown Mazeroski a fastball or curve, a dejected Terry said, "I don't know what the pitch was. All I know is it was the wrong one." Two years later, Terry was standing nervously on the mound at San Francisco's Candlestick Park in the bottom of the ninth inning of Game 7 of the 1962 World Series. The Yankees were clinging to a 1–0 lead, but the Giants had runners on second and third, with the left-handed slugging Willie McCovey coming to bat. Yankees manager Ralph Houk went to the mound to speak to his pitching ace. Terry was the American League's most winning and most durable pitcher in 1962 with 23 wins and 299 innings pitched. He also surrendered a league-high 40 home runs, the most ever given up by a Yankees pitcher in a season. Traditional strategy in such a tight spot says to intentionally walk McCovey, creating a force at any base, and pitch to the next batter, the right-handed-hitting Orlando Cepeda, also no slouch. Houk asked his pitcher what he wanted to do. "I'd just as soon get it over now," Terry replied. At this tense moment Terry could only be thinking that he had been in this situation two years earlier, facing Mazeroski. Now Terry was facing another confrontation that would end with him being a Series hero or goat. If Terry could get McCovey out, it would be his Fall Classic redemption. With two outs and the World Series on the line, Terry let fly a fastball. McCovey nailed it, smashing a blistering line drive that was heading toward right field like a bullet. But second baseman Bobby Richardson speared the ball in his mitt for the final out. "I really didn't have time to think about it," Richardson recalled. "It was just hit too hard." The Yankees were champions for the second straight season and had captured the World Series flag for the 20th time in their history. Terry, who was named the

Series Most Valuable Player, had atoned for losing the seventh game against Pittsburgh in 1960 by shutting out the Giants on four hits in a nerve-wracking Game 7 that clinched the 1962 Series for New York, four games to three.

Art Ditmar won 47 games in a span of five seasons with the Yankees, with a career high of 15 in 1960. He was traded—where else?—to the Kansas City Athletics in the middle of the '61 season. Ditmar was back in the news after a Budweiser television commercial of the 1980s incorporated the original radio broadcast of the 1960 World Series Game 7, with announcer Chuck Thompson incorrectly naming Ditmar instead of Ralph Terry as the pitcher off whom Bill Mazeroski hit his legendary home run.

Jackie Robinson played 10 years in the major leagues, batting .311. He was a six-time All-Star and played in six World Series. In 1962, in his first year of eligibility, Robinson was inducted into the Baseball Hall of Fame. He died of a heart attack in 1972 at age 53. In 1997, Major League Baseball celebrated the golden anniversary of Robinson's landmark season integrating baseball by officially retiring his uniform number 42. Each April 15th since 2009, all players across the big leagues have donned number 42 jerseys to celebrate Jackie Robinson Day.

Left-handed pitcher Sandy Koufax struggled with control at first, but when the Dodgers moved to Los Angeles he found his stride. In 1963, Koufax led the league in wins with 25, in ERA with 1.88, in shutouts with 11, and strikeouts with 308. He won both the Cy Young Award and Most Valuable Player Award that season. The six-time All-Star would go on to win two more Cy Young Awards in 1965 and '66, finishing second in MVP voting and leading the league in wins both seasons, with 26 wins in 1965 and 27 in '66. He pitched four no-hitters, and he won five straight NL ERA titles from 1962 to 1966 and led the Dodgers to NL pennants in 1963, 1965, and '66, winning the World Series in '63 and '65. He struck out 15 Yankees batters in Game 1 of the 1963 World Series. "I can see how he won 25 games," said Yogi Berra. "What I don't understand is how he lost five." Traumatic arthritis in his elbow ended Koufax's career early due to a threat of permanent disability. Despite playing only 12 seasons, Koufax—at age 36 in 1972—became the youngest person ever inducted in the Baseball Hall of Fame.

Tommy Lasorda spent parts of two seasons with the Dodgers, and following a season with the Kansas City Athletics in 1956, he returned to the minors for good. He became a scout for the Dodgers in 1960, and then a manager in their farm system beginning in 1966. He returned to the big leagues as a third base coach for manager Walter Alston in 1973, and was named Alston's successor in 1976. Lasorda guided the Dodgers to World Series appearances in 1977 and 1978, losing both times to the Yankees in six games. At the end of the strike-shortened 1981 season, the Dodgers defeated the Yankees in six games to give Lasorda his first World Series championship as a manager. He won another championship with the Dodgers in 1988, defeating the heavily favored Oakland Athletics in five games. As a successful and popular manager for the Dodgers from 1977 to 1996, Lasorda won nearly 1,600 games to go with eight NL West division titles and four NL pennants. Twice voted Manager of the Year by the Baseball Writers' Association of America, he was inducted into the Baseball Hall of Fame in 1997.

After 14 years in Brooklyn, Gil Hodges and the Dodgers moved to the West Coast to begin playing in Los Angeles. He would remain there for three seasons, until 1961. He joined the expansion New York Mets for the 1962 and '63 seasons. In 1963, the owners of the Mets negotiated a deal with another expansion club, the Washington Senators, for Hodges to become their new manager. He managed the Senators through the 1967 season, after which he was brought back to manage the perennially awful Mets. In 1969, he led the Miracle Mets to the world championship, defeating the heavily favored Baltimore Orioles in five games. His managerial career was cut short when he suffered a heart attack on Easter Sunday in 1972, two days before his 48th birthday. He died before the opening of the season and was succeeded by Yogi Berra.

EPILOGUE

Hoyt Wilhelm pitched a no-hitter against the Yankees in 1958. Forty-five years would go by before the Yankees were no-hit again, when the Houston Astros used six pitchers to no-hit New York in an interleague game, on June 11, 2003. Wilhelm threw his knuckleball for a career that lasted 21 years until 1972, when he was nearly 50 years old. He became the first relief pitcher to be elected to the Baseball Hall of Fame in 1985.

SOURCE NOTES

THERE AREN'T MANY PEOPLE ASSOCIATED WITH THE NEW YORK YAN-
kees of the 1950s who are still living, and those who are have told their
tales hundreds of times. The same anecdotes appear over and over again
in one form or another. I have tried to verify and amplify them, and
while I am not naive enough to believe I have completely succeeded,
I hope that I have situated these stories in their proper place in the
chronology of history. This book contains a great deal of information;
I've done my best to be as accurate as possible.

I wish I could list all of those who have contributed to my research,
but it's not feasible. The information contained in this book was derived
from a great many sources—websites, news media archives, and a number
of books. Sportswriters covering the team on a daily basis for newspapers
are the real heroes, serving as my boots on the ground, and I am indebted
to their work. There are so many newspaper stories that have recorded the
team's accomplishments, so many magazine articles that have profiled
the individuals, and so many books on the team and the players. I have
mentioned many of the sources and authors in the text, but I hope that
the writers, reporters, and authors from whom I have derived knowledge
of the Yankees will accept as partly theirs the thanks I can manage by
listing them here. I apologize for any inadvertent omissions.

Websites
Of the many websites I explored, none can match the comprehensive
volume of facts provided by Baseball Reference. It offers career and season statistics, schedules, results, box scores, daily standings, batting and

pitching logs, and play-by-play accounts of every game, and was relied on heavily for its extensive details. Also deserving of special notice is the Society of American Baseball Research, which is a valuable source for biographies of the players, managers, and executives. Other useful sites were:

Baseball Almanac

The Baseball Page

Bleacher Report

ESPN

The Hardball Times

Major League Baseball

National Baseball Hall of Fame

New York Yankees

Retrosheet

This Day in History

This Great Game

World Heritage Encyclopedia

News Media Archives

Associated Press

New York Daily News

New York Post

New York Times

Sporting News

Sports Illustrated

USA Today

BIBLIOGRAPHY

Allen, Maury. *Memories of the Mick*. Dallas, TX: Taylor Publishing, 1997.

Appel, Marty. *Pinstripe Empire: The New York Yankees from Before the Babe to After the Boss*. New York: Bloomsbury, 2012.

Boxerman, Burton A., and Benita W. Boxerman. *George Weiss: Architect of the Golden Age Yankees*. Jefferson, NC: McFarland, 2016.

Cramer, Richard Ben. *Joe DiMaggio: The Hero's Life*. New York: Simon and Schuster, 2000.

Creamer, Robert. *Stengel: His Life and Times*. New York: Simon and Schuster, 1984.

DiMaggio, Joe. *Lucky to Be a Yankee*. New York: Rudolph Field, 1946.

Falkner, David. *The Last Hero: The Life of Mickey Mantle*. New York: Simon and Schuster, 1995.

Ford, Whitey, with Phil Pepe. *Slick: My Life In and Around Baseball*. New York: William Morrow & Company, 1987.

Golenbock, Peter. *Dynasty*. Englewood Cliffs, NJ: Prentice-Hall, 1975.

Kahn, Roger. *The Boys of Summer*. New York: Signet Books, 1973.

Kahn, Roger. *The Era, 1947–57: When the Yankees, the Giants, and the Dodgers Ruled the World*. New York: Ticknor & Fields, 1993.

Leavy, Jane. *The Last Boy: Mickey Mantle and the End of America's Childhood*. New York: HarperCollins, 2010.

Leventhal, Josh. *Take Me Out to the Ballpark: An Illustrated Tour of Baseball Parks Past and Present*. New York: Black Dog & Leventhal, 2000.

Mantle, Mickey. *The Education of a Baseball Player*. New York: Simon and Schuster, 1967.

Pennington, Bill. *Billy Martin: Baseball's Flawed Genius*. New York: Houghton Mifflin Harcourt, 2015.

Reilly, James A. *The Biographical Encyclopedia of the Negro Leagues*. New York: Carroll and Graf, 1994.

Roberts, Randy, and Johnny Smith. *A Season in the Sun: The Rise of Mickey Mantle*. New York: Basic Books, 2018.

Stout, Glenn. *Yankees Century: 100 Years of New York Yankees Baseball*. New York: Houghton Mifflin, 2002.

Total Baseball. Baseball: The Biographical Encyclopedia. New York: Total Sports Illustrated, 2000.

Trimble, Joe. *Yogi Berra*. New York: Grosset & Dunlap, 1956.

INDEX

Italicized page numbers indicate illustrations.

Palmer, Arnold, 189
pantyhose, 213
Parks, Rosa, 127, 171
Parnell, Mel, 2
Pascual, Camilo, 139, 140
Patterson, Red, 70
Paula, Carlos, 120
Pennock, Herb, 14, 39
Perini, Lou, 74
Pesky, Johnny, 69, 85
Petty, Lee, 205
Philadelphia Athletics, 20, 54,
    101–2, 167–68, 187
Philadelphia Phillies
    glove ban complaints, 90–91
    management history, 14
    nicknames, 14
    racial integration, 127
    1949 season, 14
    1950 season, 14, 15–19, 94
    1951 season, 36, 37, 43, 52
    1956 season, 149
    trades, 108, 188
    World Series, 127
Phoenix, AZ, 24
Piazza, Mike, 223
Pierce, Billy, 115, 145, 162
Piersall, Jimmy, 57
pilots, 51, 52, *53,* 54, 90, 180
Pinelli, Babe, 152–53
Pitcher of the Year Award, 200
Pittsburgh Pirates
    racial integration, 113
    1955 season, 105, 113–14
    1956 season, 141
    1959 season, 209
    1903 World Series, 81
    1925 World Series, 197

1960 World Series, 226, 230,
    231
platooning (player rotations)
    benefits of, 9, 10, 78
    criticism of, 10, 214
    as management strategy, 2, 4, 55,
        78, 94, 99, 115–16, 123, 190,
        205, 214, 222
Playboy (magazine), 76
Player of the Year Awards, 55, 160,
    187, 200
Pledge of Allegiance, 99
Podres, Johnny, 81, 129–31, 132,
    133
polio vaccination, 60
Post, Wally, 170
Povich, Shirley, 8
presidents and presidential
    candidates, 60, 156, 211. *See
    also* Eisenhower, Dwight D.
Presley, Elvis, 135, 217
Professional Athlete of the Year,
    13, 147, 200
publicity stunts, 29–30
Puerto Rican baseball players,
    113–14
"Put Your Head on My Shoulder"
    (song), 213

R

racial integration
    anniversary celebrations of, 232
    award recipients, 38, 61, 62, 127,
        212–13, 224, 229–30
    in baseball, 58, 105, 113–14,
        120, 212–13 (*see also* African-
        American baseball players)
    in basketball, 20, 217

ABOUT THE AUTHOR

David Fischer has written for the *New York Times* and *Sports Illustrated Kids* and has worked at *Sports Illustrated*, the *National Sports Daily*, and NBC Sports. He is the author of several sports titles, including *Derek Jeter #2: Thanks for the Memories*, *100 Things Yankees Fans Should Know & Do Before They Die*, and *Miracle Moments in New York Yankees History*. Fischer is also the editor of *Facing Mariano Rivera*. He resides in New Jersey.